CW00920056

ISBN: 9781313452502

Published by:
HardPress Publishing
8345 NW 66TH ST #2561
MIAMI FL 33166-2626

Email: info@hardpress.net
Web: http://www.hardpress.net

PUBLICATIONS OF THE
AMERICAN ACADEMY OF POLITICAL AND SOCIAL SCIENCE.

The Outlines of Sociology.

BY

LUDWIG GUMPLOWICZ,

Professor in the University of Graz, Austria-Hungary.

TRANSLATED BY

FREDERICK W. MOORE,

Assistant Professor of History and Political Economy in Vanderbilt University,
Nashville, Tenn.

PHILADELPHIA :

AMERICAN ACADEMY OF POLITICAL AND SOCIAL SCIENCE.

1899.

CONTENTS.

PART I.

PART II.

PART III.

(3)

PART IV.

THE PSYCHO-SOCIAL PHENOMENA AND THE INDIVIDUAL.

PART V.

THE HISTORY OF MANKIND AS LIFE OF THE SPECIES.

SUPPLEMENTS.

THE OUTLINES OF SOCIOLOGY.*

INTRODUCTION.

Gumplowicz's "Outlines of Sociology" is distinguished from all earlier sociological works by the character of the sociological unit upon which it is based, which is the group. The author limits himself to the study of the behavior of social units, and especially to the study of the action of groups on each other and the action of the group on the individual. To compare Gumplowicz's theory with the theory of Giddings, and to use a metaphor for brevity, the former begins a whole stage. later in the evolution of life; it does not account for but assumes group life.

Starting with cohesively aggregated life, Gumplowicz makes important use of the principles already accepted concerning the influence of environment, and especially of the economic wants and the tendency of desires to grow with the opportunity to satisfy them. To these he adds, as something new, the postulates that the normal relation of unlike groups is conflict and that progress comes through the conflict of groups. Hence the important sociological phenomena are those relating to the conflict of unlike groups and to their amalgamation and assimilation.

Sociology is considered the fundamental social science, for it deals with the same subject-matter that all social sciences deal with, and treats of laws and modes of behavior in group life that are common to all the special social sciences alike. If what is general and common to all is set apart as the sphere of a particular science, then what is peculiar to each differentiated class of phenomena may be properly left to a special science working on the principles of the general science as a basis.

Further, the special social sciences, which have developed in advance of the general science, must submit to a revolution in point of view, to a revision of method and a restatement of accepted laws in harmony with the new ideas

*[The translator takes pleasure in making public acknowledgement of the important assistance rendered him by his friends Dr. A. R. Hohlfeld, Professor of German in Vanderbilt University, Dr. C. F. Emerick, Instructor in Economics in the same institution, and W. C. Branham, A. M., Co-Principal of Branham and Hughes School, String Hill, Tenn. The first named carefully compared the translation with the original and the others assisted in revising the proof.]

in sociology; while for the future, whether new social laws are first detected in general sociology or in one of the special sciences, it must be remembered that the phenomena which the latter study are social also, and that the special laws of their behavior are inherently social and must stand the test of sociological criticism.

Gumplowicz's sociology is not properly descriptive. Description falls to anthropology, ethnology, politics, history, comparative philology, the comparative study of law, religion, institutions, etc. It is considered the peculiar task of sociology to abstract the laws of the behavior of social phenomena.

The volitional element plays no part, or a negative one, in Gumplowicz's theory. Man, misled by the idea of human free will and by an anthropomorphic conception of deity, has overestimated his own influence and importance. He is most successful in art and invention, for here he strives to copy nature. In other spheres he is not infrequently found striving to preserve what nature has ordained to decay. But first striving to learn what the laws of nature are, he should next learn to adapt himself to them as best he can and to bear with resignation what cannot be avoided. Nature is unchangeable and so are her laws. The history of mankind is the history of a species as such. The fate which befalls the individual in society is not the fate which he merits always, but it is necessarily that which his group makes inevitable. Historic justice is not individual, but social.

FREDERICK W. MOORE.

ARGUMENT.

Part I.

Part I contains a survey of past progress in social science, intended to prepare the reader for the new departure in sociological thought which the author proposes to make.

He reviews the work of Comte, Spencer, Bastian, Lippert aud others, and the relations of economics, politics, the comparative study of law, the philosophy of history and the history of civilization to the science of society.

Incidentally four important propositions are laid down:

First.—Social phenomena are subject to the general law of causation as much as other classes of phenomena which have been successfully treated by the scientific method. This has been asserted or tacitly assumed by all the earlier writers; it is axiomatic.

Second.—Human acts, whether individual or social, are the product of natural forces and they excite reflection. The function of the mind or soul is secondary in point of time. In this the author differs from some of his predecessors.

Third.—Differing radically from other writers, the author denies that society is simply an organism analogous to but as high above man as man is above other organisms in nature. In his conception, society, the social group, the sociological unit, is an organism or organization entirely, (*toto genere*), different from any other. Considered as a whole it is unlike any of its parts. Its nature cannot be inferred from their nature, but more probably the nature of the individual will be influenced by it. His system begins with social elements (swarms, hordes, groups, etc.), and logically proceeds to the consideration of man, their product both in mind and body; the social process and its products; and finally the ethico-social products of the action of society upon the individual.

Fourth.—The author holds and defends the position that every political organization, and hence every developing civilization, begins at the moment when one group permanently subjects another. Subjection of some to others is the source of political organization and political organization is the condition essential to social growth. This proposition and the preceding constitute the corner stone of the author's theory.

Part II.

Part II is introductory. Beginning with the classification of phenomena and defending the unity of science, the author proceeds to a presentation of the concepts especially connected with sociology.

SECTION 1. The author takes up the triple classification of phenomena into physical, mental and social, and justifies it and the corresponding subdivision of the sciences by demonstrating that there are social phenomena subject to laws of a special character.

SEC. 2. But if science is unitary and the universe of phenomena monistic, there must be some laws at once specific enough to be valuable and general enough to apply to all three classes of phenomena alike.

He enumerates the laws of causality, of development, of regularity of development, of periodicity, of complexity, of the reciprocal action of unlike forces, of adaptation, of the essential likeness and identity of forces and events, and of parallelism, showing that each clearly applies to social phenomena, the only disputable point.

SEC. 3. Within each class the behavior of the phenomena is capable of reduction to a number of laws which are more specific, which apply to that one sphere (or even to a part of it alone) and are more fully characteristic. It is the function of sociology to find the laws of social phenomena.

Social phenomena are defined as those arising out of the relations of social groups to each other. Psycho-social are those again which result from the influence of the group upon the individual.

[*Psycho-social phenomena and psycho-social laws are thus quite distinct from social phenomena and social laws, using the word social in the narrower, more specific sense which the author gives to it here and occasionally elsewhere. But he uses the word in a more general sense also, including social in this narrower sense and psycho-social as correlative subdivisions of it.

[There would seem to be need also for a third subdivision including phenomena growing out of the relation of the group to its physical environment. Critics who will recognize the importance of the group as the social unit and the weighty significance of the antagonism existing between

*[The brackets, wherever found, indicate that the included matter has been added by the translator.]

groups will, nevertheless, show that such factors as food supply affect the size and coherency of groups and the number in a given territory. In some places he seems incidentally to allow for them. But his definition by unmistakable implication excludes them. Had he broadened his conception of sociology so as to include this class of phenomena, his dispute with Lippert would have fallen to nothing and his later reference to the origin of groups by differentiation would have been much more natural and easy.]

Phenomena that have been treated by one or another of the sciences currently called social are nevertheless properly subject to reinvestigation by sociology, for they have been treated from the individualistic standpoint, which is false. To review them from the new social standpoint and to ascertain the social laws of their behavior will be of great importance. It will be found that they all take their rise in a common ground, which is the peculiar sphere of sociology.

Sec. 4. As there must be unlike forces wherever reciprocal action is expected, the author assumes that there must have been a countless number of unlike original primitive groups. This hypothesis is then supported by arguments proving the polygenetic theory of man's origin.

Sec. 5. However, if the polygenetic theory is true, it only proves the existence of primitive groups anthropologically homogeneous. But as birth and especially training in a group are the factors which make an individual a member of a social group, these primitive anthropological groups must also have been sociological groups; and though anthropological types have become endlessly mixed, each syngenetic group, because its members have had a common birth and training and have acquired the same language, rights and religion, still continues to be a sociological unit.

Social laws, he adds, are the laws of the action and development of syngenetic groups.

[Thus, narrow as he seems to make the conception of syngenetic groups and important as such groups seem to be to his theory, he makes allowance here incidentally and specifically later for the origin of fully accredited social groups by differentiation within a given group.

[Primitive groups are unlike, *heterogen*, and so are syngenetic groups, says our author. Now *heterogen* and *homogen* are antithetical and should refer respectively to the mutual unlikeness or likeness of the parts of a given whole. But this is not strictly the way the author uses them and his meaning would still be ambiguous if it were. There are three sets of relations between unlike groups to be distinguished: those between the differentiating parts of a whole that was beforetime strictly homogeneous; those between the parts of a whole which is tending toward homogeneity by assimilation and amalgamation of its parts; and finally those between independent wholes which exhibit antagonism and conflict whenever their spheres of influence overlap. These independent wholes our author refers to as *heterogen*, unlike (improperly called heterogeneous). Sometimes, however, the adjective seems to refer to wholes whose parts are in conflict with each other and is properly translated heterogeneous. The translator has used his judgment as to the signification of the word in its context but has carefully inserted the German word in parenthesis wherever it occurred.

[A study of the relations of the several classes to each other will show a logical sequence from the conflict of independent wholes through the subjection of one to the other even up to the complete homogeneity of the new whole by assimilation or amalgamation. There is also a logical sequence from the condition of homogeneity to the condition of differentiated parts with their proper relations. Now these two tendencies are so antipodal in direction and character that it is unscientific and ambiguous not to distinguish carefully between them. But the author, as said, uses one and the same word *heterogen*, heterogeneous, to describe the two conditions indicated in the first and second classes of relations indicated above. He does not distinguish the former and therefore omits from his theory of sociology all consideration of the character and behavior of homogeneous groups.]

He shows that the failure of earlier sociologists to obtain social laws was due to their failure to start with the proper sociological unit; and incidentally he proclaims it as a typical social law that it is the tendency of every social community to make as much use as possible of every other social community that comes within its reach.

Part III.

In Part III the author treats of social elements, simple and compound, and the cause and manner of their combination.

SECTION 1. Proceeding to consider the nature of the original syngenetic group he concludes that it must have been a horde of human beings of all ages and both sexes living in sexual promiscuity. Further than this he is unable to carry the analysis; as far as this he feels justified in going, since the hypothesis of such a horde enables him to explain the origin of the mother-family which investigators have all but proven to have been universal. Uterine consanguinity is the first force to introduce order into the chaos of primitive promiscuity.

But the groups are mutually hostile and in particular in the course of their conflicts females are captured who become the property of their captors. [The warriors or the group? Are rights of individual property in movable goods recognized respecting them?]. Then the men, supported by the favorable conditions growing out of their relation to the captives, are able to resist the rule of the women and to substitute an organization controlled by the males in which the various stages of the father-family are developed down to and including the development of the rights of the children to inherit.

Highly significant in the author's opinion is the intermixture of different ethnical races which occurs here. [But this emphasis seems overstrained. Either the males as a whole subordinated the females of the group as a whole, still keeping them in the group except as they were disposed of to other groups by purchase or capture; or the original group divided, some under the leadership of the women retaining the organization of the mother-family, the rest led by the possessors of the captive females forming a new whole organized as a father-family. In either case the conflict within the original group between the two classes, males and females, with their peculiar interests, is quite as bitter and relentless as the conflict between different syngenetic groups; and it is not so important as the author represents that there should be ethnically different groups to antagonize and exploit each other.]

Not only are females and personal property captured in the raids of group upon group, but whole groups are conquered, reduced to submission and put to work on the soil they occupied, producing supplies for the conquerors. In the relations thus established we have property in land in distinction from personal property (which is a very different thing and arises much earlier), the organization of sovereignty by one class over the other, and finally the state.

SEC. 2. The state consists of two parts, the ruling and the subject classes, of which the former is inferior in numbers but superior in mental power and military discipline.

There are two sets of activities in the state. One is in the ruling class directed toward external defence and conquest, and the other arises from the conflicts of the two classes. [The differentiation of interests within each group severally is not an activity peculiar to the state !] So there are but two points essential to the definition of the state. They are the organization of the sovereignty and of the minority. The purposes commonly attributed to the state, like the promotion of justice, are simply the modes of operation appropriate to its several stages of development.

An important incident is ethnical heterogeneity. The hostile contact of different social elements of unlike strength is the first condition for the creation of rights. The relations established by force, if continued in peace, become rightful. Thus inequality is stamped on every right.

SEC. 3. The life of the state is summed up in a common industrial enterprise conducted under compulsion in which the greater burden falls on the subject class while the rulers perform services which are no less essential. [Were the author as fully impregnated with democratic ideals as Americans are his language at this point, though not his idea, would be somewhat different. For in a democratic government the ruling class is the periodically determined majority, or its representatives.]

Man's material need is the prime motive of his conduct. Efforts to satisfy wants promote progress and are perpetual; for new wants are constantly arising and social distinctions continue the antagonism between groups which began with ethnical differences.

But war, if perpetual, would defeat its own end in the utter exhaustion of both parties. Peace is necessary. One party is victor and tries to establish institutions for maintaining the inequalities, while the other tries to reduce them. So apparent peace is only a latent struggle over the body of reciprocal rights.

If the rulers are well off the subject class must rise too in order still to be most serviceable. But social facts especially provoke reflection; and the life of the subject classes is the more fruitful in ideas. Well-being and enlightenment are the leaven of progress.

Sec. 4. The ranks or classes in the state increase in number, and political organization changes to correspond. The third class in order is that of the foreign merchants, catering to material wants chiefly; the fourth is the priestly class arising by differentiation from the others and satisfying spiritual wants. The development of wants and the formation of classes go hand in hand. Material wants may be classed as primary, and intellectual or moral wants as secondary.

The power of any class in the state can be expressed in terms of human labor which it either commands directly or can purchase through its possession or control of supplies and means of promoting production. If a class can satisfy a social want it will be indispensable, and through the power it acquires in return will participate in government.

However, habit, a purely mental factor, is also a source of power; and order, custom and rights belong to the same category. But without the organization of the state the moral powers would not exist and the material possessions would fall to the physically stronger.

Sec. 5. Some social groups, like the ruling, subject and merchant classes, are original, primary, ethnical and hereditary. Others, like the priestly and professional classes, are secondary and evolutionary and arise by differentiation. Though we no longer see primary groups arising, it has not been proven that no groups ever arose genetically; though we see only the differentiation of secondary groups it cannot be asserted that all groups are of that sort. Nevertheless all social groups of whatever origin are alike active as social elements and those of the secondary sort tend by endogamy and otherwise to strengthen their coherence.

Sec. 6. The word society should properly be restricted to denote a group centering about one or more common interests. As such it may be large or small; local, national or international. The word folk should be used co-extensively with the state to denote the group held together not only by political organization, but also by common territory, language, etc.

SEC. 7. Societies are numberless; but social relations and the principles underlying social power conform to natural laws. The primary binding tie is association; all others are evolutionary. All are essentially represented in the primitive horde: association, with consanguinity, language and all that they imply, and common needs and common interests in satisfying them; and there are no social contrasts which cannot be referred to dissimilarity in one or more of these respects. So we observe the coherence of the heterogeneous and the differentiation of the homogeneous for cause. But social classes overlap and are curiously involved.

SEC. 8. The group-making factors are classified according to fundamental principles as material, economic and moral. But further, each varies according to the degree of its permanency. Permanent material, economic and moral interests make a group unitary.

SEC. 9. The power of the group in the social struggle depends on the number of group-making factors uniting its members. The number of possible binding forces increases with civilization but decreases at any time with the number of individuals in the group.

In the final analysis the intensity of the union depends upon the personal character of the individuals [*i. e.*, on their sociability. This is one of the rare instances in which the nature of the individual is taken into account]; and in times of revolution numerical strength is the test, but such times are abnormal with civilized man.

Groups struggle for their interests group-wise; the result does not depend upon individuals and success is the standard of conduct.

The means of utilizing power vary infinitely, but generally take the form of an appropriate institution or exclusive right, as *e. g.*, legislation. However it may be with the individual, society never errs in seizing and applying the right means. [This is a paradox. Conscientious scruples which would constrain the action of individuals are ineffective to guide the action of groups. But societies do err; for they perish as the result of their own mistakes, and in those which succeed there are traces, if we look for them, of choices that retarded progress or threatened extinction and therefore had to be abandoned.]

SEC. 10. The struggle must always be conducted between assemblages and they must adopt a form of organization suited to the situation. So the struggle in the interest of the great mass of the people is most difficult and the slowest to begin. Historically the means which they generally seek is participation in legislation.

SEC. 11. The conduct of the group is in utter disregard of the individual and his code of morals. His moral sense is therefore often seriously injured. [The difference between the individual and the social code of morals demands explanation. A partial explanation will doubtless be found in the current theories of individualism. But this is insufficient. There would be a remnant which can probably be best explained as due to the experience of individuals in the homogeneous group. This will be in harmony with the author's theory of the influence of the group on the individual; but it will at the same time point out an important omission in his general sociological theory, viz., the failure to give due consideration to the life of the homogeneous group.]

SEC. 12. Every right ends in an obligation, the right of those who otherwise have no rights. Though rights are constantly changing the idea of right endures and is a fit weapon for the social struggle. But it is applied indirectly. The bourgeoisie appeal to it to enlist the lower classes with them against the upper. With success the lower classes gain some amelioration and experience. This is aptly called the struggle for emancipation. It may lead to revolution or anarchy; but a reaction and a new period of evolutionary rights will follow.

SEC. 13. The natural tendency of the state is to increase in territory and power. But relative stability within and assimilation of former conquests are essential conditions to continued growth the absence of which will induce a catastrophe.

If extreme violence is necessary to subjugation and if assimilation is difficult, morals and the sense of humanity will suffer harm.

The principle applies as well to other social domains as to the political, e. g., it explains the periodical crises of economic production.

SEC. 14. Folk-states will arise. But if, falling into opposition, the weaker are subjected by the stronger the struggle for authority in the new composite state will take on added severity. Historically it is apt to centre about the rivalry of different languages for official recognition.

Part IV.

Part IV treats of the influence of the group on the individual. The processes involved and the laws are those specifically called psycho-social.

SECTION 1. The historical antithesis between individualism and collectivism disappears upon substituting social or societary egoism and sympathy instead of the alleged individual egoism and sympathy of current philosophy.

SEC. 2. To establish the claims of a socialistic philosophy over the individualistic the author notes, first, that the source of thought is in the group and not in the individual. The influence of environment on the individual is of fundamental and not simply of secondary importance; but the individual's environment is almost exclusively his group, and the power that is admittedly strong enough to change his physiognomy is *a fortiori* strong enough to change his mind. The type produced is not anthropological but social; and the factor producing it is social also. Social thoughts and efforts produce the type; but it is the social life, varying with the habitat, that produces these. Hence also the variety of social types.

SEC. 3. Pre-eminently it is the economic status which gives character to the social type, making the nobility and peasantry conservative and the merchant class progressive and giving to each of the differentiated classes also a type appropriate to its peculiar interests. But the individual is affected through his moral nature; the transforming force is moral.

The tenacity and permanence of the type is directly related to the solidarity of the group which is a function of the group-making factors.

SEC. 4. The first factor in morals is habit and acquired manner of life; the second is the conviction implanted by the group in the individual that the manner of life which it imposes upon him is proper. Thus morals grow out of the relations of the group to its members. But when different groups are united different moral codes contend; all are useless because no one is acknowledged by every individual and a new code has to be formed and enforced by the state, called a code of rights. Thus rights grow out of the union of different social elements.

There will be important conflicts between the code of rights enforced by the state and the moral code growing up in the complex community on the one hand and the moral codes of the more compact circles comprised within it on the other.   The supreme purpose of the state must be to build up a moral code for the state as a whole; indeed the ideal code is international.

Sec. 5. There are two elements in morals, the natural and the human, the former changeless, the latter changing. Though man acts as natural forces compel him to, it is his nature to reflect on his acts and to believe that he acts freely. When his behavior finally becomes such as the long experience of his social group proves to be best he calls it moral, but seeks a higher sanction for his moral ideas by ascribing events to mythical and generally to anthropomorphic origins.   Truth and fiction thus grow up together until it seems impossible to sustain morals without maintaining the truth of what is really supposititious.   Thus the conflict of ignorance fighting in the name of morality begins.

But morals is the ripened fruit of the actual development of civilization; natural science is the basis of morals, and whatever promotes scientific knowledge promotes moral science also.   Man's only standard is the visible tendency, the assumed will of nature.

Sec. 6. Rights are social creations, formed by the conflict of unlike social groups of unequal power.   But corresponding to each right is a duty or obligation.

Sec. 7. The theory of "natural rights" is untenable. Rights arise in the state only; and though there is much unavoidable evil in the state, the alternative, anarchy, is worse.

Neither is justice the source of rights.   On the contrary, it is simply an abstraction from political rights and increases in perfection with time.   But because rights are relatively fixed in the form of written law and deep seated usage, while political relations and the corresponding sense of justice suffer continuous change, rights fall into formal antithesis to justice at times.

Sec. 8. Considering the nature and form of morals and rights it is not difficult to explain the cases where morals have conformed to rights, and where rights, becoming formal merely, have yielded to well-grounded morals and new rights.

Though morals are thus changeable the individual treats them as unchanging; for his starting point in morals, though socially caused, is subjective and relatively fixed.

NOTE TO 6, 7 AND 8.   Private rights depend on the truth and merits of the claims of the contending parties; public rights on their relative power, on their might.   The one relates to individuals, the other to the state.   Much confusion has arisen from trying to apply the principles of private rights to political affairs.   [After the author's presentation of the omnipotence and omnipresence of social influences, what sphere is left for private rights as distinct from political (social) rights?   In the relations, it must be replied, regulating the conduct of individuals within a homogeneous class or group.   As the tendency of the state is to unity and solidarity in some respects at least, the sphere of private rights is doubtless not small.   So a part of the conflict between individual and social codes is due, not so much to the false ideas of free will as to the tendency to apply by analogy the rules suited to one set of relations to another and different set.   The author has not made as much of the rules of behavior governing the relations of individuals in the unitary horde as they deserve.]

SEC. 9.   Man's impotency in the contest with social necessities is illustrated by the antithesis between his desire to preserve and nature's tendency toward change and decay. Though men admire the ascetic who defies nature and despise those who follow natural necessity, human freedom in science and philosophy, in legislation, statecraft and diplomacy is shown to be merely the necessary oscillation of human choices back and forth across the line of necessity. Only those which coincide with necessity are fortunate; but as oscillation is a necessity, not all can coincide, resignation to necessity is impossible and happiness is always less than the maximum.

Some amelioration is possible, especially by learning not to overrate the value of human life.   But the greatest success is in technology, science and art, in which the object is to learn what is natural and to copy it or adapt one's self to it.

Part V.

Part V treats briefly of the history of mankind as the life of a species sociologically organized.

SECTION 1.   The task of sociology is to investigate human group-making; not to give the history of every group, which would be impossible, but to show conformity to law in the

process and to study and describe the manner of social
evolution.

SEC. 2. Conformity to law is admitted almost without contradiction in the development of art and science; but, if it
is true in these domains, it must be admitted even by those
who have hitherto denied it to be equally true of political
history in general; and if true of the great general results
it must be true of the individuals and of the social structures,
for there is a close causal connection between mental development and social, political and economic conditions.

SEC. 3. The evolution of mankind must be conceived of
not as unitary and not as polygenetic, not as genealogical
nor even as having a beginning.   But the same things take
place according to the same laws whenever the same conditions arise.   We must conceive of evolution as running its
course and stopping when energy is no longer generated.
This suggests cyclical development.

SEC. 4. Cyclical development follows from man's unfreedom and dependence on physical wants.   According to the
Malthusian law, in some groups population increases under
favorable conditions wihtout the group making progress in
any other particular or gaining any strength.   Such groups
easily fall prey to more developed communities.   The states
thus formed by conquest will enjoy general progress, in the
lower as well as in the higher classes.   Then population
may stagnate or even decline.   Being numerically weak,
the states will fall prey to some barbarian, whether external
horde or internal proletariat.

SEC. 5. There is of course progress in particular countries
and in particular periods of the cyclical process, but there is
no progress in the course of history taken as a whole.
History simply repeats itself.   There is of course progress
in invention and discovery; but it is not to be explained as
the result of a perfected human intellect.   Intellects of the
same general range of power have replaced with interest the
accumulations of earlier generations.   But even these accumulations are reduced by recurrent catastrophes of wide
reach.   The same is true of morals and philosophy.

SEC. 6. The current conceptions of justice consider man
as its object, and, owing to the belief in human free will
and to the anthropomorphic conception of deity, men try to
judge historical and natural events by the standards of
human justice.   This is as wrong as it is harmful, for the

individual is never considered in these phenomena, only the mass, and there is no criterion of his worth.   Fate strikes individuals in proportion not to their own merits, but to the merits of the group.   This is historic justice; and the crown of sociology is to recognize in human history a natural process.

PREFACE.

Two years ago I published some of my "sociological investigations," under the title of "*Der Rassenkampf*," diffidently offering them as the "first lispings of a great science of the future, sociology." The favorable reception accorded them by competent authorities at home and abroad has encouraged me to present the following "Outlines of Sociology." From the attention universally accorded to sociological problems it is evident that sociology is not an ephemeral idea, but is actually coming to be a science. I succeeded, as I believe, in laying down a few of its principles in "*Der Rassenkampf.*" In the present "Outlines," I have earnestly striven to project a complete and unitary plan of the science; to show the distinction between it and other sciences, and to call attention to the most important questions which must hereafter be subjected to sociological investigation. May this book meet with the same tolerant criticism as its predecessor.

THE AUTHOR.

GRATZ, *April, 1885.*

I. SKETCH OF SOCIOLOGICAL LITERATURE.

It is usual before proceeding to the systematic presentation of a science to give a sketch of its literature. A bibliographical introduction informs the reader how much effort has been expended on the science, how it has progressed, and what stage of development it has reached. If the sketch is also critical, and it can hardly fail to be so, the reader is also informed of the new writer's attitude toward the work of his predecessors. Such an introduction gives a comprehensive view. But it involves disadvantages of a technical nature. If every system should be described in detail, the introductory sketch would become a history of the science. The reader would have to wander through system after system, each one represented to be more or lessf alse, before learning how the writer would correct them; which is not practicable. Or should the writer make and substantiate his criticisms in the introduction itself, he would anticipate his own system; whatever followed woulu be merely tiresome repetition. This too would be impracticable; especially since the refuting arguments can be used much more effectively as the author proceeds to unfold his own views. Then he is not bound by historical sequence nor need he present the older systems entire.

Accordingly we shall mention only the most important pioneers in the domain of sociology noting, with all possible brevity, the most prominent and most general points of view in their systems and deferring criticism and refutation until we present our own system.

Young and imperfect as the science of sociology still is, a history of its literature has already been written.* But its author makes the " socialistic " doctrines his starting point, and his failure to distinguish clearly between socialism and sociology greatly diminishes the value of the work. Further bibliographical material may be found in the literature upon the development of constitutional law, politics, political economy, and the philosophy of history.†

---

* "*Die Socialwissenschaften.*" A guide to the modern schools of social science, by Friedrich v. Baerenbach, Leipzig, 1882.

† Beside the well-known works of Raumer and Bluntschli, Rocholl's "Philosophy of History," (*Philosophie der Geschichte*), may be mentioned.

Probably the first author to cherish presentiments of a "science of the common nature of nations "* was Giambattista Vico. But he adhered to Biblical tradition and did not emancipate himself from the contemporary theories of natural rights. Neither should we expect to find in St. Simon, the world reformer, an objective science of society. Full justice has been done him when it is recognized that it was from him that Comte received his inspiration.

To Auguste Comte unquestionably belongs the honor of having been the first to recognize the real character of sociology. In his "Positive Philosophy " he declared repeatedly, plainly and correctly what this science should be. "All that can be rationally proposed in our day," he says in one place, " is to recognize the character of positivity in social as in all other science, and to ascertain the chief bases on which it is founded." † The scientific character of the future sociology is thus indicated. Further, " it is the exclusive property of the positive principle to recognize the fundamental law of continuous human development, representing the existing evolution as the necessary result of the gradual series of former transformations."‡ Thus Comte conceived mankind to be subject to the law of evolution and the present to be the necessary consequence of the past. Though his conception of mankind was erroneous, as will be shown later, still both ideas are true and important; and the general principle has been maintained firmly in sociology ever since. Moreover, an admonition of broad scientific application was added: " True resignation, that is, a permanent disposition to endure steadily and without hope of compensation all inevitable evils, can proceed only from a deep sense of the connection of all kinds of natural phenomena with invariable laws." || Without such resignation, there can be no sociology.

* " *Principii di una Scienza nuova d'intorno alla commune Natura delle Nazioni,*" by Giambattista Vico. *Secundo Edizione del 1725 pubblicati con Note da Giuseppe Ferrari e la Vita dell' Autore.* Milan, 1836.

† " The Positive Philosophy of Auguste Comte," freely translated by Harriet Martineau. London, 1875. Two volumes. Vol. ii, bk. vi, cap. i.
" *Cours de Philosophie positive,*" by Auguste Comte. Paris, 1839. Four volumes. Vol. iv, lec. 46.
" *La Philosophie positive,*" by Auguste Comte, *Résumé* by Jules Rig. Paris, 1881. Two volumes Vol. ii, lec. 46.
[Generally the quotations are cited in the words of Miss Martineau. But this has not always been possible, as the author's quotations are from the résumé of Jules Rig. (J. E. Rigolage).]

‡ Martineau, *op. cit.,* Vol. ii, bk. vi, cap. i; Comte, *op. cit.,* Vol. iv, lec. 46; Rig. *op. cit.,* Vol. ii, lec, 46.

|| *Ibid.*

"If there are (as I doubt not there are) political evils which, like some personal sufferings, cannot be remedied by science," he went on, "science at least proves to us that they are incurable, so as to calm our restlessness under pain by the conviction that it is by natural causes that they are rendered insurmountable."*

Would that he had acted upon this wise principle himself. But he violated it by suggesting plans for the "practical amelioration" of "the condition of the lower classes." † The error is one for which his master, St. Simon, is to blame. It finally forced him out of the path of objective science and into the false ways of subjective politics.

How clear and precise his statement of the task of sociology in contrast with the older doctrines of the philosophy of history!

"Social science could not exist," he says, "so long as men were ignorant concerning what constitutes development; for this science studies the laws of development."‡

Yet he himself failed to apprehend its true nature, for he accepted Pascal's "admirable aphorism" that "the entire succession of men, through the whole course of ages, must be regarded as one man always living,"‖ and he misconceived the result of sociology most egregiously, saying "that this science fulfills the famous suggestion of Pascal by representing the whole human race past, present and future, as constituting a vast and eternal social unit whose different organs concur in their various modes and degrees in the evolution of humanity." § But it is false to conceive mankind to be a unit as we shall show hereafter. It led Comte into a thousand and one errors.

In his time, it is true, historical and ethnographical material was very meagre. His personal knowledge of mankind was limited; and his investigations into the laws of human development were restricted to the Teutonic and the Latin races of Europe. Indeed, France was often his sole example; the "great revolution" was to his mind the overturning of all humanity, whereas far the greater part of

* *Ibid.*

† *Ibid.*

‡ Rig. *op. cit.*, Vol. ii, lec. 47 ; Comte, *op. cit.*, Vol. iv, lec. 47 ; Martineau, *op. cit.*, Vol. ii. bk. vi, cap. ii.

‖ *Ibid. Cf.* Pascal's "*Pensées.*" Part i, art i.

§ Martineau, *op. cit.*, Vol. ii, bk. vi, cap. iii ; Comte, *op. cit.*, Vol. iv, lec. 48 ; Rig. *op. cit.*, Vol. ii, lec. 48.

mankind was not influenced at all by this local European event.

Not only were his "laws of human development" based on this narrow experience; they were also so distorted by personal predilections that they possess little value. The historical and ethnographical horizon of his time was far too narrow. His sociology was a failure from utter lack of material. The epoch-making character of his work is solely due to the brilliant generalizations (*geniale Principien*) upon which he founded it. They are the basis, as we shall see, of all the sociological efforts from his day to ours.

The prospect of verifying his laws of human development by means of numerical calculations must have been all the more enticing, to a mathematician like Quetelet, from the fact that Comte himself seemed directly to suggest it.[*] Quetelet's interest centred in the "Natural History of Society," *i. e.*, in sociology. Even his earlier work on "Man" has the sub-title "Social Physics," and he states that "it is the body social that we propose to study."[†]

His task is obviously allied to that of Comte's sociology. But the "law of the great number"[‡] which he relied on to discover the laws of social development was ineffectual. His statistical works afford material for the theory of "man" and the thralldom of human will only. For sociology they could do nothing. He made no distinction between "mankind" and the unclear concept "society;" and many of his investigations begin with errors current in the social science of his day. He assumes, for instance, that "the simplest and most natural social union among men is the family, which is found in all ages and among all peoples."[||] He did not know that the family, in the modern signification

[*] "It is clear that this education [the preliminary sociological training] must rest on a basis of mathematical philosophy even apart from the necessity of mathematics to the study of inorganic philosophy. It is only in the region of mathematics that sociologists, or any body else, can obtain a true sense of scientific evidence and form the habit of rapid and decisive argumentation; can in short learn to fulfill the logical conditions of all positive speculation by studying universal positivism at its source;" Martineau, *op. cit.*, Vol. ii, bk. vi, cap. iv ; Comte *op. cit.*, Vol. iv, lec. 49 ; Rig. *op. cit.*, Vol. ii, lec. 49. However, Comte warns against applying mathematical laws to the " complicated speculations of sociology."

[†] "*Sur l' Homme et le Développement de ses Facultés, ou Essai de Physique sociale,*" by A. Quetelet, Paris, 1835. Introduction sec. 3.

[‡] Quetelet, *op. cit.*, Introduction secs. 2 and 3.

[||] " Natural History of Society." Comte makes the same statement: " The family presents the true germ of the various characteristics of the social organism. Such a conception is intermediate between the idea of the individual and that of the species or society." Martineau, *op. cit.*, Vol. ii, bk. vi, cap. v; Comte, *op. cit.*, Vol. iv. lec. 50; Rig., *op. cit.*, Vol. ii, lec. 50.

of the word and the sense in which he uses it, is a very late social institution and an adaptation to political ends. Equally ingenuous is his idea that a " nation " " is a body composed of homogeneous elements performing their functions in unison and inspired with the same life principle;''* whereas, in truth, every nation consists of unlike elements performing complementary functions under compulsion. His theory was that social unions originate in the " preponderance of the force of attraction impelling individuals to associate." He frankly conceded, however, that " a nation is not always composed of elements of one sort. Indeed it is quite often the result of invasion and the fusion of conqueror and conquered."† But this is the " exception;" his theory is not based upon it. No wonder that he failed to get a clear conception of the laws of social development. Phenomena as common as the struggles of nation with nation seem to him against nature; and he concludes his " History of Mankind " with the enthusiasm of an Elihu Burritt, saying:

> " To the credit of mankind be it told, the nineteenth century is on the point of striking into a new path. It is recognized that there must be laws and tribunals for nations also; and that crimes practiced on a large scale by one people against another are just as much to be hated as crimes of man against man." ‡

These are beautiful effusions; but they attest the scantiness of Quetelet's sociological information. Since he wrote them the nineteenth century has witnessed, even in Europe alone, a half dozen wars: the Crimean and the Austro-Italian; the war of Prussia and Austria against Denmark; the Austro-Prussian, the Franco-Prussian and the Russo-Turkish. According to him they were all downright " crimes." Yet the victorious nations inscribed them in their annals in letters of gold, and succeeding generations exult at the thought of them. His " new path " is still a good way off. Is it not sociology that should take a new course?

Herbert Spencer's words on this point are of inestimable importance:

> " Thought and feeling cannot be completely dissociated. Each emotion has a more or less distinct framework of ideas; and each group of ideas is more or less suffused with emotion. There are, however, great differences between their degrees of combination under both of these aspects. We have some feelings which are vague from

* " Natural History of Society."
† *Ibid.*
‡ *Ibid.*

lack of intellectual definition; and others to which clear shapes are given by the associated conceptions. At one time our thoughts are distorted by the passion running through them; and at another time it is difficult to detect in them a trace of liking or disliking. Manifestly, too, in each particular case these components of the mental state may be varied in their proportions. The ideas being the same, the emotion joined with them may be greater or less; and it is a familiar truth that the correctness of the judgment formed, depends, if not on the absence of emotion, still, on that balance of emotions which negatives excess of any one.

"Especially is this so in matters concerning human life. There are two ways in which men's actions, individual or social, may be regarded. We may consider them as groups of phenomena to be analyzed, and the laws of their dependence ascertained; or, considering them as causing pleasures or pains, we may associate with them approbation or reprobation. Dealing with its problems intellectually, we may regard conduct as always the result of certain forces; or, dealing with its problems morally, and recognizing its outcome as in this case good and in that case bad, we may allow now admiration and now indignation to fill our consciousness. Obviously, it must make a great difference in our conclusions whether, as in the one case, we study men's doings as those of alien creatures, which it merely concerns us to understand; or whether, as in the other case, we contemplate them as the doings of creatures like ourselves, with whose lives our own lives are bound up, and whose behavior arouses in us, directly and sympathetically, feelings of love or hate."

"Here let me emphasize the conclusion that in pursuing our sociological inquiries, and especially those on which we are now entering [political institutions], we must, as much as possible, exclude whatever emotions the facts are calculated to excite, and attend solely to the interpretation of the facts. There are several groups of phenomena in contemplating which either contempt, or disgust, or indignation, tends to arise but must be restrained."*

As the English statesman cries "hands off" to the onlookers in political quarrels, so Spencer cries "away with sentiment," whenever a sociological investigation is undertaken. On the portal of this science he writes: "All sentiment, abandon ye who enter here." This is not merely a practical admonition, it is a *conditio sine qua non*, a stipulation indispensable in sociology, and which moreover forestalls objections raised on moral grounds.

Fortunately Spencer is in full agreement with Comte in recognizing "the character of positivity in social as in all other science." It is to him the first principle of methodology, or rather it precedes methodology. But in accepting the fundamental similarity of sociology and biology he made a well-nigh fatal blunder.

* Spencer, "Principles of Sociology," Vol. ii, sec. 434.

Comte affirmed emphatically that this similarity was an essential sociological principle.

"The necessity," he says, "of founding sociology upon the whole of biology is obvious." "The subordination of social science to biology is so evident," he continues, "that nobody denies it in statement however it may be neglected in fact." "Biology will be seen to afford the starting point of all social speculation, in accordance with the analysis of the social faculties of man, and of the organic conditions which determine its character. But, moreover, as we can scarcely at all investigate the most elementary terms of the social series, we must construct them by applying the positive theory of human nature to the aggregate of corresponding circumstances. . . . . When the social condition has advanced so far as to exclude this kind of deduction, the second aspect presents itself; and the biological theory of man is implicated with the sociological in a less direct and special manner. The whole social evolution of the race must proceed in entire accordance with biological laws."*

The whole "theory of the organic state" which flourished so luxuriantly in Germany from Rohmer and Bluntschli to Schaeffle and his "Structure and Life of the Social Body," should probably be traced back to Comte directly or indirectly; and Spencer seemed about to follow him too. "Setting out then with this general principle, that the properties of the units [which it is the province of biology to treat] determine the properties of the aggregate," he also concludes

"that there must be a social science expressing the relations between the two, with as much definiteness as the nature of the phenomena permits;"

and that

"in every case [social science] has for its subject-matter the growth, development, structure and functions of the social aggregate, as brought about by the mutual actions of individuals."†

He is an individualist and endeavors to derive knowledge of social events from the individual and his nature. If this were possible sociology must be a higher order of biology, since we get our knowledge of the individual through the latter. But we may state here that the social communities are the sociological units or elements, and that it is not possible to ascertain their mutual relations from the properties of their constituent parts, i. e., from the properties of individuals. No one starting from the latter can

* Martineau, op. cit., Vol. ii, bk. vi, cap. iv; Comte, op. cit., Vol. iv, lec. 49; Rig., op. cit., Vol. ii, lec. 49.

†" The Study of Sociology," pp. 52, 53.

reach the nature of the group. Hence biological analogies are worthless in sociology except as illustrations.

Without saying so in words or even becoming clearly conscious of it, the English philosopher seems to have felt this. At least his scientific instincts have preserved him from such obvious exaggerations as others have made in consequence of false analogies between biology and sociology. Although he even affirmed such analogies in principle, he never based anything essential upon them, he never went so far but that the core of his sociology remained sound. Whenever he used biological terms, he treated them as similes rather than as analogies. Notice, for example, how he describes the peaceful differentiation of authority in a primitive horde:

" Setting out with an unorganized horde, including both sexes and all ages, let us ask," he says, " what must happen when some public question, as that of migration, or of defence against enemies, has to be decided. The assembled individuals will fall, more or less clearly, into two divisions. The elder, the stronger, and those whose sagacity and courage have been proved by experience, will form the smaller part, who carry on the discussion; while the larger part, formed of the young, the weak, and the undistinguished, will be listeners, who usually do no more than express from time to time assent or dissent. A further inference may safely be drawn. In the cluster of leading men there is sure to be one whose weight is greater than that of any other—some aged hunter, some distinguished warrior, some cunning medicine-man, who will have more than his individual share in forming the resolution finally acted upon. That is to say, the entire assemblage will resolve itself into three parts. To use a biological metaphor, there will, out of the general mass, be differentiated a nucleus and a nucleolus."*

The passage quoted is typical. Spencer uses biological principles only to a very limited extent in investigating sociological laws. Social facts and phenomena keep reminding him of similar biological facts, as is proper; but he always connects the two distinct species by a plain " similarly it happens," without identifying them at all. It is this quiet objectivity which makes him so superior to other sociologists. Schaeffle and Lilienfeld, for example, took these analogies seriously. They followed these will-o'-the-wisps over treacherous ground. But Spencer does not confuse the nature of social and organic phenomena for an instant, notwithstanding anything which the title "Society is an Organism" might imply.† Every fact presented as common

* Spencer, " Principles of Sociology," Vol. ii, sec. 464.

† Ibid., Vol. i, pt. ii, cap. ii.

to both classes of phenomena is so general that we may concede it without detracting from the lucidity of the thought. He finds that societies grow as truly as living organisms do; though this comparison holds only because we have but one expression (growth, *Wachstum*) for two ideas, organic growth and social enlargement. If there were a special expression for each there would be no temptation falsely to compare or identify them. Likewise, nothing but want of verbal precision makes it possible to say that both an organism and a society increase in "structure" at the same time that they increase in scope. The word "structure" is biological and should be only metaphorically applied to the development of social classes, departments of government, and the like. In that case, there would not appear to be any common quality. The same criticism is true of Spencer's third comparison, that both in an organism and in society, "progressive differentiation of structures is accompanied by progressive differentiation of functions."* The thought is perfectly clear, if we interpret the words according to the nature of the respective phenomena. His comparisons with biological processes, therefore, do not make our ideas of social processes less precise.

Although such comparisons are frequent the positive inductive method of natural science is not a mere phrase with Spencer. He really applies it in the domain of sociology; whereas Schaeffle and Lilienfeld, as we shall see, misled by biological analogies, deduce sociological laws from *a priori* biological laws, regardless of consequences. For the real subject-matter of sociology their method substituted a spurious organism from another domain of knowledge.†

But Spencer attacks social phenomena directly, examines them calmly, with no predilections whatever, and formulates his results in sound doctrines and general laws. His method is correct, but still his results were only partial. He could not cut loose from the unitary conception of mankind, the *fable convenue*, the old conventional assumption of all former

---

Ibid., sec. 216.

†In the chapters of Spencer's "Sociology," treating of "Social Structures," "Social Functions," "Systems of Organs," etc. (Part II), the phenomena of organic life are always presented first, then those from social life are described. But the two sorts are kept distinct. There is no confusion. If the reader should omit the biological similes, the presentation of the sociological phenomena would be all the clearer. In the works of Schaeffle and Lilienfeld the two sorts cannot be separated, for they are made identical. Consequently the description of the sociological phenomena suffers materially.

sociologists and philosophers, although often after a calm examination he is fairly compelled by the logic of facts to attribute the beginning of social development to the mutual effects of unlike (*heterogen*) ethnical elements. The "first internal cohesion" of "small hordes of primitive men" is due, he notes, to their "combined resistance to external foes." * Of the "rudiments of political organization," he says:

"While there exist only small, wandering, unorganized hordes, the conflicts of these with one another work no permanent changes of arrangement in them. But when there have arisen the definite chieftainships which frequent conflicts tend to initiate, and especially when the conflicts have ended in subjugations, there arise the rudiments of political organizations."†

And he adduces ethnological facts to illustrate every social phenomenon arising from the contact of social groups. But when he wishes to attribute phenomena to the mutual effects of the individuals of a group, he is forced to fall back on loose logical reasoning and biological similes. Had he appreciated this himself perhaps he would have given up attempting individualistic explanations and would have, from the beginning, accepted the plurality of human hordes as not susceptible of further sociological analysis.‡ But as it is, there is a perpetual contradiction throughout his sociological investigations. On the one hand he tacitly assumes a unitary mankind descended from a common origin; on the other, where he really explains social phenomena, he goes back to a "plurality of primitive hordes." As we have demonstrated in "*Der Rassenkampf*," the assumption of primitive plurality of human hordes is the only possible rational basis; the only one upon which all social phenomena can be satisfactorily explained. We have elsewhere made it sufficiently clear that this assumption does not contradict Darwin's theories.§ Primitive plurality is often the only

* "Principles of Sociology," sec. 250, *et seq.*

† *Ibid.*, sec. 11.

‡ Though Spencer does not affirm plurality of primitive hordes to be the first natural fact in sociology, he does note incidentally that "social evolution begins with small simple aggregates."—*Ibid.*, sec. 257.

§[A part of Section 14 of "*Der Rassenkampf*" reads as follows: "Darwinism is so fully occupied with the questions of evolution and natural selection that no opportunity is found to consider the question of single or plural descent carefully. Yet, not only must Darwin's theory assume one line, but, naturally and logically, it must admit a number of parallel lines of evolution. Otherwise it must be assumed that at the moment when organic cell life began there was only one cell from which the whole animal world has developed by successive changes. Such a silly assumption is foreign to Darwinism; indeed, it has been expressly emphasized that reference is made only to the 'original forms' under which existence began, and that the question whether there were one or more individual forms was considered unessential."]

possible explanation and we shall adopt it exclusively, thus sparing ourselves the vacillation between the unitary and the plural conceptions of mankind from which Spencer suffers. Had he followed it consistently, he could have still more easily applied his formula of evolution, of which we shall speak later, to the development of social phenomena. His universal law is so ill-adapted to the development of mankind as a unit that the insufficiency of this assumption is manifest at every step. Fortunately the importance of his work is not due to the formulas which he superposes upon the facts; but to his acute observations and his method of treating them. He has command of more material than any one save Bastian; and he is enough of a positivist to test its complicated mass objectively, calmly, without prejudice, drawing conclusions regardless of metaphysical prepossessions. This has made Spencer the real founder of sociology and he will long remain its most powerful champion. Next to him stands Bastian; his superior, perhaps, in knowledge and in calmness of observation, but less skillful in presenting scientific conclusions. But before turning to this phenomenal scholar and investigator, we wish to mention several other attempts at sociology.

Monism is the thought underlying all of them. They culminate in the endeavor to find a universal law for events in the whole domain of nature. They all fail to distinguish between universal and social laws, seeking to explain social events by universal laws—which is impossible. They revive the old dispute between spiritualists and materialists. The former attribute everything to the mind's efficiency; the latter, to the effective force of matter. The first grand attempt to explain all events, natural, human and social, by a single universal law of matter, was Holbach's " System of Nature." The author is a skillful reasoner; so we find the demonstration complete in every detail, showing how those two primordial forces, attraction and repulsion, not only sustain the heavenly bodies in their paths and regulate all life and motion on our planet, but also help to establish the relations between man and man and build up every social community. Indeed there would seem to be nothing that attraction and repulsion do not accomplish.* Molecules

* " The System of Nature or Laws of the Moral and Physical World," by Baron d'Holbach. A new and approved edition with notes by Diderot, translated by H. D. Robinson. Two volumes in one. Boston, 1877. Bk. i, cap. iv.

attract one another and bodies are formed; they repel one another and bodies are dissolved; by the process of accumulation plants and metals, animals and man are made;

"in short never to separate physical from moral laws—it is thus that men, mutually attracted to each other by their reciprocal wants, form those unions which we designate by the terms marriage, families, societies, friendships, connections."*

"In all the phenomena man presents," it is said, "from the moment he quits the womb of his mother, to that wherein he becomes the inhabitant of the silent tomb, he perceives nothing but a succession of necessary causes and effects, which are strictly conformable to those laws common to all the beings in nature. All his modes of action—all his sensations—all his ideas—every act of his will—every impulse he either gives or receives, are the necessary consequences of his own peculiar properties, and those which he finds in the various beings by whom he is moved. Everything he does—everything that passes within himself, are the effects of inert force—of self-gravitation—of the attractive or repulsive powers contained in his machine—of the tendency he has, in common with other beings, to his own individual preservation; in short, of that energy which is the common property of everything he beholds. Nature, in man, does nothing more than show, in a decided manner, what belongs to the peculiar nature by which he is distinguished from the beings of a different system or order." †

The idea of explaining all human and natural phenomena by the law of attraction and repulsion has repeatedly reappeared since Holbach's day; and we shall meet it again in Schaeffle.

Comte and Spencer, as we have seen, derived sociological laws from the less remote domain of biology. The "theory of the organic state," so-called, which was current in Germany for decades, was based on Comte's ideas until, finally, Schaeffle combined it with Holbach's thought. Everybody will acknowledge Schaeffle's great intellectual power and scholarly ability. But the fundamental thought of his system, the alleged analogy between the state and an animal organism, is baleful, and all must regret that talent and experience were spent in elaborating an idea so extravagant. It is impossible to go into the details of his comprehensive work here, and it must suffice to quote the leading thought in the author's own words:

"We have repeatedly observed that not only nature as a whole, but also the several organic and inorganic bodies in it, seem to be great societies or systems whose parts, in turn, are either simple or more or less composite. Then, according to what has preceded, attraction and

* *Ibid.*
† *Ibid.*

repulsion between the elements and the outside world would impart
motion to these atomic kingdoms.   Under such circumstances, can it
be a misinterpretation to assume that the social body, which is the
realm of persons and the most universal and spiritual realm of experience, cannot accomplish the ends of its existence without the manifestation of the same double force in each of its personal elements?
Some parts would appear to be centripetal in virtue of one force, while
others, obeying the other, would seem to assert their independence of
the whole.   But, as the units of the body-social are neither simple nor
irrational, we ought not to consider the two fundamental impulses
either simple or irrational; but we can and we must explain the total
life of the body-social as the product of the multiform, reciprocal
effects of all the active social elements, of all the subjects endowed
with volition, of all persons and institutional groups of persons in a
state of attraction and repulsion.   For ethical movement is not imparted to the body-social by anything outside; but we see it arise
within from the discharge of ethical forces between the constituent
parts, both individual and collective.'' *

This language, though not quite clear, is not the mystical
language of Kantian metaphysics, beneath which clear
thoughts lie, for the illustrations are inapt. Schaeffle analyzes
the '' body-social,'' but he leaves us in doubt whether this
mystical expression denotes mankind as a whole, or only as
a state or folk.   It is unclear and intangible as Quetelet's
'' society.''   The latter uses the ''great number '' to explain
his meaning; the former demonstrates that there are social
cells, tissues, bones, nerves, etc., which makes the matter
worse.   It needs a very lively imagination to connect
Schaeffle's lengthy excerpts from anatomy, physiology and
psychology with social phenomena and social development.
Sober reason turns in despair from the endless limping comparisons.   If they contain a kernel of truth derived from
experience and acute observation, as often happens, it is
tedious to find it in the confusion of metaphors and analogies.
Of Lilienfeld, we can, on the whole, say no more than has
been said of Schaeffle.   He has the same erudition and
equally great intellectual power and inventiveness; and he
displays the same degree of industry in executing a plan
which is fundamentally wrong and in defending a cause
which is lost from the start.
The fundamental thought of his ponderous work is
expressed in these words:

* Schaeffle, ''*Bau und Leben des Socialen Koerpers.*''   Tübingen, 1875. Vol. i, pt.
5, cap. 2, concerning ''the two principal kinds of effects of reciprocally acting
ethical forces, fellowship and self-dependence, love and hate.'' [The passage
quoted does not appear in the second edition.]

"There is only one way to make human society the subject-matter of a positive science. It must necessarily (?) be classed (!) among organic beings and regarded as an organism as much above man as man is above all other organisms in nature. On no other condition is it possible to treat human society inductively and to conceive of it as an inseparable part of nature. On no other condition can dogmatic social science become positive. But on this condition it obtains a basis as real as that of natural science."[*]

The reverse of all this is true. Social science can never "obtain a basis as real as that of natural science" until the fantastic view that "society" is an "organism" has been thrown overboard and all biological analogies have been cleared away.

Lilienfeld's query whether "social organisms do not obey the same laws as all other beings" must be emphatically answered in the negative. The distinction between social organisms and organic beings is something more than a simple "preponderance of the principle of adaptation in the former and of the principle of causality in the latter." They are distinct species of phenomena and different laws control them. Laws of organic development and laws of social development are *toto genere* unlike and ought not to be confounded. When Lilienfeld further inquires whether "in relation to us, the whole of mankind does not constitute an organic being uniting in itself all social groups and related to them as the whole is to its parts," we may be sure that we are confronted with a wretched scientific blunder. After mankind has been declared to be an "organic being," what can be expected from any further investigation?

Yet in the next chapter, on "Human Society as Real Being," he solemnly protests that he

"conceives the analogy to be something more than an allegorical parallel." "If we had considered all the current scientific and popular expressions which point to a relationship between natural and social phenomena to be mere rhetorical figures, we should have trodden in the footsteps of all the doctrinaires and metaphysicians; we should have been working over the same barren soil on which in the course of centuries so many capable natural scientists have sacrificed their powers with no sociological results save doubts and contradictions."

Nobly said. But it must be laid to his charge that in spite of all he was no more fortunate than they.

He seems to think that a metaphor can be made real by

[*] Paul von Lilienfeld. *"Gedanken ueber eine Socialwissenschaft der Zukunft."* Vol. i, p. 25.

"conceiving" it to be real. "We must win the conviction," he says, "that this or that social group, this or that
state, is a real living organism like every other in nature."
He expects a great deal of the reflecting reader. We have
not been able to win this conviction even after a most earnest
study of his five volumes. There are many true and deep
thoughts, but nothing to enforce this conviction. In one
place he trenchantly criticises "metapolitics, which is busied
with generalizing from allegories, i. e., from data that are
themselves once removed from reality." "Double non-
sense" he calls it. We frankly confess that between it and
his methods we see no difference. As of Schaeffle, so we
must say of Lilienfeld, that his work contains incidentally
admirable observations; but his elaborate system is built on
a false foundation and can be of small profit to science."*

All in all, de Roberty is right when he laments that, notwithstanding Schaeffle and Lilienfeld, "social science still
has its proper course to seek."† The period of progress,
since Comte clearly outlined the social problem, was only
one of incipiency, important though it be. Among other
errors of this period, de Roberty specially mentions "setting
the phantom light of general analogies to guide the science."
He recommends above all that the "natural history of
society" be made the basis of sociology, saying that on it
alone could an abstract social science be built, but his work
is occupied with the preparatory questions of methodology.
As propaedeutics of sociology it has fulfilled its mission;
he does not claim more for it. The task which he refers to
sociology, the construction of a science of "society," based
on its natural history, has since been undertaken with great
success by a German ethnographer, Bastian.

We have already called Bastian a phenomenal character.
He has done more for the "natural history of society," as
de Roberty called it, than all his predecessors together. The
scope of his labors is great and his plentitude of deep and
excellent thoughts is beyond any man's power to reckon
to-day. We can only make a few fragmentary observations

---

* Lilienfeld's first volume appeared in 1873 and Schaeffle's in 1875. Although the
latter knew of Lilienfeld's work before his own was published, it is our opinion
that the two systems were independently conceived. Without doubt, however,
both writers were influenced by the theory of the "organic" state then prevalent
in Germany and very forcibly stated in the popular works of Bluutschli and
Ahrens.

† "La Sociologie, Essai de Philosophie sociologique," by E. de Roberty. Paris,
1881.

upon them, being wholly unable suitably to exploit the sociological treasures he has stored up.

Bastian could never succeed in systematizing his knowledge; it was too great. ⌊Whenever he made the attempt, even in his early work on "Man in History," his system was broken down at its very inception and swept away by the flood tide of his information. Significant, however, is the thought contained in the sub-title to this work: "Contribution to a Psychological Conception of the World." It recurs in all his works, and is the great philosopher's pole-star on the immeasurable ocean of knowledge, his inspiration in all his labors.

Probably this thought dates from the time when "race-psychology" first flourished in Berlin. For in his preface he says:

"Psychology ought not to be limited as heretofore to individual self-observation and the pathological evidence afforded by schools and insane asylums. Man, as political animal, attains full development only in society. Mankind, than which there is no higher concept, must be made the starting point; mankind is the unitary whole in which the individual figures as an integral part."*

He searches "mankind" far and wide for manifestations of "thought." He considers his task to be psychological. His object is to disclose the soul of the races, which are the parts, and so finally to disclose the soul of mankind, the whole. In the later works, he calls these psychical manifestations "race-thoughts" (*Voelkergedanke*).

So he is really not a sociologist; he lays little or no stress on the process of social development. Still the material which he gathers from every nook and cranny to demonstrate "race-thoughts," illustrates social development also. Bastian wanted to be a race-psychologist; but the problem he set himself was falsely proposed and impossible, and the force of facts drove him into another course; he became an ethnographer and built up a system of ethnology.

Some passages may be cited to show his views. He is a realist from the first and occupies the only correct realistic ground, materialism and idealism combined.

"If so-called materialists have hitherto vainly attempted to construct new systems," says Bastian, "if they have been unable to satisfy public expectations and have found no surcease for that longing of the human heart which has always hovered over the earthly horizon

*"*Der Mensch in der Geschichte. Zur Begründung einer psychologischen Weltan-schauung*," by Adolf Bastian, Leipzig, 1860, Vol. i, p. x.

of all races like the promise of dawn, it was because they neglected
psychology, not knowing how to rescue it from the hands of dialectic
speculation and to claim it as their own province.   They opposed the
idealist on party lines, instead of drawing his objects also within the
sphere of scientific investigation.   True science recognizes neither
materialism nor idealism, for it includes both.   Psychology, 'race-
psychology,' based on ethnographical studies, had to wait until the
other natural sciences developed, because it must build on them.   But
now that the preliminary work is done, it joins them, proposing to
swing a bridge from the narrow circle of sense to the endless realm of
ideas."*

What, then, is his attitude toward the facts of the social
world ?

"No judicious investigator," he says, "will give further heed to
enthusiastic utopists and reformers.   As soon as we learn that recognition of the causes proves development to be according to law, we
accept whatever is as right, because it has become what it is.†"

He is equipped with all the requirements of true objective
science.   He wishes to "gather up evidence" and "collect
psychological statistics" in order "to acquaint the reader
with the course of thought peculiar to the various races of
mankind."   Unfortunately (or perhaps fortunately for the
future science) Bastian plans a task immeasurably greater
than he can manage.   His plan is nothing more nor less
than "to show by statistics that exactly the same number of
original psychological elements have coursed regularly
through the heads of all races in all ages of history."   A
quarter of a century has passed since this was written and
the tireless statistician of race-thoughts has never suspended
his labors.   That his mind is still fresh and clear is proof
of its extraordinary strength; for his "statistics" have
become impenetrable forests wherein ordinary mortals lose
their way and become bewildered.

Future science will be able some day to utilize his
labors and will find them invaluable.   But it seems to us
that the laws of the "regular" course of thought might
have been made intelligible at once if he had been a sociologist rather than a race-psychologist.   The fundamental
characteristic of Bastian's investigations is the endeavor to
attribute all social phenomena to human thought.   He
accumulates inexhaustible stores of social facts in order to
unriddle man's thoughts from them and then to discover the
thoughts, the soul, of the races.   With him thoughts are

* *Ibid.*, p. x.
† *Ibid.*, pp. xvii, xviii.

always primary and deeds are an emanation from them; thought arises only under the influence of external natural phenomena, and the social world emanates from thought. The scheme of his system is: (*a*) nature, (*b*) man and thought, (*c*) society and social thought. His scientific structure culminates in the latter; his ultimate object is race-psychology. In sociology the point of view and the object must be totally different. The social process must precede; the social fact is primary. Man disappears from the foreground of consideration since he receives his thought, his soul, from the social fact. Social thought, the concept of social facts, appears in the individual human mind only by reflection.

Hence, in distinction from Bastian's system, sociology includes: (*a*) social elements, swarms, hordes, groups, etc., (*b*) man, their product, both in body and mind, (*c*) the social process and its products, (*d*) the ethico-social products of the reciprocal action of society and the individual. The social phenomenon is always primary; the thought of the individual and the ethico-social products, such as religion, rights, morals, etc., are derived. An undigested remnant of idealism still troubles Bastian and he continues to be a pronounced individualist (atomist), *i. e.*, he uses the individual and his nature to explain the nature and development of the whole.

The first volume of his " Man in History," treats of psychology (*i. e.*, the psychology of the individual) as natural science;* the second is on psychology and mythology, and treats of the relation of the individual to nature; and the third is occupied with " political psychology," concluding with a description of society. But this does not seem to us the right method for sociology. It has had little success in political science and has fallen into disrepute as " idealism " and " atomism." Yet he even attributes " property," in the traditional way, to the primitive possessory act of the savage seizing the " fruit from the tree " to still his hunger, † and he adheres to the old idealistic phrase that property is " the necessary extension of the sphere of personality in society."

Likewise the state, to cite only one more example, is derived

---

*[" *Als Naturwissenschaft*," though a part of the title, is omitted by Professor Gumplowicz.]

† *Ibid.*, Vol. iii, p. 217.

from the family, which has gradually "become a race.*
But in the later works every suggestion of idealism and the
whole rationalistic theory of the state is omitted. He studies
the "natural history of society" more and more objectively
and finally gives the most striking expression to this tendency in a "system" of ethnology.

In the ethnographical works,† also, here and there in
masses of descriptive matter which is invaluable for its own
sake, reflections crop out that are not only the results of
acute observation and clear reasoning, but are besides really
epoch-making in social science. As example we will cite the
discussion of the "ethnological conception of descent and
relationship" in the introduction to his "Ethnological
Investigations," for we shall often have occasion to refer to
it in presenting social development.

The current use of the terms "native race" and "relationship" is criticised very sharply. It is shown that in the
nature of the case they are only relative. If we know any
of the circumstances at all our knowledge reaches back such
a little way that we can never use these words in their
rightful acceptation.

"When historical analysis is not able to go further the last race may
provisionally be called native. Although classical authors described
some races as earth-born autochthons which were not known to have
had an earlier dwelling-place, in general they applied the term regardless of historical considerations. Indeed some races called aboriginal
were notoriously immigrants, and were on that account connected with
the mountains in etymology."

No criticism could be more destructive of the Biblical
theory of descent underlying every system of political and
social science than that of Bastian. He shows that

"every race tries to find the 'first man,' as the redskins call him; the
ancestor of man, or father of the race. For, as examples from Asia,
Australia, America and elsewhere show, the name of the race always
coincides with the general name for man." "No difference of origin
is allowed for," he continues, "except that the former race is said to
have sprung from the ground, into which it withdrew again before
conquerors born of birds and wild animals; or, being the offspring of
trees and vines, was not adopted into the family of the proud heaven-
descended heroes. . . . In Grecian tradition Laos sprang from the
stones, and in German the Saxons from a rock. Assyrian traditions

---

* *Ibid.*, Vol. iii, p. 265.

† "*Voelker des oestlichen Asiens*," 1867; "*Ethnologische Forschungen*," 1872;
"*Rechtsverhaeltnisse der Voelker*," 1872, etc.

are revolutionary; the Lybian repeat the myth of the Moxos,* and in Scandinavian story the first-begotten were divided into classes. But since Christianity and Islamism made the Semitic legend preponderant over large portions of Europe and Asia all racial diversity is referred to the three patriarchs who survived the flood with their father.''

The passage is typical of Bastian's ability to upset false ideas. By citing notions that recur the world over, so as to show that they are only a form of human thought, he thoroughly destroys the delusion that they ever contained any truth.

Next to the Biblical explanation of man's origin nothing is so fatal to sociology as the false views of tribal descent and kinship. By correcting them Bastian rendered sociology another very great service.

"Kinship and descent, like so many other words, have a figurative as well as a real signification, whereas they ought to be employed in the inductive sciences as technical terms with one well-defined meaning. Descent from a common ancestor implies kinship, but kinship may also arise from a union of races and is therefore the broader term. Strictly, descent should be traced through a limited number of generations, beyond which it is preferable to speak of kinship. The limit might be somewhat extended where endogamic marriages are the rule, as among the Incas, Achimenides and Wanes, and in the aristocratic circles of certain mountain peoples. But this practice is extraordinarily rare, whereas the marriage regulations among the Australians, Chinese, Abipones and many others must lead to the incessant crossing of families; for the degrees of relationship within which they prohibit marriage are even remoter than those the pope once had much difficulty in enforcing in Bavaria. The term 'descent' should be avoided as much as possible in ethnology, unless one wants to grapple with the fruitless problem of ultimate origin. And yet many an historical clue is afforded by mythical traditions of descent, whether confined to the Teutons, as those given by Tacitus, or made to embrace a wider field, whether Celts, Scythians and Illyrians are grouped under one common ancestor or the equally incongruous Galla, Waknafi and Wakamba, whose languages even are unlike, under another; or whether Grecian eponyms are represented to be brothers, or genealogical tables are projected for the known and presumptively the whole world at once.'' †

"In general, the more definitely a particular locality is circumscribed the broader is the sense in which kinship may be used. The recurrence of the same *kabong*, or brotherhoods, throughout the whole Australian continent gives a clue to the general similarity of type which continual crossing produces among savages at the same time that it prevents individualities from becoming constant.''

*[The Moxos were a tribe of Bolivian Indians who believed that they originated on the spot, and who were restrained from migration by a superstitious fear of the mountains, rivers, etc.]

†" *Ethnologische Forschungen*,'' Vol. i, p. viii.

It is important to bear in mind how relative the ideas "kindred" and "autochthonous" are, but it is equally so to have an objective conception of race and stem.

"Nationality," says Bastian, "grows out of similarity of interests and views; it is furthered by religious and political union, and especially by the assimilation of language, and attains its greatest perfection within an area enclosed by natural boundaries."

According to Bastian, the earliest precursor of the nation is the race or stem, which is "earlier than the folk," since the "incorporation" of races "into folk is determined by political boundaries." Important also is Bastian's confirmation of the fact that "the most favored regions of civilization are those in which several streams of foreign immigration meet," which amounts to saying that civilization is promoted by their union. Admirable also is his explanation of how the resulting civilization or, what is nearly the same thing, how the "national type" is related to the local conditions, *i. e.*, to "the local ethnological type," to the "anthropological province," to use his own words.

"A great variety of inhabitants," he says, "may exist in every geographical province. The range of conditions within which life is possible is wide, and circumstances may cause very great differences to arise even between adjacent varieties. Hence the dispute over stability and mutability of races is, for the most part, factitious, for both views are supported by examples, but the conditions which produce them respectively are not accurately distinguished. How far the national type produced by one cause or another shall approximate to the ethnological or territorial type will depend on circumstances. A native stock, though capable of improvement in various ways, will never change much. Even if there should be an influx of strangers indigenous to another climate and permanent political changes should result, the influence of environment would still tend to mould the type into harmony with itself. But for centuries there might be a multiple series of transitional phases; and when growth finally ceased, the resultant type, while bearing the impress of historical and geographical environment, might differ widely from the autochthonous type, which was wholly or principally the product of the geographical province, as the modern Frenchman differs from the Gaul and the pre-Gallic Kelt, or the Spaniard from the Hispanian, etc."

But, by the "original autochthons" we must understand that he means the type which is the earliest that historical investigation can discover, not an absolutely "original" type. For, as Bastian emphatically declares of the "original representatives of the anthropological province of the Celebes," the Alfores, "our ignorance of any predecessors is not sufficient proof that there were none." This is the

only worthy conception of anthropological history, and
Bastian is consistent in contending that "questions of tribal
descent have no ethnological meaning, since in the course
of a few generations consanguineous relationships become
so extended and involved as to obliterate tribal lines."
So the "voluminous question whether the Slavs descended
from the Illyrians, the Sarmates or the Veneti," seems to
him "senseless;" but the point is to learn "the elements
composing the tribe" and the processes going on in it.
Hence, in summing up the task of this "ethnological"
science, he says: "In the ethnological treatment of nationality," by which, as we know, he understands an ethnical
composite,

"we must not divert attention into wrong channels by raising unjustifiable questions about descent and preventing insight into the
springs of life ; neither may we begin the investigation with an
arbitrary hypothesis,"

Biblical tradition, for example,

"but we must proceed from the given circumstances backward,
separating out the elements so long as we have a spark of historical
light left, or so long as collateral proof still serves to guide us through
the darkness of myth."

The outlines of the science thus incidentally sketched are
not the product of *a priori* deductions and philosophical
speculations. They developed part by part as he pondered
over enormous piles of ethnological material collected in the
study and on exploring expeditions. He was forced to proceed systematically. First of all, he had to make a critical
estimate of similar previous attempts; thus he compiled his
"History of Ethnology." Its logical successor, "Race-
thought and the Science of Man" was probably intended to
be introductory to a systematic outline; but the flood of facts
makes the forecast of a system impossible. Finally, in the
"General Principles of Ethnology," he is more successful,
as much so as is possible with his overflowing information.
These three late works* best show his epoch-making
importance in sociology.

Just as Comte assigns sociology a place after biology in
the hierarchy of the sciences since it is the youngest, the
future science so Bastian begins his "History of Ethnology"
by pointing out that this science occupies the last place in

*"*Die Vorgeschichte der Ethnologie*," 1880; "*Die Voelkergedanke im Aufbau einer
Wissenschaft vom Menschen*," 1881 ; "*Allgemeine Grundzuege der Ethnologie*,"
1884.

order of development.   This external coincidence of itself
suggests that perhaps both have the same thing in mind.

Indeed, Bastian calls ethnology the "science of man;"
which would also describe sociology.   But by ethnology he
means a science, or better, that science of man which takes
races * and not individuals for the subject-matter of its investigations.   A good portion of his scientific program is thus
comprised in the name.   This "science of man" is to consider the individual only as a member of an ethnical
group.   Its identification with sociology which considers
him as a member of a social group is almost complete.
Besides, hear what Bastian says of the present position of
ethnology:

"Some inductive natural sciences like botany and chemistry have
had a plain and definite field of observation before them; and though
they could not have arisen before the new epochal age of discoveries
dawned they have since developed systematically, rapidly and fully;
whereas ethnology, which as science of man should strive for ultimate
conclusions, was incapable of such rapid progress.   It had to wait
upon the others.   First induction must become fully established in
chemistry and physics.   Progressing from inorganic matter to organic,
it must reach the limits of the corporeal in physiology.   After that,
continually supplementing its gigantic powers by the comparative
method, it might venture to invade the mental realm, transforming
psychology into a natural science and analyzing race-thoughts in the
name of ethnology."

Thus the object of ethnology in Bastian's sense is the
discovery of race-thoughts, and the means is ethnography.
Hence Bastian sees the germs of ethnology in the first of
modern geographical discoveries, and its continuation in the
ethnographical and anthropological data of the nineteenth
century.   "Firm footing was first gained" with Adeling's
"Mithridates" and Blumenbach's works.   "After that the
development of the science was only a question of time."
It was strongly promoted by a treatise on "Ethnology and
the History of Primitive Ages" and by the founding of
ethnological museums.   Then Prichard, writing in a
"religious sense," "to prove the unity of mankind and
descent from one pair" gave the science its first handbook. †

* "The problem cannot be to find a 'God in history' until man has been found
there.   The first problem concerns man in his character of ζῶον πολίτικον, political
animal, in the social state ; whence it appears that the race-thought is primary and
that the thought of the individual is secondary, first becoming clear as an integral
part of the whole in the exchange of thought through language."—" Vorgeschichte,"
p. 25.

† "Die Vorgeschichte," p. 1, and passim.

Herder, Rousseau and others contributed by discussing the philosophy of history. Men like Auguste and Amadée Thierry hastened to adopt the new points of view. Interest grew and ethnological societies were founded in Paris and London and correspondence was opened with societies, journals and museums abroad. Bastian dwells on the significance of these steps, holding the energetic development of ethnological museums to be indispensable, a *conditio sine qua non* for his future science.

"With suitable museums not only will many practical ends be realized but especially the basis of induction will be strengthened, which will be a great advantage in psychology where theoretical studies first come in contact with the domain of philosophy."*

But he does not mean the psychology of Fries, Herbart, Beneke, Fichte, Schopenhauer, Ulrici, and Fischer; nor any "witch's concoction before which the philosophers stand dismayed," but the natural science of psychology. "In it lies our hope; so far as can be seen, the last hope of mankind."†

The essential characteristic of the future psychology, which he desires should go hand in hand with ethnology, is that it does not start from the individual man. For he "is nothing, at best an idiot; only through spoken intercourse in society does he become conscious of thought, is his nature realized. The thought of society, social thought, is the primary result and the thought of the individual is won by later analysis from it."‡ These words are golden and we shall accept them as the motto of sociology. Bastian aptly criticises the current psychology by saying that "systems of philosophy generally begin with the individual and have to patch social thought together out of the tatters that have come into their hands they know not how; whereas, if the social thought were looked upon as an unmutilated garment, each individual thought would be found woven into its right place." Then he unfolds his ethnological plan " to win from social thoughts sufficient material for psychological investigation." Not satisfied with the consideration of "the thought-structures, or thought-trees of civilized races only," he demands also the assistance of the "ethnology of the savage races," of those

* *Ibid.*, p. 79.
† *Ibid.*, p. 83.
‡ *Ibid.*, p. 79.

"cryptogamic structures, so to speak, in which the processes of cell-life and growth may be more easily observed, in order that the laws discovered in them may be applied to phanerogamic complexes." "The laws governing every organism are firmly fixed within it; even ethical laws are unchangeable. Everywhere in the five continents, we see thoughts springing forth, similar where the conditions are similar or varying with local differences. As the same principles regulate the processes of cell-life in the tropic palm and the arctic fir; as the same plant may have its leaves broad, curled, or dwarfed to needles according to its habitat ; as there are Asiatic, African and American varieties of the lion, so the pantheon of the Indian national mind differs from that of the Grecian and the Scandinavian."

"In all the psychological creations of society, whether religious, social or æsthetic, there are primitive elementary thoughts indisputably recurring and passing through the same course of development, often with truly startling identity, like ghostly doubles of distant acquaintances. The organic bond is so close that one with such sharp eyes as Cuvier had for fossils might reconstruct the whole circle of ideas from the torn fragments and accidental traces."*

Accordingly, Bastian proposes three specific ethnological problems. The first is

"to determine the elementary laws of growth in race and national thoughts; to get something which will do for these what the cell-theory does for plant-physiology. . . . . The second would be to study the local influences of environment, to which Buckle in his philosophy yields a preponderating importance. . . . . The last is the investigation of what might be compared to grafting or to cultivating ornamental plants by artificial means. It is chiefly concerned with races just beginning to develop a civilization, before they cross the threshold of history. All changes due to intercourse whether with friends or foes fall under this head; all such phenomena as were formerly supposed to be borrowed. For whenever similarity of ideas was discovered, historical hypotheses were immediately recast according to that principle; whereas, according to the psychological axioms of ethnology and the methods of comparative etymology, the explanation should be first sought in the most general and elementary laws. When there is no longer possibility of finding it in them, resort may be had to historical intercourse so far as it seems reasonably certain. . . . When the work is begun in earnest, ethnology will have to arrange its investigations according to these three points of view."†

Such is Bastian's ethnological method. In his " Race-thoughts " he worked zealously to prepare suitable material and to arrange it properly according to this plan. The methodological and propaedeutic hints of the " History " come out more clearly. Carping criticism might complain of the repetitions; but deeper insight discovers here a hard intellectual struggle from the darkness of intimation to the light of cognition—the severe birth-pangs of a new science.

* *Ibid.*, p. 89.
† *Ibid.*, pp. 90–91.

Properly rejecting theories ascribing "the preponderating influence to environment," he again lays it down as the problem of inductive ethnology,

"disregarding the somewhat superficial local phenomena for which an historical or geographical explanation must he sought later, to determine first of all and permanently the uniform laws of the growth of human race thoughts. It can he done most simply by the genetic method, starting with uncivilized peoples as the lowest and most transparent organisms. How development proceeds from such germs to the most exalted mental products, must be discovered by comparing parallel series of phenomena according to universal natural principles."

This is not mere repetition. Each thought is more fully developed and more clearly expressed. As he progresses he approaches nearer to sociology. He very properly hopes "by observing uncivilized races and gaining an insight into the human mind's processes of growth" to obtain a perfect key to its "higher stages," "even to its full development in civilized peoples."* It will not always be possible, however, for

"many primary ideas are so completely eliminated as civilization progresses that their relation to current ideas is lost and they have only an archaic value. . . But others   with their offshoots, still permeate modern conceptions."

He has really projected a complete science of sociology. Indeed in spite of his peculiar views, he penetrates right to its heart as we shall see.

" Of the many series of conceptions touching the most important interests of life, not a few," he says, " concern the condition of society when it is coincident with the state or when it is promiscuously stratified into ranks, castes, guilds, parishes, confederacies, etc. But before ethnology can expect to investigate, methodically and thoroughly, the ideas prevalent under such circumstances, it must first have comprehended the social organism within which they find expression."

This organism is the state;

"and all depends on investigating its structure and biology; for, considering man's immanent social nature, the question of its origin must be postponed temporarily before the fact of its existence. . . . Society, which, morphologically, leads up to family, tribe and state, and, biologically, to kin, race and nation, exists in greater or smaller proportion wherever man does; for the conception of man as a social being is real; hut the conception of him as an individual is abstract."

Thus Bastian stands fully on sociological ground; the involuntary course of his thought proves, better than any logical argument could, the intimate connection between his

* " *Voelkergedanke*," p. 17.

ethnology and our sociology. The former is nothing but the necessary basis, the latter is the crown of the ethnological structure.

So great is the power of thought over man, that often a mere accident is sufficient to awaken a whole system of ideas in the mind. Bastian scarcely graces the portals of sociology, whereupon they open as of themselves; and the whole complex mass of problems, overruns him. Once under the influence of the sociological idea he cannot escape a storm of perplexities and doubts. Suddenly he notices that " indefinite terminology leads to various misconceptions, as when 'race' (clan, lineage, band, etc.), is used for tribe and phyle ($\phi\acute{\upsilon}\lambda\eta$), curia and phratry, $\gamma\acute{\epsilon}\nu o\varsigma$ and gens, etc."* Suddenly he sees clearly what he did not see when he wrote "Man in History," that the "family, which is the substructure of the whole development under prevailing conditions, must be abandoned in ethnology," *i. e.*, in sociology.

"Since our idea of the family is abstracted from actual conditions, it is a particularly definite concept. . . . We have the schematic forms, family and race, and think of the latter as arising out of the former because a race can be analyzed into families; but an actual unit first (?) appears in the kindred."†

The adverb "first," seems objectionable here. Sociology does not "first" begin with the kindred or horde, but begins with it as first natural fact; for it is not and cannot be known what might have been earlier. He does not clearly understand how the state arises from the first "actual" or, as we should say, "ultimate" unit, nor what the process of transition is, for he says that "even in the kindred or phratry there are traces of a half-conscious interference, which suggest to some the social contract as the origin of the state; but the state should be attributed to $\phi\acute{\upsilon}\sigma\iota\varsigma$, to nature." He discards the social contract, as might be expected, and sets the kindred first, conceding the origin of the state from it problematically. But while emphasizing the natural origin of the state, he gives no clear account of the transitions from kindred to state, which we shall treat of later in the appropriate place. However, when once the state has arisen, he understands its changes perfectly, both

* We have discussed the ambiguous meaning of "race" in "*Das Philosophische Staatsrecht*," sec. 8, and in "*Der Rassenkampf*," pp. 186, 200 *et seq.*

† "*Voelkergedanke*," p. 21. We have expressed the same thought more than once, first in "*Das Philosophische Staatsrecht*," sec. 8, and then in "*Rechtsstaat und Socialismus*," sec. 29.

as ethnical conglomerates and as social growths.   By con-
trasting it with the kindred as the " actual unit," he points
out that the

"ideal state is never realized; for the boisterously, waking life of the
race-mind [better race minds] grows more boisterous still in the effort
to unify and nationalize the currents of ethnical feeling by force of
political authority."

In view of this deeper conception of the state, the ordinary
theory of political organizations and of political rights had
to be abandoned.*   When the Semitic sphere of knowledge
was added to the classical, theocracy was added to the chief
Aristotelian forms of government, kingdom or monarchy,
aristocracy, and city state (besides tyranny, oligarchy, and
democracy or ochlocracy).   But now that the whole globe
is subjected to observation there are so many modifications
to be noticed that the previous systems would be radically
transformed were the types arranged comparatively.
    Such reflections do not belong in ethnology.   Without
observing it, Bastian has reached social and political science.
Later, in his " Principles of Ethnology,"† he realizes it and
sets forth the relation between ethnology and sociology,
saying plainly that " ethnology, as ethnical sociology or
sociology under many ethnical forms, has to demonstrate
the physiological laws of the life of social organisms."   It is
in comparing savage races and civilized states that he
develops his most interesting ideas and proves the solidarity
of "race-thoughts."   But the comparison ought to be conducted sociologically and not ethnologically.   To obtain
positive results it is necessary to treat the natural communities as such.   As he says: " Within the ethnical horizon it
is the social organism and not its components that counts,"‡
be that organism the most or the least civilized race.

"The problems which agitate the life of the most highly developed
races should be apparent in embryonic form even among the lowest
savages; and since it is so much easier to note all the characteristic
points quickly and correctly in such small and transparent organisms,
they should help us to understand the more complicated wonders of
creation and to reduce legitimate data to law."

* Cf. "Philosophisches Staatsrecht," sec. 13, 14, where we discussed the unsatisfactory nature of this theory, which rests on a one-sided conception of the state.

† " Grundzuegen der Ethnologie," 1884.

‡ " Voelkergedanke," p. 71. See "Philosophisches Staatsrecht," sec. 7.

It would be impossible to comprehend the intellectual genesis of the "more complicated wonders of creation" without resorting to the "smallest organisms."

"While modern races, like crystals clear and polished and radiant with beauty, stand out in history in such definite proportions that scientific measurement is quite possible; in the ethnology of savage races, we deal with a chaotic seething mass* which, however, applying a chemical metaphor to race-thoughts, holds primary mental elements in solution."

These are what Bastian wants. To seek through the great variety of living forms for the earliest germinal stages of the "primary mental elements" and to watch them growing into "race-thoughts" is the task of his ethnology. He has a noble object before him and, with true and justifiable enthusiasm, he proclaims the way, and the grand visions that will meet the astonished eye when it is reached.

"After we know the law of development, it is possible to take a perfected product and trace the stages backwards to the starting point, the relative beginning. Many historical principles have thus been established. Microscopical analysis may proceed even to the cellular basis of ethnology, wherein reliable facts may be obtained concerning the conditions precedent to existence, concerning the enigma of being and becoming. Hitherto the investigation has been purely philosophical; hereafter psychological inductions will be used." "Diving into the stream of thought, we shall only raise the secrets of mysticism from the dark depths; but having the skeleton race-thoughts objectively before us, we can handle, measure and study them and, by sufficient analysis, reason back to the law of development in thought itself." †

This law should explain everything, but it can be learned only from the "primary elemental thoughts of savage races and the changes they undergo."

"In contrast with narrow ideas of history and the early efforts to attribute religious and social similarities to presumed intercourse in the past, the idea must arise, as the geographical horizon was extended and material increased, that the task of ethnology is to go back to the elementary laws of development in race-psychology; and then to make as much allowance for the admitted causes and only so much as topographical reasons require."‡

We have perhaps dwelt too long on Bastian's "History" and "Race-thoughts." Yet the fundamental sociological principles and methodological suggestions contained in them cannot be overvalued. These two works are positively

---

* [*Eine wuest und verworren gaehrende Mutterlauge.*]

† "*Voelkergedanke,*" p. 76.

‡ *Ibid.*, p. 119.

epoch-making in sociology. It might have been expected that he would have carried out his ideas in the " Principles of Ethnology," which soon appeared; it might have been expected that, after collecting material for thirty years and after preparing himself by such deep reflections on the character, problem and object of ethnology and "ethnical sociology," he would have given us finally an elaborate presentation of the science. But unfortunately he has not fulfilled this reasonable expectation. Our previous remark is confirmed. The abundance of the material interferes to prevent a clear and complete treatment of the " principles " of the science.

The most that the later work furnishes seems scanty beside the plan he projected in the two former. Not that the chapters seem deficient in form and matter; but six (!) chapters treating six topics do not comprise all the points which should at least be enumerated among the "principles" of the science. Bastian treats in succession (1) geographical provinces, incidentally touching on the question of the unity of the human race; (2) implements, the first vehicle of civilization; (3) property, the foundation of political order; (4) marriage; (5) rights, and (6) religion. But what of phenomena so essential to "ethnical sociology," as, slavery, sovereignty, state and society, political economy, commerce and the like? Where is there the least intimation of the social development in local centres of civilization ? The development of single institutions, like property, gives no idea of the development of human societies themselves, which in "ethnical sociology" is the most important thing. This is Bastian's weak point. He is so absorbed with minutiæ that he loses sight of the object as a whole. There is also another mistake, mathematical, it might be called. He states the sociological problem incorrectly, and consequently cannot obtain the correct solution. Starting " from one given point," which is falsely held to be the soul, he wants to explain the social development of human societies as the result of "thought." " In the beginning was the thought." " Thought " grows and develops; all phenomena are but variegated forms of thought, changing with time and circumstances.

Strange that Faust's misgivings did not warn him.

> " ' In the Beginning was the thought,'
> This first line let me weigh completely,
> Lest my impatient pen proceed too fleetly,
> It is the thought which works, creates, indeed?' "

Had he taken to heart the deep meaning of the poet's words :

> " ' In the Beginning was the act,' ' "*

he would have come closer to the sociological problem.

Much as he afterwards tried, he never succeeded in eradicating idealistic philosophy even from his latest works.   At bottom he is always a " race-psychologist," seeking the cause of all social phenomena in the " soul " of each race, but (we speak not as combating idealism with narrow materialism) do we not daily see that it is always the act which excites reflection ?   Does not the thought follow?   The act is produced by natural forces that have no connection with the soul.   Man acts according to natural law and thinks humanly afterwards, notwithstanding the approved maxim, " first think, then act," the worth of which for the individual we would never challenge.   But social development and the behavior of communities is another thing.   Blind natural forces prevail; there is no thought, no reflection, always an onward tendency following eternal laws and manifested in the form of acts.   Then the act creates the thought which the idealist refers to the " soul " of the actor as " motive " of the act.   As the acts arising from unitary natural laws are harmonious and regular, so are the thoughts; hence the law of the regular growth of " race-thoughts," Bastian's " race-psychology."   But we would not in the least depricate Bastian's services by these criticisms.   For perhaps no one human being has done so much for science as he, and we hope his services may long be continued.

We had to say of him that, finding so many trees, he fails to see the forest or, at least, does not let us see it.   Now we come to a younger writer, who manages his material masterfully and works the great array of scattered ethnological data into great mosaics.   Julius Lippert always presents the whole object in broad lines.

He began with a special department of sociology, comparative religion, and has advanced in fact, if not in name, to sociology in the best sense of the word.   His first two books, on " Soul Worship " and " Systems of Religion,"

* " Faust." Part I, Scene iii. Taylor's translation.

were thoroughly reviewed in "*Der Rassenkampf.*" Let us recall briefly that in them he clearly and convincingly establishes a universal law of the origin and development of religion, thus laying a totally new and a sociological foundation for its scientific study.[*]

Undisturbed by the ill-natured criticisms of the *Literarisches Centralblatt*, this very productive author has since enriched science, and especially sociology, by two valuable works: the "History of the Family," and the "General History of the Priesthood."[†] He possesses a high degree of talent for tracing the development of social or psychosocial institutions through the history of all races and ages. His history of the family is a model of sociological composition.

"Every man considers his family organization the normal human form and is prejudiced in favor of the writer who thus treats it. But that is not looking at history objectively."

he says significantly in beginning. Then after gratefully recognizing the services of Bachofen, the discoverer of "mother-right," and showing us the original mother-family, "organized upon the basis of mother-love," he goes on to show the rising "father-right" and the older father-family, "not resting on the principle of kinship or any consciousness of it, but on the principle of might, sovereignty and possession."[‡] Finally he shows the latest phase of development, the "younger father-family," "in which the terms father and son have come to imply consanguineous relationship."

He raised Bachofen's theory of mother-right, which several writers have since accepted, beyond all further doubt, adducing "rudiments in use and custom," and "allusions in myth and saga." In this way he threw much light upon primitive groups and the organization of human societies in which "stranger and enemy are synonymous terms" and "all are strangers who are not united by ties of blood or marriage to the same small organization."[§]

[*] "*Der Seelencult in seinen Beziehungen zur althebraischen Religion.*" Berlin, 1881 ; "*Die Religionen der Europaeischen Culturvoelker.*" Berlin, 1881.

[†] "*Die Geschichte der Familie,*" Stuttgart, 1884. "*Allgemeine Geschichte des Priesterthums,*" 2 vols., Berlin, 1883, 1884. [The scope of this work includes the study of both the priesthood and priestcraft.]

[‡] "*Geschichte der Familie,*" p. 5. We developed the same thought in "*Rechtsstaat und Socialismus,*" sec. 30.

[§] *Cf.* "*Rassenkampf,*" p. 195 *et seq.*, "*Rechtsstaat und Socialismus,*" sec. 19.

He discovers that there was a prehistoric variety of the family in Germany "later than the one with maternal succession," one in which the man is "lord of herds and slaves," "the woman belongs to the man as a part of his possessions" and "her children are his not simply if and because he begat them, but because the mother is his."* This "ancient family" goes hand in hand with a "developed system of slavery," for the latter "proceeds undeniably from rising father-right" in the older sense."†

He shows various stages intermediate between the older and the younger father-family.

"Whether the old union shall be preserved or dissolved into separate families, depends on occupation and property-relations largely; but eventually the question arises everywhere."‡

Later, we shall consider whether he has made it perfectly clear that the motives he alleges are sufficient to produce the change; but it must be recognized that he was the first, so far as we know, to prove that this is the course of development and to attach importance to it.   He was the first to call attention to the contrast between the older family and the younger one in which we live.   This is no ordinary service, for the problem was a difficult one.   "Have we any idea," he asks justly, "we who are wont to think that family relations are natural and have always existed, have we any idea by what tortuous, weary paths mankind reached this form of existence?"§ He has pointed them out with great clearness. The task of the future will be to investigate each stage of the long way in detail.

Lippert's third sociological problem, the priesthood, surpasses, if that were possible, both the others in scope and difficulty; for it is intimately connected with almost everything that is important sociologically.   The priesthood, as a body, has always and everywhere striven to control all spheres of social life ; so that its history necessarily involves consideration of the most important of them : religion, custom, rights, sovereignty, state and society, etc.   He did not shrink before the difficulties of the task but has produced a

* "*Geschichte der Familie*," p. 95.

† *Ibid.*, p. 141.

‡ *Ibid.*, p. 221.

§ *Ibid.*, p. 216.

significant sociological work which is a pioneer in several directions.

He starts with the same theory that the root of all religions is in " soul-worship " and that religious ceremonies are derived from religious conceptions.

" Especially is it a fact," he continues, " that the unseen is not thought of as a natural force, even when manifested in a natural effect ; but it is conceived to be a personal spirit analogous to the human soul. The savage is utterly unable to comprehend a natural force; but as soon as he begins to think logically every death suggests the idea of a personal spirit. It is only by grasping this fact firmly that we can see how religious observances, however complex, originate in human logic and how the unity of the latter explains the essential similarity of the former even to the remotest corners of the earth."*

This citation indicates the plan of the work and justifies the method of general treatment adopted. At bottom, Bastian's thought is the same; but his terms, race-soul and race-thought, are less clear than Lippert's plain " unity of human logic." Since human logic, when stimulated by one and the same fact, soul-worship, can not conceal its character even in the complex texture of religious observances, it must be universally demonstrable that the principle underlying them is unitary; and this Lippert has succeeded in doing by describing the life of the groups individually. For though soul-worship originated everywhere in the most primitive human logic, its development varied with the kind and degree of social life in each group. It would be impossible for us here to present the development of the priesthood in detail, the world over, as he does or discuss the purely sociological questions involved. But his view on the question fundamental to all sociology, the origin of political organizations, must be presented because it differs essentially from that which we have hitherto defended and upon which we base the present work. While we hold that every political organization, and hence every developing civilization, begins at the moment when one horde permanently subjects another; and while we do not hesitate to recognize that the most cruel and barbarous conquerors are the blind instruments of human progress and powerfully promote civilization, nay even found it; Lippert sees nothing but the victory of " barbarism " over "civilization " in the undeniable fact that states are founded by conquest. He holds

* "Geschichte des Priesterthums," p. 13.

that civilization begins and grows in "peaceful" companionship within the primitive horde, defending the view warmly and decrying the opposing view attributed to the "school-books." We are free to confess that his views enlist our sympathies; we would gladly accept them in preference to our own if we could be convinced of their truth. But we will reserve the discussion until later, simply citing some of his statements here.

"Mexican history," he says, "is full of tales of invasion, but in every case dominion fell to the rude sons of barbarism; not one of the conquering races, Toltecs, Chichimechs, and Aztecs in turn, brought civilization to the charming land of Anahuac. Rather, the old tragedy was oft repeated. The races which had been hundreds and perhaps thousands of years in rearing a civilization in their upland valleys are the 'good house-wives' of history, of whom nobody speaks. But the Bedouins, repeatedly breaking in from the wilderness of barbarism, often beaten off, but finally victorious, made civilized man with all his skill their slave, and they are praised as the creators of it all. In the school-books they are called the founders of civilization, as if they had brought it from the wilderness. The sympathizer with those quiet and ceaseless workers, the lineage of peace, must be satisfied if the object of his regard is not accused of the most profligate 'corruption' which a healthful breeze from the desert must needs blow away. Fortunately the conquerors do not always want to destroy all of it. They are ready to adopt the most serviceable parts and even to increase and extend them by the power of organization."*

Lippert makes no secret of the fact that his judgment is influenced by sympathy with the conquered; which makes his opinion the less objective. Moreover, he concedes to the "rude sons of barbarism," a "power of organization" sufficient to "increase and extend" the civilization of the "lineage of peace." We are thankful for both the confession and the concession. Later we shall have occasion to show that "power of organization" is an invaluable trait of the "rude sons of barbarism" and that the "lineage of peace," after being powerfully organized, will add not "sand upon sand" but block upon block, "to rear a civilization." But reserving the discussion, let us hear further evidence in support of his views.

Historians have generally followed Garcilasso de la Vega in dating the beginning of Peruvian civilization from the

* *Ibid.*, Vol. i, p. 288. [Lippert distinguishes between the nomads and the Bedouins. As characteristic of the latter, he mentions "changeable abode, irregular migration, constant search and strife for booty, and, what distinguishes this stage from the earlier, everything is looked upon as booty. No animal is wild and strong enough to escape; no treasure which another has stored away is safe; nor any fruit which another has cultivated; and the best booty of all is man himself." "*Culturgeschichte,*" Stuttgart, 1886, Vol. i, p. 152.]

time when the Incas conquered the ancient Peruvians and founded a kingdom. Lippert discards this conception and agrees with the views of the English traveler Hutchinson, who is "convinced from personal inspection that we are here dealing with a civilization that began long before the time of the Incas and progressed gradually." "This opinion will doubtless gain ground," says Lippert; and he believes himself justified in considering that the government of the Incas, as well as that of the Toltecs and Chichimecs, was "the dominion of an energetic conqueror over races that had already founded a settled civilization." This may be the case, however, without justifying Lippert's theory. Everywhere we see repeated instances of civilized states subjected by more or less "barbarous" conquerors; as China was by the Mongols and Roman Italy by the Goths and other German tribes. The Incas were not necessarily the first conquerors, the Anglo-Saxons, of Peru; they may have been its Normans. This argument alone is not sufficient to confirm Lippert's theory of the *generatio æquivoca*, the problematic genesis, of civilization.

Again, ancient Egypt is cited. "The historical events" seem to Lippert not "essentially different from those which welded the Peruvian state together." But they may be explained in more than one way and, it seems to us, justify Lippert's views less than the Peruvian and Mexican cases cited.

"As there the low country on the holy lake, so here the rich delta lands of the holy river between desert and wilderness first invited to permanent occupation. The races in the delta, pressed by the nomadic hordes to the border of the sea, had to sustain life in permanent settlements by provident labor; they subdued the waters and made the first stride toward civilization, learning to feel their higher human value in comparison with the barbarians."

Let us not forget that Lippert is here speaking of the "object" of his "sympathy:"

"We may assume," he continues, "that there was in antiquity a like number of small tribes leading a pastoral life and cultivating a piece of land incidentally, as many modern Africans do, yet never leaving a certain definite territory. The fertility of the inundated lands permitted such an arrangement and the 'red-land' of the desert remained the home of the nomads."

After this rather apodictic description of the settlement of the "lineage of peace" on the lowlands of the Nile, he goes on somewhat doubtfully:

"Naturally we do not know how the lowland races of antiquity became politically united. But the union might very well be due to the advance of the nomadic hordes which even to-day sweep over the plains and neighboring deserts. Certain it is that in historical times, as well as in prehistoric Mexico, tribes of higher civilization have been united politically under the sovereignty of tribes of younger civilization; among whom the tribes spreading over both plain and desert must doubtless be reckoned."*

However much we may sympathize with Lippert's theory, is this statement of the facts sufficient to convince us of its correctness? He is unable to explain "how the prehistoric lowland races became united politically." We should explain, though only by analogy from historical experience, that political union and organization were in all probability due to subjection by the "sons of barbarism." This is not a pleasant explanation either to Lippert or to us; but it seems to be the only correct one. We hold that sociological laws prevail unchanged whether we have historical evidence of the fact or not. Applying Lyell's geological method† to sociology, we should say that the "sovereignty" of the "rude sons of barbarism" was necessary to organize the "lineage of peace" and to cause the succeeding development of civilization. As Lippert concedes that he knows no explanation, he should not take it amiss when we say that his theory is simply an interpretation of the facts dictated by sympathy with one party and consequent antipathy toward the other. But we leave the question unsettled. It is possible that in some lands civilization arose from the subjection of one tribe to another and that in other lands it was autogenetic in the "lineage of peace." However, autogenesis is contrary to the experience of historical times and needs to be established beyond a doubt.

This indication of the contents of Lippert's work must suffice. It is not possible even to trace the course of his investigations into the development of the priesthood, much less to do justice to the many historical and sociological questions which he treats from new standpoints. He is master of the art of giving life and artistic shape to the sociological material which others have collected; with that we must stop.

* "*Priesterthum*," Vol. i, p. 380.

† *Cf.* "*Der Rassenkampf,*" pp. 172 *et seq.* [Lyell's "Principles of Geology" has the sub-title "An Attempt to Explain the Former Changes in the Earth's Surface by Reference to Causes now in Operation."]

Comte, Spencer, Bastian and Lippert are the leaders in sociology. What others have done is of secondary importance and will be mentioned incidentally as the discussion proceeds. But we must speak of several whole branches of science which concern sociology more or less intimately and co-operate to prepare the ground for it in various ways.

First in order are economics and politics, in which it was very difficult to get an adequate conception of society. What Mohl, Gneist and Stein did in this direction, we have duly commended elsewhere;* it is only necessary to recall that these scientists conceived society to be preponderantly economic. Especially Stein has only "economic" groups of men in mind though, to be sure, he is thinking of their relation to the state as political power "above society." This simple economic conception of society, partial as it is in view of social questions, pervades political economy so thoroughly as to make it in common speech the "social science." Carey's "Principles of Social Science," wherein he handles political economy simply, had the same effect. Baerenbach, in his bibliographical sketch of the "social sciences," treats political economists chiefly, noting their relation to the "social questions" in particular. Likewise Menger, discussing the "Method of the Social Sciences," treats the method of political economy alone, which he looks upon as pre-eminently, $\varkappa\alpha\tau$' $\dot{\varepsilon}\xi o\chi\dot{\eta}\nu$, the social science. In spite of this narrowness, the great sociological importance of political economy should not be overlooked. It was the first science that recognized that men's actions, which alone it considered, were controlled by economic laws. Seeing that the regular transitions from one economic phase to another were determined by external factors, political economists were forced to accept the idea of development in accordance with law. What is still more important, political economy had in the nature of the case to treat not individuals, who might evade every rule and law, but social groups: landlords, manufacturers, merchants, artisans, laborers, agriculturists, etc. So political economy became the best fitting school for sociology; and economic thought led the way to sociological thought.

The connection between political economy and sociology nowhere appears so prominently as in Carey's works. But this is due to this versatility. His field of view extends far

---

* "*Philosophisches Staatsrecht*," sec. 12; "*Rechtsstaat und Socialismus*," sec. 15–22, 28.

beyond the merely economic events of social life.   The man who defended the unity of science in Comte's sense and strove to demonstrate it in all the phenomena of life, could not be content to consider economic events exclusively.   He made very instructive digressions on various sociological matters.*   .

The socialists also were pioneers in sociology.   They pointed out that the relations between the laboring and the property classes, between large and small industries, etc., develop in conformity to law.†

Next to political economy, the science of comparative law has accumulated the most valuable sociological material and awakened the most fundamental ideas.   Since every domain of social life fashions its own rights, this science embraces the whole social order and every domain may be considered from its point of view.

Sporadic attempts at scientific comparison long since demonstrated that, among the most various peoples of ancient and modern times, similar rights rise and develop analogously to a degree that is inadequately explained by assuming historical relationship and transfer of ideas.   We have seen how Bastian protests and offers instead an explanation based on race-psychology.   In any event reflective comparison must suggest that rights develop according to law; and from this idea it is only a step to a "Natural Law" and a "Natural Science of Rights,"‡ as Post called his earliest writings.   In them he presented the physical idea that "the world's history is the unfolding of material forces by the specialization of universal types."   But as he worked at the problem incessantly year after year he emancipated himself from this idea so that, in another series of writings, he made a very objective compilation of interesting material for a comparative science of rights.§   The subtitles of these works are characteristic of the general course of his ideas.   While the first, in 1875 and 1876, were introductory contributions to a "universal comparative science of rights," he offers in

* "Principles of Social Science," Philadelphia, 1857–67, 3 vols.   *Cf.* Stoepel's introduction to the German translation of Carey's "Unity of Law."   Berlin, 1878.

† *Cf.* "*Rechtsstaat und Socialismus,*" bk. ii.

‡ "*Naturgeschichte des Rechts,*" 1867; "*Naturwissenschaft des Rechts,*" 1872.   *Cf.* "*Philosophisches Staatsrecht,*" p. 168 *et seq.*

§ "*Geschlechtsgenossenschaft der Urzeit,*" 1875.   "*Ursprung des Rechts,*" 1876; "*Anfang des Staats- und Rechtslebens,*" 1878 ; "*Bausteine fuer eine Allgemeine Rechtswissenschaft,*" 1880–81 ; "*Die Grundlage des Rechts und die Grundzuege seiner Entwickelungsgeschichte,*" 1884.

1880–81 material for a "comparative ethnological basis" for the science, and in his latest work, in 1884, attempts to construct "a universal science of rights on a sociological basis." Thus we see that from all sides, ethnology, political economy, and comparative law, scientific ideas tend toward sociology and help to establish it.

However, traces of his "physical" views of the science still appear. In most of his works he advances the idea of "species-organism," an order of structure higher than natural organisms. We can not accept any such idea, because there is no reality behind it; but we shall not dispute with him, as he uses the term less and less frequently and drops it altogether in his latest work.

With this correction, we can accept his views of the development of juridical and political life. "There are definite laws," he writes, "for the development of every organic structure within the human race and above individuals," for the development of human communities, we should say;

"and they can be discovered by comparing the corresponding periods of development of all the species-organisms which are living or have lived on the earth. It is the first task of the future political and juridical science to determine them."*

He distinguishes several phases in the history of the "species-organism," the first of which he calls a "kith and kin,"† or "peace" confederation.

"The most primitive form of organization in the life of the human species is the confederation of kith and kin, a number of men leagued together, on the basis of common blood, for (?) offence and defence."

This forcibly recalls the "social contract." We should substitute in its stead the simple "primitive horde" as the first natural recognizable fact. It is neither an "alliance," which implies a previous state or act of separation, nor an "offensive and defensive" alliance, which would imply a "social contract." Yet, with a slight correction, the "kith and kin" confederation might stand as the most primitive social formation, if Post's statement of its development into higher social forms could be accepted. But that is difficult, for he neither explains development nor shows on what it is based, but presents it as spontaneously following an inner law.

* "*Ursprung des Rechts*," p. 7.

† [*Geschlechtsgenossenschaft*=kith and kin confederation.]

"Every form of organization," he writes, "proceeds from this and can be traced back to it. The kith and kin confederation is the normal form of organization in hunting and nomadic races and by growth from within outward is often extended beyond the narrow circle originally included until it has become a system of tribes or a race with institutions considerably developed."

This is not clear. Such development never takes place by "growth from within outward." Besides Post takes no account of the motives and factors impelling it. "When the kith and kin confederation adopts a settled life its old constitution decays to a certain degree." * How it becomes settled does not worry him. "It takes place," "the confederation decays," he says, content that there is some "law" behind the changes. But such statements are unsatisfactory, to the sociologist at least. Although Post's services in the domain of juridical science must be recognized and although he has industriously collected suitable material and tirelessly incited to sociological investigations, his treatment of social development is not thorough; it shows that he has no clear idea of what social development is. Even his latest work on the "Basis of Rights and the History of their Development," though clearer and indicating progress in every direction, is still unsatisfactory on this point. We can overlook his old hobby, that "the human race, like every organic race on our planet, constitutes a biological organism;" † but we must reproach him for retaining, even in his latest work, the fundamentally false views of social development criticised above, especially as the literature of the subject ought to have helped him to make many corrections. He says, *e. g.*, that

"a number of individuals descended from a common parent or parents, affords a nucleus from which a tribe may arise. As the offspring grow up, the procreative process is continued and the tribe becomes a union of tribes. After a number of generations, we speak of a race, then of a people, then of allied peoples."

But what scientific proof does he offer? The same naïve idea underlies the Biblical story and leads with infallible logic back to Adam and Eve. Or is it a scientific explanation of development to say that "with the decay of common tribal life the mutual rights and duties of the individual members are differentiated," ‡ and that after the "gradual

* " *Ursprung des Rechts*," p. 11.
† " *Grundlagen und Grundzuege*," p. 16.
‡ *Ibid.*, p. 75.

decay of original universal common life,"* the "human individual by degrees becomes endowed with rights,"† which
"slowly develop in times of peace." ‡   These are simply
vague propositions about unclear ideas; consequently they
make nothing clear.§

But we must be grateful for the material which Post has
accumulated, in spite of its defective presentation.   He also
deserves full recognition for tirelessly disseminating the idea
of a "natural science of rights" of a "comparative ethnological science of rights," and finally of "social science."

He conceives the social problem quite in Bastian's sense
however.

"The great fundamental thought of modern social science is to discover
the essential nature of the human mind from what it has deposited in
the several domains of race-life.   Sociological jurisprudence searches
for the essential nature of the human juridical consciousness in what
it has deposited in the juridical views and institutions of all races of
the earth."

With Post as with Bastian, the "mind," "consciousness," is the primary, the world-moving principle, so to
speak, the object of all investigation ; and social phenomena
are only means of exploring this inmost cause of all that
happens.   We shall soon have opportunity to demonstrate
our own view that what happens of natural necessity is
primary and emits "mind" as flowers do   fragrance.
"Juridical institutions" are not the deposit of juridical
consciousness.   On the contrary, the latter is deposited
from the former.   History begets the mind, not the mind
history.

Political economy and the comparative study of rights and
religion concern particular domains of social life and hence
anticipate parts only of sociology.   There are other branches
of philosophy, however, which have treated the supreme
problem of sociology itself, or at least its most important
principle, though not under that name.

Here we will mention only the philosophy of history.   It
treats of the historical development of mankind; its object
is to seek the "philosophical idea."   It is clear how close

---

* *Ibid.*, p. 76.
† *Ibid.*, p. 83.
‡ *Ibid.*, p. 87.
§ This sentence might also be cited : "Nevertheless, as the tribal state
gradually develops, differences of rank also appear." *Ibid.*, p. 102. If everything
developed gradually without our needing to know why and how, we should be
done with sociology at once.

it approaches to the supreme problem of sociology; and the
sociological importance of its literature is apparent at once.

Pretty much everything written on this subject before
1876 is summed up in R. Rocholl's prize essay. Rocholl
has mastered the art of letting all the philosophers of the
world speak through him, while he betrays not a single
original thought to the acutest reader. A whole volume,
and nothing original ! He understands how prizes are won.
Whoever is curious to see all that philosophers would
interpret into the history of mankind should read this book.
It makes the reader dizzy; or, he thinks that Rocholl is
exhibiting a fools' gallery. In fact, the philosophy of history
was an untimely birth. The ''idea in human history''
was spoken of before anyone half understood what human
history was. For, what is the bit of Mediterranean history
compared with all the actual history of man on this planet
which the philosophers knew nothing about? How childish
any opinion of the whole when they knew only the least
part!

Yet the stimulus of their sociological ideas is considerable.
The most important difference between sociology and the
philosophy of history is that the latter would deliver an
opinion on a whole which it did not know; whereas sociology,
being aware that the whole can never be known, will judge
only of a process which is the same here and everywhere,
which transpires in the same way to-day before our eyes as
it transpired thousands of years ago. Sociology declines in
advance to interpret the whence and the whither and the
wherefore. This is its claim to decided pre-eminence over
the philosophy of history, from the ill success of which it
learns valuable lessons.

The transition from philosophy of history to sociology
was more direct in France than elsewhere. In Germany
the so-called history of civilization intervened. The history
of human civilization from its beginning to the present day
is almost, at least might easily become, sociology. Kolb,
Henne am Rhyn, and especially Hellwald, have accomplished much in this field, correcting many things that the
philosophers had spoiled. They introduced a wholesome
soberness into the conception of human development. The
indefatigable Hellwald makes use of all sorts of anthropological and ethnological material, extending the horizon of
the history of civilization even to the ultimate beginning of

prehistoric time. The investigations of Lubbock, Tylor and Caspari in this field are especially helpful; and in anthropology and ethnology Waitz-Gerland, Perty and Peschel have contributed their share of valuable sociological material.

Thus, there is no lack of sociological material, and Comte, Spencer, Bastian and Lippert have imparted the breath of life to sociology; may it never lack for disciples to labor in it and cherish it unremittingly.*

* [For a sketch of the sociological writings of Gustave le Bon, see Appendix A.]

II. FUNDAMENTAL CONCEPTIONS.

1. THE THREE CLASSES OF PHENOMENA.

It is an old saying that division and classification are means to knowledge. The more appropriate the means, the greater is the profit that may be expected from their use. To this end that which has been characterized as the "world of phenomena," all the phenomena that surround us, has been repeatedly classified. But with increasing knowledge, the plan of classification has to be changed; deeper and deeper grounds of division are discovered, approximating nearer and nearer to the very essence of the phenomena. A superficial examination served to distinguish animate from inanimate nature. According to another very common classification, the phenomena that were perceived by the organs of sense were put in one class and those that were perceived by the mental faculties were put in another; the former were called material, the latter mental phenomena.

As knowledge advanced, inanimate nature was divided into inorganic and organic. Then another class, composed of phenomena which were referred to the soul of man as source, was co-ordinated with the organic and characterized as psychic. Thus three classes, inorganic, organic, and psychic,* were obtained. It is apparent from the terminology itself what phenomena are included under each class; and it is just as clear that this classification is intimately connected with a given stage of human knowledge, with the knowledge of the distinction between inorganic and organic matter. It seemed desirable not to call organic matter simply "inanimate;" for the inorganic inanimate had to be distinguished. But there was also a growing conviction that all of man's actions, his whole behavior, at least all the phenomena affected by him, have their basis in a soul (*psyche*) which is found in man and is peculiar to him. If convictions change on this point, if it is discovered that there is no such soul, that man's thoughts, and the whole

---

* To cite one example among thousands, Ruemelin in his essay on the "Laws of History" ("*Reden und Aufsaetze*," *neue Folge*, p. 118) speaks of the "phenomena of inanimate nature, of the organic and of the psychic world." We shall recur to this essay later in another connection.

of his so-called spiritual life, is only a manifestation of the physiological functions of his organism, that basis of classification will be dropped; the psychic phenomena will be included with the organic.

Thus classification is a means of promoting knowledge; and knowledge acquired is, in turn, the basis of new and more accurate classifications. But it often happens that phenomena are forced upon our attention which we cannot immediately identify with any class hitherto known; we are not sure how to classify them. In such cases, we include them in some class already constituted, in spite of the differences, or we make a sub-class for them; or, finally, having found some characteristic which is peculiar to them, we proceed to constitute a totally new class. A recent instance is furnished by the " social " phenomena. It was observed that they differed from other phenomena; there were many reasons why they should be recognized as a special class. But nobody knew exactly what to do with them. They could not be included with either the organic or the inorganic; they presented the characteristics of neither the animate nor the inanimate; they did not seem to be purely psychic, for they did not emanate from the individual soul; indeed they appeared to sweep whole aggregates of men, in spite of will and consciousness, along with them. So they presented a problem of classification, the solution of which was attempted in various ways.

It was perceived that especially those phenomena which are manifested in the state, political revolutions, party conflicts, political endeavors, etc., are social. Some attempted to class them all with " organic " phenomena. It is really so comfortable in old quarters, where everything is familiar, that people will cramp themselves a little, if necessary, in order to avoid the trouble of moving! Hence arose the " organic " theory of the state. Schaeffle has shown that all the so-called social phenomena are in reality nothing but " organic functions of the social body," which has cells, tissue, nerve, muscle, flesh, bones and blood, just like every animal organism. There are still people, not only in Germany but in France, who accept this literally; we do not.

There were others who were less imaginative and more reflective, yet abhorred the overthrow of old and familiar arrangements no less than the former. They represented that everything that takes place in connection with the state

is manifestly done by man—for who else could do it? But
whatever man does issues from the soul within him. Hence
social phenomena are psychic. To be sure, a social occurrence is different from an individual thought or feeling. But
the difference can be disposed of by making a sub-class,
"psychic" is "psychic." Thus that estimable scholar,
Ruemelin (again from many examples citing the one we
have first at hand), treats social phenomena as psychic and
"social laws as a special kind of psychic" laws.*

But we can no more consent to subordinate social phenomena under the psychic than we can to reckon them as
organic. Rather it seems to us proper to divide the phenomena which we perceive into three classes: physical,
mental and social.

We classify social phenomena apart from all others
because the ends of scientific investigation will be best served
by treating them separately. They constitute a unique
group, distinguished by several fundamental traits.

It is certain that they cannot be perceived by the senses,
and there was thus much reason for reckoning them with
mental phenomena. But social phenomena happen only
through the co-operation of a number of men, of an aggregate; whereas mental phenomena, strictly so-called, are
inseparable from the mind of the individual. They originate
in it and are limited to it. Thus all conditions of the soul,
all scientific activity and each artistic manifestation of the
human mind, all works in art and science—so far as the
mind perceives them, all thoughts and ideas which, issuing
from the human mind, are perceived by the mind, are
mental phenomena. But all relations of men with one
another, all their economic, political and juridical relations,
for example, are social. A number or aggregate of men is
their distinguishing trait. It is not necessarily present in
mental phenomena in the real sense, but without it a social
phenomenon is unthinkable.

As the classification of phenomena is only an aid to
knowledge, and as the world which envelops us is strictly
one and unitary, so, it is conceived, there is only one
science. For, as we have shown elsewhere, † the object of
science is to discover the laws that control the sequence and

* "Ueber sociale Gesetze," in the Tuebinger Zeitschrift für die gesammten Staats-
wissenschaften, 1868, pp. 134, 118.
† "Philosophisches Staatsrecht." Vienna, 1887, sec. 1. "Rechtsstaat und Socialismus." Innsbruck, 1881. Part i, sec. 1.

the development of phenomena.   Yet the division of science into parts devoted to particular classes of phenomena is common and has been recognized as proper.   It satisfies the need of a division of scientific labor.   The division into "natural" sciences and "mental" (or moral or ethico-political) sciences is the best known and the most usual.   It is parallel with the classification of phenomena as physical and mental.

The natural sciences dealt with the phenomena of organic and inorganic nature and with the physical laws governing them.   The mental sciences sought for the laws controlling the human mind.   Then, when Comte and Quetelet classified social phenomena apart for scientific study and asserted that they too were controlled by fixed laws, the question of defining social laws arose.   It was not easy to explain what they were.   Yet, if there is a science of social phenomena, if there is such a thing as sociology, we must be able to give a clear positive definition of social laws.

In order to define them we must recall what a natural law is.   Applying our idea of a natural law in general to social phenomena, we shall get an idea of what a social natural law, or, briefly, a social law is in the abstract.   Finally, we shall test the objections commonly raised to the existence of social laws.   If they can be refuted we may enter the domain of social science.   For to this we must hold fast: without social laws there can be no social science.

When we find the same phenomena time and again occurring together or in the same order, we say that it is due to a law.   Obviously, we are using an analogy.   When an act of legislation directs how a thing shall be done, it is uniformly done in the prescribed way.   When, in nature, we see a phenomenon repeatedly occurring in the same form, we conceive that it is the result of some higher will incorporated in a "law," and we speak of the law of the phenomena without hesitation.   We thus acquire for a series of phenomena an easily intelligible expression, a simple formula.*

The question then arises: Can such laws be stated for social phenomena also; in a word, are there social laws? We ought to answer in the affirmative if there are social phenomena which constantly occur together or in the same order, so that we may ascribe them to an hypothetical higher will, to a "law," as we do physical phenomena.   That the

* Mill, "System of Logic," Bk. iii, cap. iv.

mutual deportment of social groups, the formation of social communities, their development and their decay so occur, history and experience prove undeniably.   Hence, we may direct investigation in the social domain with a view to formulating the social laws of those phenomena.

.This matter is so simple and self-evident that there would seem to be no need of wasting any more words over it. But, unfortunately, it is not acknowledged by everybody. The formulation of social laws, *i. e.*, natural laws of social development, is violently opposed by some who are anxious to maintain man's free-will in its integrity.   For it is feared that a death-blow would be dealt it, if natural laws of social development were generally accepted.

The struggle between these two principles, whether to apply natural law or free-will to social phenomena, is well portrayed by Ruemelin's experience.   His candor deserves special recognition.   In his earlier years this scholar was inclined to accept natural law in social phenomena which, as we have seen, he made a sub-class of the psychic.   He expressed this view in an academic discourse ''On the Concept of Social Law '' * in 1868.   After defining natural law in general to be ''an elementary expression for the uniform behavior of force in each and every case,'' he questioned ''whether this idea of law which is taken originally from the processes of inanimate nature is also applicable to the processes of animate nature,'' and answered in the affirmative, though with no great assurance.

'' As a result, we have found three kinds of forces,'' he said, '' physical, organic and psychic; no other kind can be conceived co-ordinate with them.   Social phenomena are a sub-class of the psychic.   There are two kinds of psychic phenomena, the psychological and the social.''

He seems to concede almost without reserve that the phenomena of political economy are social.   Since this science '' starts, expressly or tacitly, with the hypothesis that man has a strong inclination to supply himself plentifully and at the least possible cost with the means of satisfying his desires,'' it '' seems quite proper that the fundamental propositions concerning competition, the movements of prices and wages, and the circulation of money should be called laws.   They fulfill the requirements exactly. They indicate the elementary and uniform behavior of psychic forces in a mass '' or aggregate.

As to whether the so-called statistical laws should be recognized as social, Ruemelin has serious doubts.

* "*Ueber den Begriff eines socialen Gesetzes.*"   *Tuebinger Zeitschrift*, 1868.

" Psychology," he argues, "considers the psychic forces observable on typical individuals to be characteristic of the class ; social science observes the same forces operating in aggregates of individuals and notices the changes thus produced. Hence social laws should express in elementary form the behavior of psychic forces in aggregates."

But he is not certain that statistical laws satisfy these conditions. Some weighty objections prevent him from recognizing that everything proclaimed by the statisticians to be law is social; and he is right perhaps. He sees in the reasoning of the statistician, Quetelet, especially, "significant truths and serious misunderstandings compactly woven together;" and in that, too, we will agree with him. He closes his "Search for Social Laws" unsatisfied. "The return was not great." But that is no occasion of reproach. "The youngest sciences are always the hardest," so he comforts the sociologists. "They treat problems that others had quite overlooked or had not the means to grapple with." He has the "highest opinion of the future of statistics, of the scientific value of a methodical observation of facts, if continued and developed." In short, he does not give up hope that real social laws may thereby be discovered, though he does not conceal his misgivings. This was in 1868.

Ten years later he spoke again on the "laws of history," and described the observations he had made in the meanwhile. The riper scholar's disappointment is undisguised. The hopes he had cherished a decade before had been completely dissipated. The serious doubts he had entertained had been fully verified.

"I thought that there must be" social laws, he says almost sadly, "and that statistics would be especially helpful in discovering them. I have had the task constantly in mind for many years ; I have sought for them not simply in statistics and in the theory of society, but in history and in philosophy too. I have fallen upon numerous cases of uniformity, upon rules of experience of comprehensive import, upon positive causal connections ; but never upon any thing answering to the formula for a law, never upon proposition expressing the elementary, uniform behavior of psychic forces in an aggregate."

Then he explains why his search was futile. He is "inclined" to believe "that the problem was not properly stated and that what he sought is not susceptible of being found." The ultimate cause of failure he discovers in the fact that "physical and psychic phenomena differ from one another even as incomparable quantities."

"Between material existence and motion in space on the one hand, and feeling, thought and volition on the other, there is a chasm which cannot be filled and has not yet been bridged." Hence, "it would be strange if one and the same concept of law were applicable to both."

Thus we see Ruemelin coming again in his later years full sail into the sea of dualism; and it ought not to seem remarkable that, in following out the fundamental opposition between mind and matter, he should dispute the possibility of law in the province of the former since "man's free-will" prevails there. Then come the old arguments on the old theme.

"Whoever denies freedom of the will is bound to show natural laws determining will and excluding choice. It is said by some, for example, that the strongest motive must of necessity determine the human will. If this were something more than worthless tautology(?); if it were only explained what beside the will could make a motive the strongest!"

Strange prepossession! Why should not external circumstances make a motive the strongest? and how can a *deus ex machina* named "will" strengthen a motive, *i. e.*, an external factor? The external factor works with the force inhering in it in the given conditions as the steam does in the locomotive. Must the will still mediate that the force of the steam may overcome the force of inertia? No more in the case of man is this putative mediation and assistance of will necessary to strengthen a motive which is in and of itself the stronger already. Man differs from the locomotive only in having consciousness, *i. e.*, an inner sense which, like an inner eye, sees the internal processes, becomes conscious of them, observes the conflict of motives, and the victory of the stronger. In common experience this perception is mistaken for free-will; the coming consciousness of the overbalance of the stronger motive, for the act of choice. All this was long since known; but it will not for a long time yet convert the adherents of dualism and free-will. The force of mental inertia and conservatism cannot be so easily overcome.

Those who persistently maintain the dualism of mind and matter cannot possibly accept social laws in the sense of natural laws of social development. Hence Ruemelin is thoroughly self-consistent in discarding them and every "law of history," too. He is perfectly logical when he says:

"I must characterize the theory as self-contradictory and incomprehensible which imputes to the individual human soul freedom of the will, in the sense of rational or irrational self-determination within the broad scope of given natural conditions(?), while necessity is recognized in the history of mankind or of single ages and peoples. Psychological indeterminism and historical indeterminism stand and fall together . . . If the complex aggregate of social relations into which I have been put determines all my thinking and doing or allows me only the narrowest scope of individual independence, it is of no use to discuss freedom and accountability further. But if I am able of myself to initiate new series of operations, to mould and assert myself in spite of the opinions and usages of others, then no logic can prevent a community as a whole from acting freely and striking into paths which have no causal connection with the past. Necessity will then signify no more than the universal limits of human activity, will be restricted to the unavoidable influence of the community on the individual.''

Persistence in the traditional dualistic view is also largely due to the mistaken idea that '' the necessity of natural law '' would negative '' conscience '' and all rational activity.

'' Or we are told,'' says Ruemelin, further, ''that the will is determined by necessity, being the product of two factors: the concrete circumstances and the individual character, which is itself the product of inherited faculties, training and course of life. If conscience and reason are included among the inherited faculties and it is conceded that they co-operate in their way in the act of willing, the answer may be accepted. But then it is merely a quarrel about words to speak of the deterministic character of natural law and the necessity of willing.''

As if reason and mental effort could not be, were not actually the product of natural processes! As if we could not speak of the natural development of reason, mental effort and will, i. e., of mental effort the product of motives!

After traversing such errors, Ruemelin reaches the principle which, as a true dualist, he believes he has '' established,'' viz.: '' that psychological and physical laws are wholly different in form and nature and cannot be expressed by the same formula.''

As has been said, the logic is correct; but the premise, free-will and self-determination, is false. Possibly Ruemelin is justified in saying that the constraint exercised by society upon the individual has not yet been demonstrated to him by obvious proofs.

'' I cannot convince myself,'' he says, '' that investigation into the relations between society and the individual has ever led a single step beyond showing an intimate and universal reciprocation of influences, in which each is giving or receiving, active or passive, all the time, in varying degrees.''

But insufficient proof does not alter the fact of unfree-will; and it would better have become a philosopher to take the matter in hand himself than to assume the attitude of defence by throwing the burden of proof on others.

Had Ruemelin done so without prejudice (his dualism greatly embarrassed him), he would have given up the false premise of free-will and all that it entails; and he would not have discoursed at length on the way men of genius make the world's history. Such things should never have been said at this late day in a German university, and by a lay professor. The standpoint which he occupies is purely and simply theological.

Dualism of mind and matter is a fundamental principle of religion. Religion is a necessity to the masses; their temperament demands it. So free-will and self-determination, the necessary consequences of dualism, are integral components of every religious system; and we have no thought of combating them here. Moreover modern philosophy and modern natural science have spared us the trouble of establishing monism, which is as correct and true as, for the temperament of most men, dualism is necessary. We are not writing for this majority. They may leave our book unread. We turn to the adherents of monism; our problem is to work out its consequences in the social domain.

2. UNIVERSAL LAWS.

Modern natural science has successfully demonstrated that even the "human mind" is subject to physical laws; that the phenomena of the individual mind are emanations from matter. But in the domain of social phenomena unchangeable natural laws have not been completely demonstrated. Between "mental" phenomena subject to the laws of matter, and the social world strode the conception of human freedom to distract and confuse. It seemed to order and control social relations according to its own choice. In the domain of mental phenomena, in the narrower sense of the word, monistic natural science has in part demonstrated the unconditional sway of natural laws and in part shown the presence of other factors to be impossible. Dualism, driven from this domain, has retired to the domain of social phenomena, whence it must be dislodged. To this task the distinction which we have drawn between mental and social phenomena is essential; for it is an old rule of strategy to

divide the enemy and grapple with the scattered sections
separately.   The critical question concerning monism is the
existence of universal laws valid for social as well as for
physical and mental phenomena.   If such laws exist, the
monistic theory is true; if such laws cannot be discovered,
monism is an unproven hypothesis, like dualism.

As we have seen, their existence is hotly denied; and
doubtless the earliest defenders of monism in the domain of
social phenomena gave occasion for the denial.   For with
great zeal and less discretion some thought it simply necessary to transfer to the domain of social phenomena the laws
that had been discovered in the domain of physical phenomena, the laws of attraction and repulsion, of gravitation
and the like.   Others seemed to see in the shapes which
social phenomena assumed structures similar to animal
organisms and they thought that the laws valid for the
latter might be accepted as valid for the former also.   We
have already pointed out the impropriety of these assump-
tions and we shall criticise them more in detail hereafter.

But in spite of such errors, there are universal laws which
prevail alike in the physical, the mental and the social
domain; and the existence of the science of sociology can be
justified only by proving their existence and validity.

Before calling attention to some of them, we must answer
another question: How far, in general, can we expect to find
laws common to phenomena so unlike as physical, mental
and social phenomena are?   Plainly we ought not to go too
deeply into the characteristics of the species; for where the
peculiarities begin the common traits end.   Where the
physical nature commences the laws common to the mental
and social domain cease to apply.

Of course it may be objected that the universal laws will
be taken from such a high sphere of abstraction that every
idea beyond the concept of mere existence will have been
sacrificed.   Such laws, though easily found, would lack
significance; and we shall try to find our universal laws
close to where the three classes of phenomena become differentiated, in the sphere of the modalities of existence.   Having found them here, we shall consider our task complete.
It was the great error of our predecessors that they sought
universal laws in the lowest sphere of one class alone, even
among the differentiated physical phenomena.   We ought
not to commit the same error; we must not seek to generalize

the physical laws of organic life and extend them to the domains of psychic and social phenomena as they did. But we may and indeed must discover the universal laws of the modalities of existence of all being. We must be satisfied to possess in them the keys which, to use Bastian's expression, "unlock in all directions."

Let us now proceed to give examples of such universal laws.

(a) The Law of Causation.

The law of causation is just as true of social as it is of physical and mental phenomena. Every social phenomenon is the necessary effect of anterior causes. No social phenomenon originates in the nothingness of individual whims. The principle of sufficient cause is true also. Every social phenomenon whether political, juridical or economic, must have a sufficient cause in one or more social agencies. The effects must also be equal or at least proportional to the energy of the causes alike in the social, the physical and the mental domain. The deed of an individual will never create a social condition nor change it, however much appearances may deceive us. One social condition is produced by another. The task which falls to the writer of pragmatic history is to point out the true connection in each case.

(b) The Law of Development.

Parallel with and perhaps emanating from the law of causation is the law of development. Each social phenomenon is a momentary phase in a period of development; though often the end of the period may be beyond the reach of calculation. Every political organization, all rights, every economic relation suffers change. We can distinguish the beginning, the process of growth and often the decline and decay.

But of course manifestations of the law in the social and in the physical domain must not be confounded. Cells, germs, stalks and fruit; or eggs, embryo, lungs and digestive organs can not be found in social formations. Such analogies lead away from the truth; they becloud scientific vision and give incorrect results. The order of development in the social domain is from one social phenomenon to another.

If we would obtain reliable scientific results in sociology, this distinction must be observed rigorously. No digression to manifestations of the law in other domains can be allowed.

(c) Regularity of Development.

Development does not in and of itself involve the idea of regularity; the sequence of like or similar phases might or might not be uniform in all cases. But actually progress is regular; it conforms to law everywhere. We admire the regularity of development in the whole compass of physical nature. It dominates mental phenomena. It is found to be true of the state, of rights, of political economy, and of language which must also be included with the social sciences since, according to the definition given above, language is a social phenomenon. The great honor of discovering it in the domain of social phenomena is shared by the historical schools in the several departments.

(d) The Law of Periodicity.

In all domains of phenomena, regularity of development passes into periodicity. Wherever we can watch the whole process, we find a period of existence extending from the origin through the phases of growth and perfection to decline and fall. Of course the manifestation is different for each class of phenomena. Sap flows, the trunk grows strong, the organs develop, etc.; or, thought arises, is confirmed, is spread abroad and gains consideration—then loses influence and is recognized as nothing; or, a social relation arises in small proportions, is extended over larger aggregates, procures ever greater recognition, exercises decisive influence on great masses, is then broken up and supplanted by other relations and disappears leaving no trace. It is one law valid everywhere and universal.

(e) The Law of Complexity.

In physical nature we always find the elements in combination, never single. Likewise in the mental domain we meet with combinations only. Our conceptions, our thoughts and our mental powers, too, are complex. So also are all the social phenomena about us. They are structures composed of simpler parts. Every state, every people, every tribe is complex in a great many respects. Every principle of right is a composite of views, conceptions, ideas and principles. Every common economic interest is made up of conditions, activities, relations. In every language there is an endless variety of philological elements.

But further, what is complex may be analyzed. Analysis of physical phenomena will give the elements of matter. Analysis of mental phenomena will disclose ultimate concepts and the simplest mental functions. In the social domain it leads to the simplest social structures thinkable, from state and people to primitive horde; from developed institutional rights to the beginning of actual relations; from the most complex economic interests of the community to the satisfaction of the simplest needs; from a literature in the fullness of bloom to the simplest expression of thought by sound and gesture.

(*f*) *Reciprocal Action of Foreign* (*heterogen*) *Elements.*

Another result of complexity is that phenomena of every class show the reciprocal action of foreign (*heterogen*) reacting elements. Although there is an endless variety of cases in each particular domain, yet the law seems to express the first and most important impulse to development in each and every one of them. The significance of this force in social processes was surmised long ago, but it was erroneously interpreted by individualists and atomists as the reaction of man upon man and was designated as love or hate, as sociability or mutual hostility (*bellum omnium contra omnes*). The error in this conception will appear as we proceed. Specific reciprocal influence of man upon man cannot be affirmed in a universal law. What holds true between man and man in one group is not necessarily true in another group. Here it may be love and sociability and there hate and thirst for strife. First one and then the other relation was assumed to be normal according as attention was confined to one group or directed to the deportment of group toward group; but neither assumption was correct, because neither was universal. To find a law valid in all times and places for the reciprocal forces inherent in social phenomena we must take, not the individuals, but the social groups as the elements. Thus the law of the reciprocal action of foreign (*heterogen*) elements will be found universal. Social groups exhibit reciprocal effects which are fundamentally the same always and everywhere; they arise from the same exciting causes and obey the same law, though manifested in various forms and ways according to time, circumstances and the peculiar qualities of each.

A more specific expression for the universal action of

foreign (*heterogen*) bodies upon each other might seem desirable, but there would be danger of getting entangled in empty analogies and of falsely generalizing formulas valid only in special domains of phenomena.

Suppose we desired to speak of the "absorption" of foreign (*heterogen*) elements as a general principle. Perhaps the universal law is manifested in this way on much of the physical domain. But it is not so manifested in social phenomena. Applied to them the statement would be an empty analogy. On the other hand, the manifestation of this law on the physical domain, especially in inorganic and vegetable phenomena, has been described as a "struggle for existence." Obviously this is an illustration borrowed from animal and social phenomena. It does not describe physical phenomena. So if we would have a law common to all domains of phenomena we must modestly be content to speak of the reciprocal action of foreign (*heterogen*) elements. The more precise statement of its manifestation on the respective domains must be left to special formulas.

(*g*) *Adaptation to an Obvious End.*

One thing might be affirmed to characterize this law;more precisely, and that is universal adaptation to an end,— though in a very definite, technical sense. For the universal effect of the reciprocal action of foreign (*heterogen*) bodies is to favor further development of the phenomena concerned; which may be expressed by saying that, universally, phenomena in this state are adapted to the end of further development.

This law has been abundantly demonstrated throughout the physical domain. The botanist knows "to what end" the leaves serve the plant. The zoologist knows "why" the respiratory organs of birds and, in general, "why" all animal organs have their peculiar qualities. Among mental phenomena, also, the adaptation of means to the ends produced has been recognized in many cases. On the social domain, to be sure, the law is much questioned. The more warmly it is defended by conservatives, Manchester men, and optimists, the more violently is it opposed by revolutionists, socialists and pessimists. But on one point, at least, there seems to be no dispute; every social growth, every social entity, serves a definite end, however much its worth and morality may be questioned. For the universal law of adaptation signifies simply that no expenditure of effort, no change of condition, is purposeless on any domain of phenomena.   Hence the inherent reasonableness of all social facts and conditions must be conceded.

(h) *Identity of Forces.*

The reciprocal action of foreign (*heterogen*) elements obviously proceeds from forces immanent in them or arising from their contact.   These forces never change their character.   They are identical, as we wish to say.   Those operating in the domain of physical phenomena have always been the same that they are now. ） So of mental forces; thought, feeling, volition, each has moved man and controlled his actions in the same way always.   Likewise the social forces, the causes which we must conclude from the effects that follow on the social domain, have ever been the same.   Thus the identity of forces is a universal law.   We encounter it in every domain of phenomena.

(i) *Similarity of Events.**

A necessary consequence of the last law is the perpetual similarity of events on all domains of phenomena.   It has long been recognized of physical phenomena.   Nobody doubts that the sun's warming powers acting on moist ground age after age have produced and always will produce the same effects in vegetation that they produce now. Nobody doubts that ocean waves breaking on a rocky coast have always produced the same effects that we see to-day. So, too, nobody doubts that man's mental faculties have produced the same effects in all times and climes.   Always and everywhere men feel and think and plan; even the sensible products of these mental processes are the same.   They differ only in form with changing time and circumstances. The Kamtschatkan sings his native song, and so does the Frenchman; thousands of years ago the Chinese thinker philosophized just as did more recently the sage of Koenigsberg; the architect of the pyramids projected his artistic plans and so do the modern European artists.   Thus the perpetual similarity of events in the mental domain is obvious. But people are much less conscious of similarity in the social domain, though it is no less a fact.   The identity of social forces could not be discovered because individuals instead of

* *Cf. "Der Rassenkampf,"* pp. 172 *et seq.*

natural social groups were taken to be the true elements of social phenomena. But when the true social forces are recognized, the perpetual similarity of social events must also be apparent. Rights, states, languages, religion, etc., have always and everywhere arisen in ways essentially alike. Economic events are controlled by the same forces; they have always been alike in essence, though often differing in form.

(j) Law of Parallelism.

In every domain we find some phenomena which are similar but we do not know the ultimate cause of their similarity. In the physical domain such phenomena are ascribed to identical forces directly. But in the mental domain the tendency is rather to attribute the similarity to some alleged connection between them; and in social phenomena it is considered the result of consanguinity or of some historic relationship. But actually there is something fundamental at the bottom of all these similarities which we must refer temporarily to a law of parallelism, since we do not know more precisely what it is. By resorting to this law we guard ourselves against obviously false and erroneous explanations.*

The reason why parallel physical phenomena are referred without question to identical forces, whereas such an explanation of parallel mental and social phenomena is anxiously avoided as long as possible, is partly found in the widely accepted theory of monogenism. The descent of all men from Adam and Eve afforded a very plausible explanation. But if it is rejected as too absurd, the only course left is to refer the countless mental and social parallels also directly to a law of parallelism common to all domains of phenomena.

The existence of universal laws is one of the most convincing proofs that the whole world of phenomena rests upon a single simple principle. It is a weighty argument for monism, a thorough refutation of dualism. Consideration of these laws shows how untenable it is to refer phenomena to two principles, matter and mind, since the modalities of

*"According to the psychological axioms of ethnology, when cases exhibiting similarities occur, the strictly universal and elementary laws are first applied. When there is no further possibility of finding the explanation in them recourse is had to such historic relationships as can be established. But the daily swelling mass of ethnological parallels will soon have converted the most obdurate. For since such an interpretation of parallels has come to be reckoned *a priori* reliable, no one can fail to accept it who is not stone blind."—Bastian, "*Vorgeschichte der Ethnologie,*" p. 91.

existence are the same for all and point to one simple principle only. Whether it be called nature, or God, or the great unknown world-moving principle matters not. We have presentiments that it is omnipotent, omnipresent, perhaps even omniscient. But we are not in condition to know its essence. Since, however, there are laws which are universally prevalent and valid, we must conclude that this one principle pursues, so to say, a consequent and self-consistent policy; that it reveals itself always and everywhere in the same form and in the same character for all kinds of phenomena. This necessary conclusion is of unending significance to science.

3. CONCEPT, FUNCTION, SCOPE AND IMPORTANCE OF SOCIOLOGY.

It is almost unnecessary to remark that universal laws like these are not *a priori* cognitions but the result of an exhaustive examination of all spheres of phenomena, inductions obtained by long mental exertion. In propounding them at the beginning of our discussion, we are reversing the natural order of cognition, to be sure; but this provisional anticipation of the results of an investigation is simply didactic strategy.

These universal laws govern phenomena of all kinds, it has been said. But for each particular kind they are manifested in a particular way. We might call this quality of special adaptation their " specific energy." An example will make the thought clear. Adaptation to an obvious end is a universal law. It is manifested in plants by the equipment of the several organs and the manner of their growth; and the botanist is able to formulate a whole series of special laws for plants. In the social domain, the same law will be manifested differently. For example, a horde, before starting on a raid, will organize by choosing a leader; and other illustrations may be given. Hence the sociologist may speak of special social laws to designate the adjustment of universal laws to the peculiar nature and conditions of social phenomena. Obviously special laws will be more numerous than universal; for the latter generalize the conditions common to all phenomena, whereas the former take account of those common to small numbers of phenomena.

The function of sociology consists in showing that universal laws apply to social phenomena; in pointing out the peculiar effects produced by them in the social domain, and finally in formulating the special social laws.

As we have to deal with social phenomena exclusively in what follows, we must get a clear idea of what they are; we must distinguish the domain of social phenomena from every other; we must explore it and learn the most important groups upon it.   In so doing we shall come in contact with the special sciences which are occupied with the special groups and which are very properly designated the '' social sciences '' in general.

By social phenomena we mean the phenomena which appear through the operation of groups and aggregates of men on one another.   The aggregates are the social elements. We must assume that the simplest and the original social elements were primitive hordes, of which, for reasons that have been explained elsewhere,* there must have been a great number in remote antiquity.

The combinations of the simple social elements into greater associations: tribes, communities, peoples, states and nations, are just so many social phenomena.   There are also psycho-social phenomena, such as language, customs, rights, religion, etc., arising from the action of social elements with or upon the individual mind.

The province of sociology embraces them all.   Sociology must investigate them and show the social laws of their development.   Many groups, it is true, have been isolated and made the subject-matter of independent sciences.   But that should not hinder sociology from subjecting them to a new examination from the standpoint of social science, especially since they have generally been studied from an individualistic standpoint.   Sociology should make their social origin and development perfectly clear.

It has just been said that mankind is the substratum of all social phenomena; hence, it is the real subject-matter of sociology.   But it is clear that the character of the science will be determined ultimately by our conception of the natural history of mankind.   According as our conception is correct or false will sociology be a success or a failure. The smallest mistake in the beginning will avenge itself in hundred and thousand fold greater errors in the end.

Hitherto a very gross misconception has prevailed in social science concerning the natural history of mankind.

* *Cf. '' Der Rassenkampf.''* p. 56 *et seq.*

The character of human phenomena has been completely falsified by conceiving mankind to be genealogically a unitary genus, by supposing lineal descent from a common stock, and explaining varieties of race and type as successive offshoots from it. This fundamental misconception set the whole social science on the wrong track. Not only were all right points of view, resulting from the fact of original plurality and variety of races, lost from consideration, but many false ones were presented which produced nothing but errors.

Closely connected with this, indeed resulting from it, is another error. It was conceived that culture and social relations generally, whether of mankind or of particular peoples, develop spontaneously as a plant or animal develops. It was conceived that one and the same group passed through different stages of culture, from the hunting stage to the pastoral, to the agricultural, to warrior life and so on down to industrialism by simple transitions in virtue of an inner law and tendency to develop. But the law of persistence applies to social groups as much as it does to anything else in nature. Social groups persist in their actual social condition and cannot be made to "pass" into another without adequate social cause.

Therefore, we must remember not only that contiguous groups are diverse in origin, but also that they have been undergoing different courses of development. We must also remember that every social group persists in a given condition until forced out of it and into another through the action of some other group, and such action is pre-eminently called social.

In other words, each alteration in the social condition of a group must always have a sufficient social cause, which is always the influence of another group.* This is a law, and can be amply illustrated from history and experience. An important proposition for the methodology of sociology follows from it, viz., whenever an alteration in the condition of a group is perceived we should inquire what influences exerted by another group produced it. It follows, also, that a rapid and varied development and frequent social changes occur only under the continual reciprocal influence of many foreign (*heterogen*) groups, that is, in states and systems of states.

* [*Und ein solcher [zureichender Grund] liegt immer in der Einwirkung seitens einer anderen Gruppe, i. e.*, the influence of another group is the only sufficient social cause.]

This brings us very close to the definition of a social event or process. When two or more distinct (*heterogen*) groups come in contact, when each enters the sphere of the other's operations, a social process always ensues. So long as one unitary, homogeneous group is not influenced by or does not exert an influence upon another it persists in the original primitive state. Hence, in distant quarters of the globe, shut off from the world, we find hordes in a state as primitive, probably, as that of their forefathers a million years ago. Here, very likely, we are dealing with an elementary, primitive, social phenomenon or, better, with a social element, but not with a social process nor with social change.

But as soon as one group is exposed to the influence of another, the interplay of mutual forces ensues inevitably and the social process begins. When two distinct (*heterogen*) groups come together, the natural tendency of each is to exploit the other, to use the most general expression. This, indeed, is what gives the first impulse to the social process. This tendency is so inherent in every human group, so natural and indomitable, that it is impossible to conceive of groups coming together without displaying it, without generating the social process.

The course of the process depends upon the natural constitution of " mankind " and the tendencies peculiar to all human hordes and social communities. Since these factors differ only as one individual or, at most, one species from another and everywhere exhibit the same generic characteristics the process is essentially the same everywhere.

True, the human race is composed of an endless variety of species; the different hordes and tribes are combined in many ways and produce a variety of social formations or collective entities which in turn act upon one another; even the influence of time and place yields a diversity of effects: so that the social process nevertheless presents endless variety and individuality of development. But the differences are transient and local. It is the task of sociology— and by no means an easy one—in the midst of diversity to find the controlling social laws, to explain the miscellaneous variety of social development by the simplest forces in operation and to reduce the countless shapes it assumes to a simple common denominator.

All social laws, indeed all universal laws as well, have one characteristic in common: they explain the becoming, but never the beginning of things, the ultimate origin. This limitation must be insisted upon the more emphatically since the human mind is given to inquiring after the genesis of things. It desires knowledge of the first arising, the ultimate origin—a tendency fatal to science; whereas with all the laws cognizable it can apprehend only the perpetual becoming.

Hence none of the questions about the ultimate origin of human associations belong in sociology, if indeed they belong in any science whatever! Sociology begins with the countless different social groups of which, as can be irrefutably proven, mankind is constituted. The question how they came to be does not belong within its forum.

As we begin by limiting sociological discussion to the becoming of things, excluding discussion of ultimate origin, may we be allowed to point out that the discoveries which are recognized as the greatest achievements of science all lie in the same field. The Copernican discovery applies only to the motion of the planets in their orbits, without inquiring how they came to exist. Harvey discovered the circulation of the blood, a process continually going on under our observation. And we certainly do the great Englishman no wrong in expressing the opinion that when, centuries later, the problem of the "origin of man" shall have long since been laid aside, his investigation into the laws of the becoming, into the "struggle for existence," "adaptation" and "heredity," must still be lauded as an imperishable service to science.

We are unwilling to close this section without emphasizing the importance of the knowledge of social laws to historians and statesmen.

The view that history can be raised to the level of a science only by taking account of the natural and social laws of development is still violently opposed though the reasons for it have been presented many times. We could cite innumerable examples to show how very much history has suffered from ignorance of social laws on the part of the most eminent historians. The most common error, one into which almost every historian has fallen, especially if he is treating of a single nation, is to regard the phenomena as peculiar to one people; whereas did he know social laws he would recognize that they are more general.

How long is it since in every history of Germany, in every

treatise on the philosophy of German history, political particularism was ascribed to an individualizing tendency inherent in the German people? Particularism was considered a virtue in its day. But Prince Bismarck has thoroughly counteracted the tendency and violently disputes its virtue.* If the writers were not so absorbed in one aspect of their subject, if they considered the laws governing all historical changes, they would recognize that, as a universal fact, periods of disintegration and particularization alternate with periods of integration. If they recognized that periodicity of development is a natural, necessary and universal law they would come nearer to the truth of many matters, their results would gain in scientific value.

Or what shall be said when a distinguished historian like Curtius writes: "The acquisitive impulse deeply inherent by nature in the Greeks, excited them at an early period to a many sided activity."† Is this tendency natural to the "Greeks" alone? What of the "Semites," of whom Curtius relates that "the Greeks cherished a national hatred against them!"‡ Was the "acquisitive tendency" less "deeply inherent by nature" in them? or had it "excited" them less "to a many sided activity?" Or why did the Spaniards go to America, the English and Dutch to India, if not to "get gain?" Have we not here a general social phenomenon and a general social law? and is it not a scientific error to consider general social phenomena peculiar to the people among whom they have been accidentally recognized?

Take another example from Curtius:

"According to the usual conception of the Greeks, who felt the need of assuming an author for every great historical work, without caring to distinguish what had previously existed from what subsequently ensued, the whole political system was regarded as the legislation of Lycurgus."§

But to ascribe to a single legislator the creation of a body of juridical and political regulations which have been accumulating for centuries is not peculiar to the Greeks. It is a psycho-social phenomenon common to all peoples; and will not truth and science suffer if no account is taken of the fact?

* [*Nun, Fuerst Bismarck hat diesen. . . Individualisirungstrieb gruendlich ausge-trieben* (sic) *und geht ihm noch immer gewaltig an den Leib.*]

† "The History of Greece." Translated by Ward. Bk. i, p. 15; Cf. "*Griech-ische Geschichte.*" 6th Edition, Vol. i, p. 123.

‡ Curtius-Ward, *op. cit.*, p. 59; *Cf.* Curtius, *op. cit.*, Vol. i, p. 44.

§ Curtius-Ward, *op. cit.*, Bk. i, p. 208; Curtius, *op. cit.*, Vol. i, p. 44.

How much the science of history will improve when historians discern that all the alleged individual peculiarities of the peoples they describe are manifestations of general social and psycho-social laws! Similar examples of false and narrow views could be cited without number from the best historians. But we prefer to give in precise terms the general cause of error in the conception of historical phenomena. It is asserted that

"history, however it may be defined and classified, will never be reduced to a bare natural science or sociological discipline. For it is not simply the product of telluric and anthropological natural forces and the momentum of social masses. There is a third factor, the power of individuality, which is not susceptible of calculation by the rules of either natural science or sociology."*

In so far as individuals are concerned, to be sure, history can proceed "neither like natural science nor sociology." But in so far as history portrays the individual it is pure art. For art deals only with individuals, in contrast with science which deals with what is universal, what accords with law and is schematic. The individual might be typical; nevertheless the historian is generally in error if he thinks that he finds anything individualistic in the history of a people, a nation or a tribe, or in the actions of social groups, however considered. Only single personalities are properly individualistic; when treating them the historian may yield to his artistic impulses. But when he has collective wholes to present, where he has to show how they live and move, the effort to "individualize" is short-sighted and erroneous; the science of history can and should "proceed according to the rules of both natural science and sociology." For the behavior of collective entities is determined by "natural and sociological" laws and not by the motives and natural qualities of individuals.† It will be some time before this is realized; but the recognition will come only through sociology.

Important as sociology is for historians, its significance in politics is greater still. For though hitherto politics has not been reckoned a science at all sociology will give it a scientific character.

---

* I may certainly be allowed to cite as typical of the opinion of historians in general the objections made to "history as a natural science" by the distinguished R. von Krones, in reviewing "*Der Rassenkampf.*" The prevalent conception of the task of historical composition could not be defended more forcibly than it is done in the words quoted.

† [*Individuelle Motive und Beschaffenheiten.*]

At present politics is strife after power.   Each state, party and faction, every man even, is striving after power with all the means at command.   Material means are supplemented with as cogent reasons as possible.   Such reasons and arguments are called the theory of politics.   But where is the criterion of their correctness?   From the standpoint of success, when the fact has been accomplished, the policy which succeeded is recognized as right.   Yet it is not so much ideas and arguments as greater might that makes the project prosperous.   So ultimately, greater might is the better policy— as things stand now.

Sociology must give quite another turn to politics; though, indeed, it will develop political science rather than practical politics.   That is to say, the social laws which sociology is to formulate from its observations on the processes of history include also the laws of the development of political life. When they shall have been correctly formulated from the past, they must be verified in the present and the future. They must control the course of political development now and hereafter as unequivocally as they have hitherto.   But when reliable laws have been formulated, political machinations, tavern politics and ignorant gossip will give place to political foresight and sober calculation based upon positive sociological knowledge.

These words will provoke a sceptical smile—and certainly not without some reason.   Similar promises have often proved to be vain talk if not charlatanry even; and usually people who talk of calculating future politics scientifically are not taken seriously,   Did not Auguste Comte speak of a *politique positive*, a positive science of politics, which, " instead of pronouncing absolute judgment and suggesting ameliorations," should rather create " a body of scientific conceptions such as has never been outlined nor even suspected by any philosopher before?"   Yet how many false and erroneous notions he held!   And Thomas Buckle! How little he recognized the truth about the development of political relations in modern times!   Claiming to have obtained final cognition of the "laws of history," he prophesied cessation of war and universal perpetual peace, yet how has his prophecy been verified?

In one point, however, the old sociologists were clearly right.   With presentient mind they suspected the existence of social laws and asserted the possibility of a social science.

It is true they did not pass the point of conjecture. They never advanced to the true principles of the science, much less to a knowledge of social laws. Nay! they did not even find the starting point of the way which leads to the principles. The point of departure is polygenism. The way is the investigation of the natural relations of distinct (*hetero-gen*) groups of men to one another. We entered upon it in "*Der Rassenkampf*" and we wish to continue in it here.*

Being the science of human society and social laws, sociology is obviously the basis of all the special sciences treating of parts of human society, or of particular manifestations of associative life. Anthropology, the science of man as an individual being, falls within the scope of the universal science of society as a species within the genus. So do ethnography, embracing the description and comparison of existing tribes and peoples; political science, the science of the state, treating of social communities which are the result of disciplinary organization; comparative linguistics, or philology; the comparative study of religion, rights, art, etc.,—sciences of social institutions which satisfy the psycho-social wants of man; finally political economy and other sciences treating of institutions which the material wants of man as a social unit have produced. It is perfectly natural that all these sciences should have taken shape long before the science in which they should afterward find their basis. This is the normal course of man's developing knowledge.

It was so in natural science in the narrow sense of the word. Botany, zoology and mineralogy took shape before geology and paleontology, though the latter are the foundation

* It gives me great satisfaction to observe that the reviewers have recognized the great importance of my starting point and have declared it at all events worthy of note. Alfred Koenigsberg writes in the *Neue Freie Presse*, Vienna, August 9, 1869: "His hypothesis that mankind is descended from many pairs is the egg of Columbus. It explains almost every historical event in the simplest and most unconstrained way, especially that primitive phenomenon, the conquest of a weaker tribe by a stronger; and the organization of society with division of labor. It suggests what Stephenson, the father of railroads, said upon inspecting a good locomotive: 'how hard it must have been to hit upon it; it is so simple!'" The reviewer for the *Rassegna Critica*, Naples, 1883, No. 9, says: "There are two points in this book which especially deserve praise . . . . to wit, the unqualified assertion of naturalism and the fact that, contrary to custom, neither the individual nor the psychology of the individual, but the social group, is made the element in the interpretation of history." Similar notices of approval appeared in *Globus*, 1884, No. 4; *Ausland*, 1884, No. 2; *Journal des Economistes*, October, 1883; Ribot's *Revue Philosophique*, May, 1884, and in many other critical periodicals. These critics have caught the idea of my book and it cannot be my fault that Professor Alfred Kirchhoff, in Zarncke's *Literarisches Centralblatt*, Leipzig, complains that he does not understand what I mean. However, Professor Kirchhoff is a geographer, appears never to have meddled with sociology, and is conversant with neither the literature of the subject nor the questions here under discussion. Judging from the fact that he notices the book under the rubric "ethnology," he considers sociology a geographical discipline.

of the former.   Similarly the art of healing is earlier than physiology.

The explanation is very simple. Things, institutions, relations encountered in concrete form are the first objects observed and investigated.   The most convenient hypothesis or crudest explanation suffices for a time to account for their origin.   For instance we live under laws constituting a body of rights.   The nature of the phenomenon is investigated; the rights are explained, interpreted, compared with others, and their history is traced out.   But provisionally their source and origin was satisfactorily explained by saying that the lawgiver proclaimed them.   Similarly the explanation of the origin of religion is that God revealed it to His prophet, the founder.

With the progress of knowledge and reflection, ideas concerning the origin of the subjects-matter of the respective sciences undergo changes.   The new conclusions come in conflict with the earlier explanations.   Thus the comparative study of law showed that rights arise historically in the collective or " folk " mind; and religion, similarly studied, was found to emanate from exigencies of man's spiritual nature, and so on.

Moreover as knowledge broadened the germs of all the psycho-social institutions were eventually found to be in close proximity to one another and the different social sciences met on a common ground—though the common designation was not at once applied.   The subject-matter of each science in turn was discovered existing in every people in a greater or less degree, and in a more or less forward state of development.   Consequently men were forced to regard the differences in psycho-social phenomena among various peoples and to compare psycho-social products.

The first step was the comparative study of law, especially of customary law, then of religion, language, art and philosophy.   This prompted and aided investigation of the common ground whence the fountains of all the sciences seemed to spring.   This common ground was at first designated history of civilization, ethnography, or ethnology, Bastian's term.   But in fact it may most suitably be called social science.

It discloses the true source of all those psycho-social products that had previously become subjects-matter of special sciences.   But it does this only because it comprehends the

substance of human societies.   Hence we must recognize in
sociology the philosophical basis of all the sciences claiming
to be "social;" and it will fall to the lot of sociology to
demonstrate the relation of each of them to their common
basis, and their connection with each other upon it.

4. THE SUBSTRATUM OF SOCIAL LAWS.

Laws are revealed objectively.   Substrata are necessarily
presupposed.   It is by the forms in which bodies appear, or
in which forces manifest themselves in and on bodies, that we
are able to discover laws.   The law of gravitation cannot be
conceived apart from a body which falls—on which the force
of gravitation manifests itself.   To speak of attraction is to
call to mind the bodies on which attraction acts.

So the question arises: What are the substrata of social
laws?   What are the media through which force is manifested when we infer social laws from its behavior?   Obviously the medium is not the individual, on whom a psychical
or a physical law may be manifested, but not a social.   It
has sometimes been thought that " mankind " was the substratum; but erroneously, for there must be heterogeneous
(*heterogen*) elements wherever reciprocal action and an
interplay of forces is expected.

If mankind is conceived to be a unit, the condition necessary for the action of opposing forces is by supposition
absent.   Besides, nowhere on the earth, and at no time
either in the present age or in remotest antiquity has mankind been found to be a simple substance. It always consists
in a countless number of distinct (*heterogen*) ethnical elements.   Hence I was led to seek the starting point of sociological investigation in the hypothesis that there was
originally an indefinitely large number of distinct (*heterogen*)
ethnical elements;* and it gives me satisfaction to note that
good authorities consider the polygenetic hypothesis established.   Indeed, Bastian, the highest authority in this matter,
declares that " it is self-evident," and that my efforts, in
"*Der Rassenkampf*," to " reconcile it with Darwinism,"
were superfluous.

* "The concept of force," says Caspari, correctly, "presupposes relations to
another foreign opposing force which is called resistance. Force apart from
resistance of every sort were a forceless force, unthinkable nothing. Whoever
speaks of force must at the same time conceive of mechanical resistauce or he
contradicts himself. Hence every philosophical investigator who had been educated in natural science, and had studied mechanics, understood that we must
continually suppose an original plurality of discrete force-media, force-centres,
or force-atoms (Democritus), monads (Leibnitz), reals (Herbart), dynamides
(Redtenbacher), etc."—"*Kosmos*," Vol. i, p. 9.

But since the hypothesis is so fundamental to the whole system of sociology it is not enough to state what authorities accept it. I must also take pains to bring before the reader as much scientific material as possible in support of it.

First of all may I be allowed to cite Carl Vogt, another authority of the first rank in natural science, to vouch for the "original plurality" and the "constancy" of human races: *

"No man would certainly have doubted the specific difference in mankind" says this investigator in his "Lectures on Man," "if the unity of the human species had not to be defended at any price, if a tradition had not to be supported in opposition to the plainest facts—a tradition which has been the more venerated because it runs counter to positive science." †

"As far as our traditions go, however far back they reach into the remotest antiquity, we observe that wherever peoples migrated and discovered unknown countries, they found human beings, who appeared to them not less strange than the animals and plants they met with. . . . The larger islands, as well as all parts of the continents under the hottest and coldest climates, were by navigators or conquerors always found inhabited."

Then Vogt reminds his readers that

"even religious legends, which have for their object the origin of mankind and the history of a privileged race, even these legends indicate that at the creation of the first pair the world was already peopled, an indication given even in the Bible. . . . The only fact from which we can start is that of the original dispersion of mankind upon the earth, and the original difference of races spread over the surface of the earth. However much we may indulge in theoretical speculations on the origin and differences of mankind, however weighty proofs may be adduced for the original unity of the human species, this much is certain, that no historical nor, as we have shown, geological data can establish this dream of unity. However far back our eye reaches we find different species of men spread over different parts of the earth."

"Not merely the difference of races, but also their constancy in the course of time, is perfectly established. We have endeavored to show that these characters may be traced back beyond the historical period up to the pile-works, the stone-period, and the diluvial formations. The Egyptian monuments show that already under the twelfth dynasty, about 2300 years before Christ, negroes had been imported

* It may be added that among the earlier natural scientists the following accepted polygenism: Cuvier, Buffon, Lacépède and Burdach. The philosopher Whewell in "Traces of Divinity" holds the negroes to be a distinct race, of different extraction from the other races of men. Bory and Vierey also accepted polygenism and Perty says : "The far greater probability is that men of diverse natural capacities have arisen in different parts of the earth and at various times, all very remote from ours."—" *Ethnographie*," p. 386 (1859).

† "Lectures on Man : His Place in Creation and in the History of the Earth." By Dr. Carl Vogt. Edited by James Hunt. London: 1864. Lecture viii, p. 222, "*Vorlesungen ueber den Menschen ; seine Stellung in der Schoepfung und in der Geschichte der Erde.*" By Carl Vogt. 2 vols., Giessen: 1863. Vol. i, p. 284.

into Egypt; that slave hunts had, as now, taken place under several dynasties, as proved by the triumphal processions of Thothmes IV., about 1700 B. C., and Rameses III., about 1300 B. C. There are seen long processions of negroes, whose features and color are faithfully rendered; there are seen Egyptian scribes registering slaves with their wives and children; even the down growing in bunches upon the heads of the latter may be distinguished. There are also seen many heads presenting the characters of negro tribes inhabiting the south of Egypt, and which the artist distinguishes as such by the superadded lotus-stalk. But not only the negroes, but also the Nubians and the Berbers, as well as the old Egyptians, are always depicted with those characteristic peculiarities which have been preserved to this day."

Vogt also cites the conclusions of Broca, Morton and Jomard, who identify the modern Fellah-type with the Egyptians of the time of the Pharaohs, and then he continues:

"The same constancy of characters can be traced in the other races with which the Egyptians came in contact. The Jews are as easily recognizable as the Tartars and Scythians with whom Rameses III. was at war.

"In the same way we observe upon the Assyrian and Indian monuments the characters of such races as still inhabit these regions, so that the constancy of race characters is everywhere rendered evident."[*]

Though Vogt concedes a "certain flexibility" to the "natural races" of mankind in virtue of which they "show certain changes when transplanted into different media," yet the change never exceeds a very small maximum and does not obliterate the essential race-marks. Hence Darwin is not justified in concluding from single demonstrable examples of unimportant alterations due to change of environment that they will continue until eventually the essential traits have been lost and the race has been changed.

"We thus infer that all instances which have been cited of change in races of pure descent by the mere influence of changed media, immigration into foreign countries, etc., are insignificant and do not affect the essential race-characters. These modifications, therefore, which we by no means entirely deny, do not in any way explain the differences in the human species. . . . In accordance with the facts," says Vogt finally, "we must assume a fundamental difference of races as our starting-point."[†]

We must confine ourselves to these quotations from Vogt. It would lead us too far should we follow the forcible argument in which he not only shows the harmony between Darwin's theory and polygenism but also demonstrates that the latter follows necessarily from the former.

[*] "Lectures on Man," Lec. 15, pp. 423–26.
[†] *Ibid.*, Lec. 15, pp. 435–36.

His two most important theses, the constancy and the original "plurality and diversity" of human races, have found striking confirmation in the progress that has since been made in anthropological and craniological investigation.

Efforts were made to find the types of all the known races. It had been assumed upon superficial examination, that each race represented a genealogical unit in which a fixed anthropological type was transmitted from generation to generation. But when scientists undertook to determine the typical peculiarities exactly, it was found impossible to assign a single type exclusively to any one historical race whatever. The investigators would then have been content with a "mean type" for each race. But, says Virchow, "such a variety of individual differences was accumulated among the civilized peoples of Europe that to many it seemed impossible to set up even a mean type for each."*

In his embarrassment he proclaimed, a decade ago, that "science demanded" that the "original type" of each race be discovered; and he spared neither labor nor pains in the search. If after all he did not find it among the Germans, where he looked first, it was not his fault. The simple fact is that not a single historical race ever consisted in a genealogical unit.

After laborious and unsuccessful investigation he concludes that

"the assumption of a simple original Germanic type is as yet entirely arbitrary. Nobody has proved that all Germans once had the same shaped skull, or, otherwise expressed, that they were from the beginning one nation (!), the Suevi and Franks being its purest types. If Germans and Slavs belong to the same Indo-Germanic stock, if Slavic brachycephaly and Germanic dolichocephaly do not prevent assuming the common descent (?) of Slavs and Germans, it might seem that mesocephaly and even brachycephaly among the admittedly pure Germans would be a favorable circumstance. The great hiatus becomes filled and original relationship is more easily comprehended after actual intermediate members have been discovered. If the Germanic nation once had a common fatherland in the far East, it is very probable that these differences were brought thence into the later home."

We see with what reserve and reluctance Virchow notes that the German race lacks anthropological unity. He demands further investigation.

"Perhaps it will appear that, as the measurements in our schools in my judgment indicate, different Germanic stocks have in fact existed

* "*Beitraege zur physischen Anthropologie der Deutschen,*" 1877.

here in Germany for ages, moving side by side from east to west, and spreading out towards the west."

To the sociologist the "different stocks" which the anthropologist's craniological material leads him to conjecture seem plain and natural from the beginning. To call them "Germanic" is simply national prejudice. There were many different stocks all about; and in time a "Germanic" unit arose as they came into closer contact and took on a common civilization.

But the anthropologist's concession that "the common type" of the Germans "is not so simple as it has hitherto been assumed to be" is of value to us.

The farther craniological investigations were pursued, the stronger grew the conviction that there was nothing which could be called a "unitary type," even in the remotest tribes, whom the current of migration does not touch, who have no intercourse with others, and who are apparently beyond the reach of every other agitating force of history. Among the old Frisians, even, there are several types; and Virchow is forced to assume that "possibly other tribes were there before them, whom they subjected and whose blood was mingled with theirs." Whether the craniologist examines modern Finns and Lapps, or wild Veddas from the interior of Ceylon, or the skulls from old Trojan graves, the fact of intermixture appears with equal clearness.*

But while Virchow, who started to find an original unitary type, reluctantly notes that there is none and, with disillusioned resignation, concedes an original plurality of types for all the tribes he has investigated, the distinguished craniologist, Kollmann, has proved with scientific certainty that original plurality is universal.

As early as 1883 it was apparent to him that "traces of different anthropological elements can be shown in every race. Many centuries have elapsed since the peoples of Europe were racial units, and now no dale, however remote, contains a pure race." But the latest results prove abundantly that racial differences are not due to a later process of differentiation. It has existed unchanged since diluvial times.

"An extended comparison of diluvial and modern skulls," writes Kollmann, "shows that osteological race characteristics have not

* Virchow. "*Weddes und Alttrojanische Schaedel und Graeber.*"

changed. Since diluvial times the influence of natural selection has
not caused man to 'vary' in the Darwinian sense. His race-marks
have withstood external influences with great tenacity, persisting in
spite of them. These important conclusions contradict the current
view that man is undergoing a continuous process of change. But it
must be conceded upon closer examination that the evidence I have
adduced admits of the construction I have given it, to say the least."

Then he cites the opinions of prominent naturalists to
show that not only do many animals have permanent types,
but unquestionably the men of the Nile valley also, according
to Cuvier, and even mankind since the flood, according to
Ruetimeyer.

"All the evidence man has left in his burial places," he continues,
"shows that he belongs to the latter class of beings, having a permanent type. The osteological characteristics of race and even of variety
have not changed in all the time he has wandered over Europe. . .
The universality of this rule is forcibly illustrated by the difference
between Papuans and Malays, to mention only one example. Since
time immemorial they have lived side by side in similar regions without change of habitat. Yet they are different still. As for Europe,
both prehistoric and modern, it can be shown that the number of different races has always been rather large and that they have always been
intermixed." "Owing to penetration," says Kollmann, "representatives of many races live and, for thousands of years have lived, side
by side everywhere in Europe. Hence, each people and state contains
different races in different proportions. This conclusion I drew after
comparing more than 3000 European skulls."

Indeed craniologists who are moved to defend the unity
and "purity" of their own races cannot withstand the
undeniable facts. Hoelder, for example concedes five
different "types" within the "Germanic stock." That
is, he finds five among his specimens to-day. It is not
impossible therefore that once there was a greater number
and that other investigators may be able to recover more of
them.*

"Hiss and Ruetimeyer, using rigorous scientific methods, have
shown that at least three different races have lived in Switzerland
since the period of the lake-dwellers began."†

* To social science it is a matter of indifference that craniologists like Kollmann compromise with the alleged Darwinian doctrine of unitary descent by
granting that a period of dispersion and of differentiation from a "common
stock" may have "occurred in pre-glacial times." It is enough for social science
to start with the facts of the post-diluvial period. It gladly leaves the pre-glacial
hypothesis to the defenders of an alleged Darwinian standpoint—to save the
"common stock."

† Cf. articles by Kollmann on "American Antochthons," Zeitschrift für
Anthropologie, 1883; "Statistics on the Color of Eyes and Hair, taken in the Swiss
Schools," 1881; "Craniological Material from Swiss Burial-places," 1883; "The
Value of Pithecoidal Forms and the Effect of Correlation on the Face of the
Human Skull," 1883.

These same "anthropological differences," to use Koll-mann's term, may also be noted among the American aborigines.

"Formerly it was believed that a single race extended over the whole continent from Cape Horn to the great northern lakes. . . . Decisive facts to the contrary were first adduced by Andreas Retzius. . . . He showed that there were two different races in America, a brachycephalic in the west and a dolichocephalic in the east."

In Virchow's opinion, also, the evidence shows "that the autochthonous population of America is not a racial unit." Kollmann showed from his investigations on American skulls that

"the various cephalic indices, from extreme dolichocephaly to extreme brachycephaly, are scattered ever the whole continent. . . . The autochthonous population, north and south, is composed of the same races, though their relative proportions differ. . . . Hence we must speak of American races. . . .

"I will add that there is no prospect of finding racial unity even within a smaller region. It might be thought that individual tribes in the north or the south would consist of dolichocephalic or brachy-cephalic persons only. . . . But the Mound-builders and Cliff-dwellers in their day were composed of the same races that occur later. Even they consisted of several races, like the men of the first diluvial period in Europe, or the Reindeer-hunters, Lake-dwellers, Germans and Celts."

Kollmann's theory of "penetration" is thoroughly con-firmed by the observation of his disciple Passavant in west Africa.* The first place he visited on the African continent was the French possession of Gorée, the black population of which belongs to the Seres and Joloff tribes.

"It is extremely hard for the beginner to distinguish the blacks by their physiognomies," writes Passavant of his first experience there. "At first all the faces appeared alike. Only after several weeks of practice did I really succeed in taking account of individual differ-ences."

This accords with the well-known fact that the countless differences really to be found in men escape superficial observation almost completely. It also explains the whole previous history of anthropology, especially the circum-stance that mankind was at first divided into only three or four races, distinguished by the crudest, most striking traits, such as the color of the skin, whereas, after a more intimate acquaintance, we become conscious of countless differences.

* "*Craniologische Untersuchungen der Neger und Negervoelker.*"

Cuvier, as is well known, divided mankind into three races: Mongolians, Negroes and Caucasians. Blumenbach distinguished five types and made five races to correspond. Lacépède and Dumerit added a sixth. Bory discovered fifteen races even and Desmoulins sixteen. But Waitz found this number insufficient and declared that theoretically there ought to be no division into races lest he be compelled, in spite of ethical scruples, to recognize a great number— several hundred in fact. Fortunately the American investigators were not influenced by such insipid considerations. They carried the subdivision courageously forward unconcerned about the Bible and European ethics.

The catalogue of human races accepted by Morton, Nott and Gliddon ran into the hundreds without being complete; there is nothing to prevent the increase of the number as anthropological knowledge increases. Passavant's investigations among the negroes afford further proof that this may be expected in the nature of the case.

The first subdivision of the African Negroes into four grand races: Negritos, Congo Negroes, Kaffirs and Hottentots, he says

"is the fruit of our exploring expeditions; it is connected with the progress of ethnographic knowledge." "Undaunted explorers have gradually brought a population which may be estimated at 151 millions so far within our knowledge that we can now distinguish several large ethnical groups."

There are "at least three Negro races" in Africa, he says, besides the Berbers and the Bedjas or Ethiopians.

"There are, besides, some tribes intermediate between the Negroes on the one hand and the Berbers and Bedjas on the other. There are some also in which different stocks and types are so mingled that they cannot longer be ascribed to any one in particular."

According to Passavant, instead of the one black race, we should have seven ethnical groups in Africa. But what of the material of each group? The Negritos "differ so among themselves," says Hartmann, "that the current conception of the negro with woolly hair, flat nose, thick lips and raven black skin must be entirely disregarded."

Endless differences still! But it is well understood what they consist in and why closer observation makes it necessary to increase the number of "races." "Racial characteristics are pre-eminently anatomical," says Kollmann. ". . . Physical or material traits must be apparent on the bones."

Relatively few races were recognized by scientists because " laborious investigation is needed in order to show specific characteristics on the bony framework of the skull.'' *

But is it worth the trouble ? Are not all these " differences'' capricious sports of nature, endless and ever changing, without rule or law ? Modern craniology answers the question decisively.

" The skeleton,'' says Ruetimeyer, " seems to preserve its acquired shape more tenaciously than any other organ; so much so that a cross does not produce a third form, but the two elements persist side by side. The effect of crossing on the skeleton might be called mechanical rather than chemical.''

Vogt also maintains that race characteristics are permanent on the skeleton, and Passavant considers the " shape of the skull to be a constant and inheritable race-characteristic.''

" There is a mass of evidence,'' he says, " showing that race-types are maintained continuously or reappear by reversion.''

" If the characteristics of different varieties did not resist external influences with such extraordinary obstinacy,'' says Kollmann pertinently, " complete uniformity must have long since prevailed among men everywhere; for intermixture has been continuous and prolific. But craniological evidence shows that there is no uniformity and every unprejudiced observer confirms it.''

Elswhere he says:

" Life in the drawing-room may reduce the ligaments and the muscular strength and make the hands and feet small; but the characteristics of his race, which the individual bears in himself as heir to an ancient heritage, remain undisturbed in spite of tall hat and patent leathers.''

If, then, race-characteristics are constant and the number of human races or varieties is still undetermined, it follows obviously that when man's existence on earth began and before races had mingled and " penetrated,'' there were countless distinct (*heterogen*) human swarms, severally representing the various race-characteristics which have persisted unchanged in penetration.

The conclusion is imperative. If race-characteristics pass from generation to generation only by inheritance; if no new ones arise and only the old ones appear over and over again; if they are countless to-day and penetration and inheritance are still spreading them (though many may have disappeared forever); if they prove to be as permanent and ancient as the

* "*Craniologische Graeberfunde in der Schweiz*,'' 1883.

tombs; must we not conclude that there was in the beginning a countless number of distinct human hordes, each one an individual race or society ?   Only a mind warped by Biblical traditions and modern conceptions of the family would insist on substituting first '' pairs '' instead of hordes.

It may be said that it is exaggeration to speak of countless hordes since even the anthropologists and craniologists who accept polygenism use modest numbers.   But to how few traits they limit themselves or are confined by necessity ! Who will believe that the race-characteristics are all confined to the skull and the skeleton though that is almost the only place where anthropologists may look ?

Obviously there should be corresponding differences even in the finest features of the face and in the minutest convolutions of the brain, which are as yet wholly unknown. Some are entirely inaccessible to such investigations as we apply to the bones; others are too delicate for our sense-perceptions; others still are on organs and parts of the body, like the nose and ears, which suffer complete decay so that no comparison can be made with the past.   Yet nobody doubts that the racial differences in these members are important. So it is not too rash to suppose that a far greater number of human varieties now exists and, since types are permanent, always has existed than anthropology has any means of knowing.   These considerations, we hope, will still further justify us in starting upon our sociological investigations with the polygenetic hypothesis.*

5. CONCEPT AND ESSENCE OF SOCIAL LAW.

The facts cited show plainly that existing '' races '' are not simple and mutually exclusive in the anthropological sense; moreover every means of investigation fails to disclose racial purity in prehistoric times.   Yet, reasoning deductively from the mixed to the unmixed and from the composite to the simple, we must infer that races once were pure.   The logical conclusion must be accepted as the working hypothesis, at least, of a scientific investigation.   But anthropological changes have not affected the social relations

* It has already been stated that Bastian considers such a justification superfluous since polygenism is "self-evident."   But the fact that Alfred Kirchhoff, a professor of geography who calls himself a "wicked Darwinian," writing in the *Literarisches Centralblatt*, declares this theory irreconcilable with Darwinism, proves that the correct conception of Darwin's theory has not been so widely diffused as could be wished.   Hence the above explanation seems to me still necessary.

of either the ancient or the modern human groups of which we treat. Sociologically they are distinct groups still. Sociological dissimilarities are independent of the structure of the bones and skull. They consist in very different factors. Once the distinction between native and alien may have answered to differences purely anthropological. But ever since the dawn of history the native has been distinguished from the alien simply by social status and relations which he and everybody else recognizes as necessarily correlative with and consequent upon sociological or, really, social factors.

Birth and training are social factors. The latter, especially, imparts the language, morals, ideas, religion and usages of the group and causes the individual to appear to himself and to others to belong to it. All together bind the members to each other by a common interest, which is patriotism in its earliest form.

The simple syngenetic groups are affected by a great variety of interests, political, economical, national and intellectual in such ways that several elementary groups become united in one; primary social complexes are followed by secondary and these by others of successively higher orders. The same regular processes which took place in the simple groups in virtue of their social nature occur in all the others; combinations and cultural changes only modify or complicate them. These processes, which we shall call social since their source is in social elements, are the content, as the groups, simple and compound, are the agents of social history.

Social processes exhibit great uniformity. Though time and circumstances modify them they remain essentially the same. So for each instance of uniformity in the social domain, as elsewhere, we formulate a law of the cause and call the law social.* Hence a social law is an inference from concrete social occurrences presenting the norm of the

* De Tocqueville was impressed by the thought that peoples, however distant and unrelated, must develop according to some law. "When I perceive the resemblance," he says, "which exists between the political institutions of our ancestors, the Teutons, and the wandering tribes of North America,—between the customs described by Tacitus, and those of which I have sometimes been the witness,—I cannot help thinking that the same cause has brought about the same results in both hemispheres; and that, in the midst of the apparent diversity of human affairs, certain primary facts may be discovered, from which all the others are derived."—"Democracy in America," translated by Henry Reeve, edited by Francis Bowen, Cambridge. 1862. Cap. xviii, pp. 441-42.—The ethnographical horizon has been much extended since, and de Tocqueville's conjecture is confirmed. Sociology may attempt to distinguish the *faits générateurs* the "primary facts.'; "Ethnology has irrefutably proven," say Achelis, "*Ethnologie und Geschichte*'

development and reciprocal influence of social elements, *i. e.*, of the syngenetic groups.

The only way to prosecute social science is to discover social laws where ethnical or social elements come in contact and to demonstrate their validity. So long as the investigation was conducted in any other way, no attempt to discover or found a social science could succeed.

It was recognized that there must be regularity of development and that the laws of development must be demonstrated, were a philosophy of history or a social science to be founded. Comte and Carey insisted upon this repeatedly. But no one knew where to look for conformity to law. Some, like Voltaire, sought for laws of the development of mankind. But if mankind is taken as a unit, it is obvious that development must be either upward or downward; that there must be either progression or retrogression. Rousseau and others accepted the latter alternative. Assuming a primitive happy state of nature, they went on to prove man's growth in corruption. But the greater part, including nearly every writer on the history of civilization, taught the contrary, laboring to show upward progression from original savagery to successively higher forms of civilization. Both parties were wrong; both erred in treating " mankind " as a unit of development. The mistake was general; but the position cannot be maintained unless the field of view is materially limited. Generally it is confined to the narrow stream of European civilization running through Greece and Rome to France or Germany. The development discovered here is attributed to mankind as a whole. Comte, for instance, locates a period of polytheism between primitive fetichism and modern(!) monotheism and asserts that " it was under its reign that mankind(!) rose to settled monogamy." * It is clear what a tiny fraction of mankind the statement applies to. Comte took no thought of the rest; it would have vitiated the orderly development of " mankind " and its elevation to monogamy.

But a few sagacious statisticians led by Quetelet escaped the self-deception. Unsatisfied by this fancied regularity, they sought to discover laws of orderly development by

—*Ausland*, No. 4, 1881, "that certain phenomena of associative life are perfectly similar among peoples who are entirely unlike and who have never heen related in any demonstrable way whatever. Hence . . . the nature of the human race (species) is manifestly one and universal in spite of all differences."

* Comte-Martineau, *op. cit.*, Vol. ii, p. 195; Comte, *op. cit.*, Vol. v, p 220; Comte-Rig., *op. cit.*, Vol. ii, p. 230.

other means. Quetelet is conscious that there can be no science of man unless man's whole conduct depends on fixed laws just as the phenomena of natural science do; and he regrets that philosophers have never perceived it.

"Either from a distrust in their own strength," he says, "or a repugnance in supposing it possible to reduce to fixed laws what seemed to flow from the most capricious of causes, it has hitherto been deemed expedient by learned men to abandon the line of inquiry employed in the investigation of the other laws of nature as soon as the moral phenomena of mankind become the object of research."*

He also surmises correctly that if we would discover the laws controlling man's behavior we must disregard the individual.

"It is of primary importance to keep out of view man as he exists in an insulated, separate, or in an individual state, and to regard him only as a fraction of the species. In thus setting aside his individual nature, we get quit of all which is accidental, and the individual peculiarities, which exercise scarcely any influence over the mass, become effaced of their own accord, allowing the observer to seize the general results."

After giving the well-known illustration of the particles of chalk-dust which form a circle only when seen from a distance, he continues: "it is in this way that we propose studying the laws which relate to the human species: for, by examining them too closely," by examining the individuals, he means, "it becomes impossible to apprehend them correctly, and the observer sees only individual peculiarities, which are infinity." † That is, in place of the false and discarded subject-matter, the individual, he substitutes a vague and incomprehensible "human species," "society," or "social body." This is his error. He never discovered what the real subject-matter of observation should be; and consequently all his efforts to found a science were a failure, as we shall see.

How could Quetelet discover conformity to law? His concept suggests nothing concrete, nor even anything measurable. But every concrete object in nature is limited, and none but limited objects can be observed scientifically. His terms suggest something unlimited, undefinable, as unfit for concrete observations—the foundation of all science—as time

* "A Treatise on Man and the Development of His Faculties." Edinburgh, 1842, p. 5.
† Ibid.

and space. It must be resolved into concrete units first. He wisely discarded the " individual," but he failed to find the real unit.

He had recourse to the " great number," as has been said. It is the magician's wand with which he conjures a finely plastic scientific subject-matter out of the unyielding " human species," " society," or " social system." Using a " great number " of cases, he finds laws prevalent where formerly blind confusion reigned. The operation is very simple; if it were only as sound !

Any convenient phenomenon may be observed and a record made of the frequency of its recurrence in equal periods of time. If the several totals are compared, either they will seem to conform to law or they will not, one or the other. In the former event, the statisticians proclaim the " law of the great number;" in the latter they keep silence. Generally some law is discoverable; for everything in the world is amenable to number. Anything can be counted. At some limit, which must eventually be attained, numbers always give certain proportions; and this property of numbers seems to have been communicated to the enumerated articles.

Take any rare occurrence in ordinary life. Say a lunatic climbs a tower and jumps to the street. Within the memory of man the like had not happened in that locality. It stands alone. No law can be discovered on it. If it is never repeated it eludes all statistical treatment. But possibly it may re-occur. If we could find only one other instance in a long series of years, even that would be enough to show " conformity to law;" the event will occur once in so and so many years.

Obviously the opportunity for making ratios is far greater when the events enumerated occur daily and hourly, as many in human life do. Births, marriages, deaths, in fact the majority of demographical phenomena must occur with great regularity; and statistics win an easy triumph. But have the laws governing natural phenomena been explained when the regularity of their occurrence is confirmed ? Here number is an indication or proof that there is conformity to some law; and that is all.

Statistical results are wholly insufficient for formulating and explaining the least law of " mankind," " society," " the social system." In a word the " law of the great number '' is a law of number and not of the phenomena enumerated; whereas social science wishes especially to learn the laws of social phenomena. Granted that statistics are a very important means of investigation; yet counting phenomena and computing ratios is a process purely arithmetical. It has no identity with the discovery and explanation of the laws of the behavior of phenomena.

Quetelet's statistical investigations are a great boon to science. But he did not demonstrate social laws as he proposed. He mistook the laws of number for the laws of social phenomena. His self-deception originated in his unclear concept of the subject-matter of social science. His indefinite and incomprehensible ''mankind'' could not be subjected to rigid and exact scientific treatment.

In one of his later works, the ''Natural History of Society,'' he tried to improve by distinguishing several social communities from one another. But he got no clear idea of ''race,'' ''nation,'' and '' state.'' On the contrary he did what would not have been expected of him: he assumed the individual to be their source and so prevented apprehension of their true substance as effectually as the individualistic and atomistic tendency in politics does.

Spencer's philosophy and sociology is, as we have said, a significant advance upon Quetelet, Comte and the historical philosophers. He too argues that social science is both necessary and possible. *   But he does not insist, as Comte does, that the subject-matter of social laws is mankind developing as a unit; rather he always speaks of the development of social aggregates. Nor does he, like Quetelet, use the ''great number'' to solve the problem of regular development. He thinks he has found the solution in his formula of evolution.

As evolution stands in a certain though distant relation to social phenomena, it might be accepted as a '' universal law.'' But we cannot accept it as a ''social law.'' In every science, according to Spencer's theory, if we trace the history of particular things backward we shall find that their constituent parts were once in a state of diffusion. And if we trace their history forward from any point we shall find concentrated conditions instead of diffuse. Hence he concludes that the formula for the law of evolution must include both processes, concentration and diffusion. Every

* Spencer, '' Study of Sociology.'' International Science Series, caps ii–iii.

perceivable thing, as he states it, is in a state of continuous change; it is either becoming or passing away.   The former state consists in the integration or concentration of matter and the dissipation of motion, which he calls evolution. The latter consists in the disintegration of matter and the absorption of motion, which he calls dissolution.*

He demonstrates its validity for all classes of phenomena with great acumen.   But the connection between the universal formula and the concrete phenomena is so loose that we gain no explanation of them from it.   Applying to everything it explains nothing.   It is not really a law of the phenomena.   It says no more, at bottom, than that motion is universal without disclosing why.

In the social domain, especially, the defect is glaring. The formula fits the social processes in a certain figurative sense, but does not explain them.

"While there exist nothing but small, wandering assemblages of men, devoid of organization," he says for instance, "the conflicts of these assemblages with one another cannot work changes in structure. But when once there have arisen the definite chieftainships which these conflicts themselves tend to initiate, and especially when the conflicts have ended in permanent subjugations, then arise the rudiments of political organization."†

The process uniting social aggregates into political organizations is remotely analogous to his law of evolution to be sure; but we must still have recourse to the law that "solicitude for the means of subsistence"‡ forces each social aggregate to try to make every other social aggregate coming within its reach serve that supreme end.   This law fully explains why the stronger of the "small wandering hordes" aim to subject the weaker and get their services; and it shows the necessity for all the "structures" or variety of organization which culminate in the "state."   The "universal law" of evolution applies to the process; but Spencer fails to emphasize the "social law" which explains it.

But Spencer offers many just observations upon social phenomena and processes.   The formula of evolution does not prevent a correct conception of them and in so far it is harmless and superior to other universal formulas.   The most significant part of Spencer's sociology however is his demonstration that psycho-social phenomena develop with

* "First Principles," secs. 94, 97.
† "The Principles of Sociology." Vol. i, sec. 11.
‡ [*Lebensfuersorge.*—"Solicitude for the means of subsistence."]

regularity.   Herein he displays a natural talent and master-
ship unequaled save by Bastian.   Let us notice this feature
of his social psychology briefly.

Ethnographical and prehistoric investigations conducted
in all climates and regions of the earth have established the
remarkable fact that changes in social phenomena from
period to period are consequent and logical, in a word, are
evolutionary.   Thus the investigation of the prehistoric
material showed a developing series of utensils from bone to
stone, to bronze and to iron.   The entire series could not be
illustrated in the history of one people but had to be constructed out of the relics of peoples from all regions of the
globe.   Many groups, moreover, had continued permanently
on some one stage without any development whatever.   In
all the domain of social life, religious, moral, juridical or
cultural, it is the same.

The philosophizing human mind finds a logical and
strictly regular development from fetichism through anthropomorphism, polytheism, monotheism to the atheism of
free thinkers.   But scarcely would any one group illustrate
the whole series; and how many groups still pray to fetiches,
conceive their God in human form, people their heaven with
throngs of deities or recognize only one Jahve as they did
thousands of years ago! while, on the other hand, there
were occasional free-thinkers and atheists even in antiquity.

Spencer's sociological and Bastian's "ethnological"
works abound in examples of apparent psycho-social development reconstructed out of the contributions of various
peoples, times and lands.   The first available explanation
might seem to be the hypothesis that mankind is a unit;
and this explanation has often been offered.   But man's
actual condition is unlike the constructed development.
Take any series of psycho-social phenomena whatever and
the several phases prevail as generally to-day as at any time
in the past.   Yet how inviting it is to a nineteenth century
European to construct a "social development" from the
condition of unregulated "free love" to polyandry, polygamy and, finally, to the "most beautiful flower of human
development," monogamy.

Not only is this method relied upon by Spencer repeatedly
and used by Bastian in compiling his "manifestations of
race-thoughts;" even Lippert uses it in his thoughtful presentation of the family and the priesthood, etc.   Indisputably

such series exhibit logical sequence and (logical !) "con-formity to law." But the development is not social and must not be taken for it. The development of social institutions ought not to be confounded with the development of mankind itself, with social development in the stricter sense. Psycho-social progress never takes place uniformly throughout mankind. Rather there is always such a great variety of human conditions that types may always be found for a logical series. Not only thousands of years ago but to-day there are communities living in unregulated free love, and tribes and races in which polyandry, polygamy and monogamy did and do prevail. Bastian wants to found a "science of man" upon a law of the manifestation of "race-thought," upon a case of psycho-social development, as we should call it; and Spencer constructs his sociology out of similar cases.* To a certain extent they are justified. Psycho-social investigation furnishes valuable material. The "examination of the mental creations of aggregates to find the laws of the human mind's growth," may be considered an integral part of sociology, or ethnology, the word Bastian prefers. "Whenever the local surface colorations are penetrated and analysis is vigorously prosecuted, uniform fundamental conceptions are disclosed."† But sociology, the "science of man," is something more. Social and psycho-social must be sharply distinguished. The former comprehends the relations between groups and communities of men. The latter the manifestations of "race-thought" in the domain of religion, morals, rights and civilization. Only the laws of the relations of distinct aggregates of human material to each other are social. In distinction, the laws of the "mental creations of aggregates," to use Bastian's language, may be suitably designated psycho-social.

* Bastian, "*Der Voelkergedanke*" *passim*, especially the conclusion.
† *Ibid.*, p. 178.

III. SOCIAL ELEMENTS AND THEIR COMBINATIONS.

THE PRIMITIVE HORDE.   (*Promiscuity*,   *Mother-right*,
Marriage by Capture, *Paternal Family*,
Property, *Sovereignty*.)

As individual consciousness, long dormant, does not awaken until the mind has passed through the early stages of development, so also political reflection is not aroused until after stock and folk and other complex social phenomena have been developed. In natural science we are confronted at the outset with composites which have to be analyzed, and so, too, modern social science has to work laboriously back to the primitive horde, reconstructing the originals of modern social communities out of scattered vestiges in traditions and survivals, but deriving great assistance from living examples of wild, "uncivilized" hordes.[*]

The so-called "mother-right" is an instance. There are vestiges of it still among civilized peoples, and its former diffusion is confirmed by its presence among contemporary uncivilized races. It is the Ariadne's thread of sociology, leading through the complex social communities of present and historic times back to the primitive horde.

The type of "family" presided over by the "father" existed in Europe even at the dawn of history. The Greeks and the Romans considered it the primeval form, established by nature, the true germ of all later social forms. They followed the tradition of the Asiatic races and European science accepted the current view.

Only recently has ripened reflection and acute observation discovered that the "father-family" was preceded by a period in which a very narrow consanguineous group flocked about the mother as its founder. The evidence collected by

[*] Darwin gives the following graphic picture, from personal observation, of a horde politically unorganized: "The astonishment which I felt, as I first saw a troop of Terra-del-Fuegians on a wild and rugged coast, I shall never forget; for the thought flashed through my mind at once : Thus were our forefathers. These men were absolutely naked of clothing and covered only with paint. Their long hair was twisted together, their mouths bedriveled from excitement, and their expression wild, amazed and suspicious. They possessed scarcely any skill at all, and lived like wild beasts] on whatever they could catch. They had no government, and had no mercy toward those not of their own race."—"Descent of Man," Vol. II, p. 356. *Cf.* "*Rassenkampf*," p. 195 *et seq.*

Bachofen, Giraud-Teulon, McLennan,* and more recently by Lippert, Dargun and Wilken, must be considered conclusive. Even in the Germanic law Dargun has recently shown undoubted traces of a former "mother-right."

Hitherto it has sufficed to prove that historically, or rather prehistorically, there was a "mother-family" and resulting "mother-rights," which survived for centuries. But it is more important, in our opinion, to show that the "mother-family" is the necessary consequence of the constitution of an earlier group. Not only is this necessary to a proper conception of the "mother-family," it will also help us to understand the nature of what for the present we must assume to have been the primitive horde. The very fact that the former existed confirms the existence of the latter.

Such a horde cannot be conceived of simply as new, or as proceeding directly from the hands of "a creator;" for in distant parts of the world there are hordes that are primitive still. It is a group of men who are still dependent upon the simplest animal impulses, whose conditions of life and social constitution show no social change. Its life moves upon the plane of the simplest and most common impulses inherent in man.

The satisfaction of hunger and thirst, the first necessity, engages the men of the primitive horde and constitutes a great part of their life work. The satisfaction of the sexual impulses is the next strongest factor.

The simplest form of sexual relations is promiscuity, transient connection within the horde according to accidental encounter or stronger momentary attraction. It is still exemplified in the conduct of contemporary uncivilized tribes.†

No fathers are recognized because, as a rule, they are unknown. The bond of kinship between the men and their own children is lacking and the only tie of blood other than kinship with the common stock, which binds the whole horde together, is through the mother. Under this primitive system there could be no other family than the "mother-family." The children were hers; she exercised authority over them and over the "family"—hence "mother-rule" and "mother-right."

* "Kinship in Old Greece."
† For historical cases see Post, "*Geschlechts-Genossenschaft der Urzeit*," pp. 16 *et seq.*, where the earlier literature on this subject is cited.

This type of family organization had nearly disappeared at the dawn of history. But numerous traces of it persisting in tradition have been collected; and further proof is furnished by the aetiological explanation of the subordinate position of woman where the opposite system prevails.

A conspicuous case is the Biblical narrative, which treats the woman as a secondary creation of God since she was made of the rib of the man; a circumstance tending to justify his authority.

This is perhaps one of the earliest examples showing that no actual ruler is ever at a loss for a theoretical explanation of his "right." When woman lost her authority, she also had to make the best of a descent from the insignificant rib of a man, as the political philosophers in the new order of society alleged. They who suffer the injury must also endure the ridicule. Later the subject classes were traced to an inferior descendant of Noah; while the ruling classes were called the descendants of his privileged, first-born, son. These are all genealogical tricks and aetiological lies of the historian.

It is recognized that mother-rule everywhere gave place to father-rule; but the natural forces which produced this revolution in the original constitution of society have never been pointed out so far as we know. Yet marriage by capture or, more exactly, exogamic connection explains it fully.

The universality of woman-stealing both in the present and in the past is fully established, and the custom has been well described by ethnologists. But too little weight has been given to the circumstance which constitutes its real essence: the wife must always be stolen from another horde.

This is self-evident when we consider the condition of a horde living in primitive promiscuity. Within the horde woman-stealing is impossible. It must be from without; and to this form of it the gynecocratic constitution gives abundant incentive.

In the raids of unrelated hordes the woman has been and in many cases still is more valuable than cattle or any other form of food-supply. In the gynecocratic horde an exceptional position can be claimed for her, for the captor can hold her as his individual property; whereas the native women are common and occupy a ruling position protected by custom.

The foreign woman has no share in their privileges; belonging exclusively to her "lord," she must serve as his slave. This is greatly to his advantage; it was the beginning of his "emancipation" in the primitive horde. No wonder that the advantages which this innovation secured caused it to spread so that, when the historical period opened, traditions of woman-stealing are universal. Recollect, for example, the rape of the Grecian Helen by a prince from Asia Minor, with which Grecian history begins; and the rape of the Sabine women, from which Roman history starts. Herodotus, the father of European historiography, begins characteristically by reciting the rape of Asiatic women by the Greeks, and of Grecian women by the inhabitants of Asia.

Woman-stealing readily developed into the institution of marriage by capture, the universality of which is fully attested by the countless survivals still persisting.*

But as the custom spread the mother-family and mother-right necessarily declined; the native women could not maintain their position in competition with the foreign. The charm of the new and strange alone would have assured the latter a certain preference; but it also afforded the man an opportunity, certainly not unwelcome, to escape from a condition which had become unnecessary, burdensome and "unreasonable," though the innovation must have been a rude offence against old and sacred customs.

Thus mother-rule was overthrown, and with it fell mother-right and the mother-family, while the sovereignty of the men was extended over the native women also. They had to adapt themselves to the inevitable; the good old custom disappeared and a new ethico-legal institution prevailed: father-hood, father-family, father-right.

But its significance for the social development of mankind was increased by one of the attending circumstances, the mingling of unlike [heterogen] ethnical groups. The process has been continuous and universal and the intermixtures are interminable in number, variety and degree. Together with political, judicial and other institutions, they have produced an endless number of differentiated social unities.

However, rape was not the only occasion of early intertribal hostilities; the plunder of property must also have been an incentive just as it always has been and still is, not among the uncivilized tribes alone.

Simple plundering raids are carried on at irregular intervals

---

* Post op. cit., p. 54 et seq. Dargun, "Mutterrecht und Raubehe," p. 78 et seq.

as necessity dictates and circumstances allow. But they
generally lead to expeditions for the permanent subjection of the foreign horde and the acquisition of territory.*

These latter conditions are the most favorable for the
development of civilization, as has been explained elsewhere.† Yet the proximate basis of the evolution is the
institution of property which develops in connection with
them also.

We have already seen that property developed concur-
rently with the control of one group of men over another
and, in fact, as a means to uphold it.‡ But a few remarks
must be added here, partly for the sake of greater clearness,
and partly because of some recent works which were written in ignorance of our explanation.

In the first place property in land is, in our opinion, the
only form which serves as an instrument of control. "Property" in movable goods should be distinguished from
property in immovable goods. What is there in common
between the unlimited possession and free disposal of chat-
tels and that juridical relation in virtue of which a person
may keep a piece of land exclusively for his own benefit?
Yet for these fundamentally different conceptions the European languages use but one term, with consequent indistinct-
ness and confusion of ideas in science.

Common property (*Eigentum, proprium*) is a contradiction in terms; yet even separate or private "property" has
been discussed as a simple concept and what might be true
of property in movable goods has been applied without distinction to property in land, a very different thing. This is
certainly a great mistake.

To justify private property as the natural right of the
individual to the fruit of his own exertions sufficiently
explains property in movable goods, including the product
of the land which a man's own labor has tilled, but does not
explain property in land or in the fruit of another's
labor; while to trace its origin to the actual possession of
weapons, ornaments, etc., an attempt which Dargun has

* Some idea of the behavior of primitive stocks can be gotten from the modern
Bedouins who, however, have made considerable progress. A recent French
traveler writes: "To fall upon caravans of strangers, to drive off flocks, capture
goods, kill and massacre the defenders, especially if they are inhabitants of cities,
such are the virtues which he rates highest. All these ignoble heroes of Bedouin
legend we would send to the galleys as highway robbers." Gabriel Charmes,
"*Voyage en Syrie.*" *Revue des deux Mondes,* August 15, 1881.
† "*Der Rassenkampf,*" p. 231.
‡ "*Rechtsstaat und Socialismus,*" p. 344.

recently renewed, leaves a gap between movable goods and immovable which no analogy can bridge over, for they are totally different.   No doubt individual property in movable goods has always existed, for the conditions of human life require it.   But the conditions of property in land are quite different.   Land is not the product of human labor, and its use is temporary; it can be occupied, detained or possessed only in a limited and figurative sense; it might be possible to defend a small portion of land against trespassers; but it would be impossible to defend the larger tracts which alone are under consideration here.   Property in land is not a physical fact and cannot be explained by physical facts: occupation, labor, etc.   To say that land is occupied or possessed, as is currently done, is to use a metaphor or a legal fiction.   Land, by its nature, admits of only one relation to man, the enjoyment of its use, the common enjoyment of many.

Hence the first form of property in land must have been its common use, and further, it must have been used by such a group or horde as we meet with everywhere in the beginning of social evolution.   The evidence supporting this conclusion is abundant.   Even the primitive hordes of modern times use land in common.*

Thus, in the nature of the cases, common property in movable goods is impossible, but so-called common property in land is real and original.   What is commonly called private property in land is never real, much less original; it is purely a legal relation; presupposing a complicated social organization.   It presupposes, first of all, an organized control, with power to compel obedience.   This is necessary that the individuals of the ruling class may procure from the subject class the labor power to till their lands and make them useful; thus they prove their property.   Without power to dispose of the labor force of others it would be merely a name, with that power it becomes valuable.

A second presupposition is the possibility of excluding some from the enjoyment of the product in favor of others. The organized whole must protect the movable goods thus acquired; for if they were left exposed to every aggressor it would not be worth while to raise them.   In a word, property in land is a legal relation which necessarily presup-

---

* "Man does not have property in immovable things upon this stage."—Lippert, "*Priesterthum*," vol. i, p. 35.

poses governmental organization and the guarantee of legal protection.

Thus the "common property" which the primitive horde is said to enjoy in the land on which it has settled is simply common use and not real ownership, for the word "own" contains originally the idea of separateness. Laying aside our complex, advanced legal relations, and speaking of primitive conditions, we must take "ownership" to be separate ownership and its antithesis is unseparated, not-own, *i. e.*, common. It was a much later and over-refined jurisprudence which transferred the idea of separate owner-ship to a juristic person composed of a number of natural persons, and it would be an unseemly transfer of modern legal conceptions to speak of the common property of the primitive horde.

Passing on from the use of the land in common, we first recognize the beginnings of separate immovable property when one horde has overpowered another and uses its labor force. As soon as there are subjects who are excluded from the enjoyment of certain goods which their own labor con-tributed to produce, in favor of the ruling class, and when the members of the ruling class are protected in their enjoy-ment of them by the well-organized whole, then there arises separate or private property in immovable goods. Not only did this form of property arise with the organization of con-trol and by means of it, it was at first the sole object of the organization, which, moreover, contains the germ of the state. So long as the organization continues in a nomadic condition, and lords and slaves alike have no abiding place, we do not call it a state. We apply that term only when a permanent dwelling place has been adopted and the organi-zation asserts its sovereign right of property over the land it occupies against all other social communities.

THE STATE.

The state is a social phenomenon consisting of social elements behaving according to social laws. The first step is the subjection of one social group by another and the estab-lishment of sovereignty; and the sovereign body is always the less numerous. But numerical inferiority is supple-mented by mental superiority and greater military disci-pline. There is a double life in the state; we can clearly distinguish the activities of the state as a whole, as a single social structure, from those emanating from the social elements.

The activities of the state as a whole originate in the sovereign class which acts with the assistance or with the compulsory acquiescence of the subject class. The movement is from within out; it is directed against other states and social groups. Its object is always defence against attacks, increase of power and territory, that is, conquest in one form or another; and its motive, in the ultimate analysis, lies in human providence, in the impulse to secure conditions favorable for existence [in *Lebensfuersorge*] to use Lippert's apt expression.

The activities within the state are seen in the several social elements and arise naturally from the positions which they occupy in the state and to each other.

The motive of each is essentially the same as that which animates the state as a whole. They seek conditions favorable to existence and therefore endeavor to increase their power. In particular, the superior class seeks to make the most productive use of the subject classes; as a rule this leads to oppression and can always be considered as exploitation. The subject classes strive for greater powers of resistance in order to lessen their dependence.

These are the simplest and most fundamental efforts and they account for the internal and external development of the state; while differences in the history of different states are due to different local and ethnical conditions.

As the commonest things of life are often the most difficult to understand, so it is that political scientists to this day have no clear conception of the state; each has his own definition and scarcely one is correct.

Modern scholasticism has made the theory of the state endless and fruitless. ''Volume I'' of a work on the definition of the state has appeared in Berlin * already and there is a ''history'' and a methodology of the subject. Who will write a theory of the theory of the state? Some use general terms, calling the state a '' politically organized national person ''† or the '' highest form of personality,'' or the '' organism of freedom.'' Others solve the problem by using a metaphor, by calling it a '' living being,'' an'' organism,'' etc. But Knies justly remarks that '' it is a sad proof

* Von Rotenburg, "*Ueber den Begriff des Staates.*"
† Bluntschli, '' The Theory of the State.'' (Clarendon Press) bk. i, cap. i, p. 23.

of unclear thinking to discuss scientific conceptions in metaphors.'' * Schulze made great progress in the method of
defining the state by insisting that ''it is a question of
separating the essential from the unessential in the pleni-
tude of social phenomena;''† and after methodically
searching for its historical characteristics he concluded that
it is the ''association of a settled folk in an organic
community under a sovereign power and a definite constitution for the purpose of securing all the common ends of a
folk's existence, above all for the establishment of law and
order. ‡
But his definition can be improved by eliminating superfluous parts. The idea by no means clearly expressed in
the words '' an organic community '' is included in the preceding phrase; for a '' folk,'' and much more, a ''settled
folk,'' is '' an organic community.'' Indeed a '' settled
folk '' is a state; no further '' association '' is needed to make
it one. It is superfluous also to mention a '' constitution,''
for a written constitution is not essential and an unwritten
constitution is a prerequisite of a '' settled folk.''
If nothing but the universal and essential characteristics
of every state were incorporated into the definition, an
agreement could be easily reached for there are but two.
First, there are certain institutions directed to securing the
sovereignty of some over the others; secondly, the sovereignty is always exercised by a minority. A state, therefore, is the organized control of the minority over the
majority. This is the only true and universal definition; it
is apt in every case.§
But many definitions of the state predicate its end,
declaring it to be a union or community for securing the
common weal, for realizing justice, etc. All this is wholly
inadmissible. No state was ever founded with one of these

* Knies, " Statistik als Wissenschaft," 1850, p. 90.
† Schulze, "Einleiung in das Deutsche Staatsrecht," 1865, p. 116, sec. 25.
‡ Ibid, sec. 32.
§ Elsewhere in his book Schulze gives almost the same definition. In section 41 he
says that " it is observable that in all actual states men are subject to a sovereign
power and that, as members of the body politic, they are even held by physical
compulsion to certain lines of activity." And in section 49 : " The presence of a
supreme controlling power is essential to the notion of a state." Von Ihering, in
"Zweck im Recht," Vol. I, p. 130, defines the state to be "society as possessor of an
orderly and disciplined power of compulsion." But he tries to define the "state"
by the less clear term "society" and, besides, adopts the untenable French view
of "popular sovereignty." Continuing the argument, he again defines the state
as "organized social compulsion." Properly understood this is nearly correct.
But we had already ("Philosophisches Staatsrecht," 1876) defined the state to be
"the organized sovereignty of some over the others;" and as " sovereignty " is
more specific than "compulsion," our definition is the clearer of the two.

ends in view; and there are many which are states though
they have never exhibited even a trace of such a purpose.
The truth is that in the course of time under favorable conditions every sovereign organization necessarily acts in
harmony with these ends; thus any state may serve them,
indeed after reaching a certain stage of development every
state does endeavor to advance justice, welfare, etc. But
the definition must not be confined to states at one stage of
development only; it must apply regardless of the stage
which has been or ever will be attained. Moreover, the
affirmation of such ends conceals the fact that the single
object in organizing a state was to establish the sovereignty
of some over the others, and that the results which necessarily followed were not foreseen, much less intended; they
cannot be referred to the intention of the founders who followed their own immediate advantage, as all men do. High
above egoistic human efforts social development is the product of natural law.

There is still another universal characteristic of the state,
although it has hitherto been wholly overlooked; there are
always ethnical differences between the ruling class and
the ruled.

We called attention to it for the first time in our former
publications; "authorities in political science" solemnly
ignored it; but they could not refute it. The world moves,
nevertheless.* States have never arisen except through the
subjection of one stock by another, or by several others in
alliance.

This is not accidental; it is essential, as we have already
proven. No state has arisen without original ethnical heterogeneity [*Heterogeneitaet*]; its unity is the product of social
development.

Spencer without specially emphasizing ethnical heterogeneity confirms our position when he says that "no tribe
becomes a nation by simple growth." Instead of the naive
conception that a family gradually grows to be a tribe and
the tribe becomes a folk, he holds that there must be a combination of several tribes; to which we add that, with perhaps a few unknown exceptions, tribes are united only by
the forcible subjection of one to the other. Spencer also
goes on to say that "no great society (nation) is formed by

[* Playing on the words attributed to Galileo while under ecclesiastical sentence
for his astronomical views.—*E pur si muove.*]

the direct union of the smallest societies ; " * by which he evidently means that a great nation necessarily comprises several smaller ones and includes a multitude of ethnically compound groups; it is a group of the nth power, so to speak.

Let us observe the necessary result of founding a state, *i. e.*, of subjecting one community to another or to a union of several others. It has already been pointed out that it is due to the effort to secure conditions favorable for existence. But the efforts which men naturally make to better their condition require the services of other men; if this were not so, states would never have been founded and mankind would have developed along quite different lines or not at all. It will be readily conceded that civilized men cannot live without the services of others. But there is no man known to history nor can any be thought of so uncivilized as to be able to renounce the co-operation of his kind.

The services which are needed are not easy; and the farther back we go the heavier they necessarily were. Their alleviation is an infallible characteristic of progressing civilization; we can observe it in the development of current industrial relations, and the struggle for it is the real subject-matter of so-called social legislation (*Social politik*). How men must have had to labor and indeed must still labor without the knowledge and the means of civilization! †

Many governments still commute death sentences to labor in the mines expecting to profit by this act of grace; and once the conquered were similarly condemned to slave-labor in the interest of the victors. Men never have treated their fellow-men (using that word in its most primitive sense) so severely; and why should they do violence to their natural feelings when strangers have never been lacking whom it has always been meritorious to prey upon. United under the leadership of the eldest and the mightiest they have imposed the yoke of servitude upon the stranger in hard-fought battle.

* "Principles of Sociology." Vol. i, secs. 257, 260. 456; *cf*. secs. 448, 451.
† The naval captain, Pantero Pantera, said of labor in the galleys in "*L'Armata Navale*," 1614: "High wages will supply a galley with soldiers and sailors, but free-men cannot be persuaded to submit to service at the oars, to be fastened to the chain and to take without possibility of resistance the bastinading and other inflictions incident to labor in the galleys." Yet, if the galley was to move with precision, the rowing must be controlled by chain, bastinado and all. Therefore he advised that convicted criminals be sentenced to this slave's work. Such was labor in the galleys even so late as the seventeenth century. "*La Fin d'une grande Marine*," by Jurien de la Gravière, "*Revue des Deux Mondes*," November 1, 1884.

Thus nature laid the foundation of ethnically composite states in human necessities and sentiments. Human labor being necessary, sympathy with kindred and tribe and deadly hatred of strangers led to foreign wars. So conquest and the satisfaction of needs through the labor of the conquered, essentially the same though differing in form, is the great theme of human history from prehistoric times to the latest plan for a Congo state.

Notice the condition thus established. The one party commands; the other labors and accommodates itself to superior force. As every war must cease raging and the weaker party must give up fruitless opposition, so nature helps to make the situation peaceful and lasting. But peace and permanence are the elements of order, out of which come habit, custom, rights.

The hostile contact of different [*heterogen*] social elements of unlike strength is the first condition for the creation of rights; the conditions established by force and accepted in weakness, if peaceably continued, become rightful. Inequality of power is essential, for contestants of equal strength would wear themselves out in mutual conflict or, more naturally, would unite and subject a weaker. Moreover inequality is stamped on every right; the husband orders his wife, the parent in the strength of his years commands his minor children, the owner excludes all others from enjoying the fruit of his property: all these are rights expressing the orderly relations of unequals. It is an error and a delusion to think that rights have been or can be equally distributed. They arise only in the relations which exist in the state; they express them and measure their inequality.

Let us now examine more closely the nature of political relations. Universally there is a ruling minority and a subject majority, this is the essence of the state as it is the essence of sovereignty.

But what is the ruling minority disposed to do? There is but one thing it can wish, viz.: to live in better circumstances with the services of the subject majority than it could without them. The result is a common industrial enterprise conducted under compulsion in which the greater burden, all the unfree service, falls upon the subject class though the rulers freely contribute their no less valuable share in support of the political community. Thus compulsory labor is organized through the organization of sovereignty and the whole body of rights.

The kind of industrial labor depends upon the nature of the soil, the climate and the material resources of the state. If the subjected population was roving over rich agricultural lands it will be compelled to till the soil and the conquerors will settle among them so as to exploit both land and people to the best advantage. The agricultural states of Europe still bear traces of such a compulsory organization of labor wherever an exclusive nobility has settled among a numerous agricultural population, spreading itself like a net over the whole land.

But a huge swarm inhabiting an extended prairie and pasture land will adopt a different social organization. The captives taken on many a plundering raid will be distributed among the members to perform the heavier work of tending cattle, transporting tents and the like. The nomadic state thus organized will fulfill its political functions as truly as the settled state of the large property owners. In the latter case the lord upon his manor or in his castle manages the peasants and vassals settled about him, satisfying their simple necessities from the produce of the fields and reserving the surplus for himself. In the nomadic state the master from his chieftain's tent rules over his numerous following, who tend his herds and enjoy a simple subsistence out of the increase; the rest of which, after the richer subsistence of his family is deducted, is added to his accumulated wealth and capital.

The organization will be different still where a narrow strip of coast like Phoenicia, or a group of islands like Venice, make agricultural or pastoral pursuits impossible. The superior speculative talent of the ruling class must suggest another method of utilizing the services of the subject class; they will be put to ship-building and employed as sailors, so that the rulers may seek distant coasts and win wealth and power in navigation and foreign trade.

Labor must always be organized under compulsion; the training and the discipline of the state are necessary. It demands of the laboring class, in the beginning at least, untold sacrifice of life and health; but finally in a rising civilization they become participants in the material and moral possessions.

The life of the state is summed up in this common though

unequal labor.   In it the state performs its task and fulfills
its mission, if task and mission can be spoken of where
blind impulse rules on every hand; out of it comes the highest
moral possession of mankind, civilization.*

THE STATE AS INDUSTRIAL ORGANIZATION.

The motive force in the establishment of primitive political relations was economic as has been seen; higher material
welfare was sought.   But this force never fails; the innermost nature of man keeps it in ceaseless operation, promoting the development of the state as it laid its foundation.
Investigate the cause of any political revolution and the
result will prove that social progress is always produced by
economic causes.   Indeed it cannot be otherwise since man's
material need is the prime motive of his conduct.†
This necessity incited men to exploit the services of their
fellows, and nature supplied a great many different groups
whose natural antagonism is still an important factor in
developing political relations; for human labor could not be
exploited without violence, and ethnical and social contrasts
promote the disregard of all human considerations, facilitating the satisfaction of human needs and maintaining the
everlasting struggle.   Thus the two fundamental social
processes are satisfaction of needs and exploitation of the
services (*Dienstbarmachung*) of foreigners, two apparently
unimportant means with which nature accomplishes so much.
Moreover the evolution cannot cease; for nature has provided that man's needs shall not stand still; higher and
"nobler" wants are constantly awakened; while at the
point where natural ethnical distinctions [*Heterogenéitæten*]
would disappear artificial "social" distinctions arise to per-
petuate the antagonism of human groups.   Human desires
never fail and there are groups differing in stature, color and
odor, in diet, morals and religion, or in possessions, conditions, calling, occupations and interests.
Only in the course of social development they rise to
higher stages and meet us in new forms as the need for
the bare means of subsistence with the most primitive is transformed in the higher stages into the necessity for satisfying

* In addition see " Organized Sovereignty and Civilization." "*Der Rassenkampf*,"
pp. 231 *et seq*.
† " The real motive force is the actual need.   The only reason for formulating it
in fixed law is to give it recognized legal basis," says Bruns on the Development
of the Roman Law, in Holtzendorff's " *Encyclopædie*," p. 91.

ambition, love of glory, the interests of a dynasty and various other ideals; and the life and death struggle between hordes anthropologically different [*heterogen*] becomes a contest between social groups, classes, estates and political parties. The great sociological difficulty in describing the course of development arises from the fact that there can be no leaps. Though social development like every other case of evolution is gradual, the transitional phases are innumerable and imperceptible and overtax the resources of science. The only alternative is to treat a small number of examples chosen more or less arbitrarily, which is all we can endeavor to do here.

It must not be forgotten that here, as elsewhere, the same phenomena are found sometimes contemporaneously, sometimes in sequence. There is a social development in time from the simplest satisfaction of necessities and the rudest struggle for existence up to the highest needs of a refined civilization and the system of rights developed in political strife; while its counterpart with all the imperceptible gradations and vivid contrasts can be seen in the cross-section, so to speak, of a state on the highest plane of development; for if we look at its inner structure we see the proletarian toiling for his daily bread in the sweat of his brow, and all the countless stages to the uppermost rung of society, to the statesman struggling for position or for principle. Moreover, what is true of the desires is true also of the means of satisfying them.

This in passing. Let us now turn to a closer analysis of the social evolution founded upon and promoted by organized sovereignty. Equality prevails only in the most primitive hordes. In them alone are needs satisfied without the subordination of one man's labor to another's ends; in them alone there is neither command nor obedience, lordship nor dependence, chieftain nor subject. Equal misery is the lot of all.

" When Rink asked the Nicobarians who among them was the chief they replied, laughing, how could he believe that one could have power against so many ? " And there are many similar examples. Among the Haidahs " the people seemed all equal;" Among the California tribes " each individual does as he likes; " among the Navajos, " each is sovereign in his own right." *

* [Add " as warrior."] See Spencer, " Principles of Sociology," Vol. ii, sec. 471 and sec. 466.

"Groups of Esquimaux, of Australians, of Bushmen, of Fuegians, are without even that primary contrast of parts implied by settled chieftainship. Their members are subject to no control but such as is temporarily acquired by the stronger, or more cunning, or more experienced, not even a permanent nucleus is present." *

Plainly the subjection of some to the service of others is opposed to the feeling of equality, of solidarity, of consanguineous relationships. Even the ruling classes of Europe exhibit the same feeling. "The nobleman in a peasant's cottage is the peer of the commander of the Palatine's army" ("*Szalchcic na zagrodzie równy wojewodzie*"), say the Poles. This is the equality of the syngenetic group. †

The primitive horde emerges from this condition of uniform independence and uniform misery only when a strange horde comes within its reach as the result generally of migration or a plundering raid. If it subjects the strangers its wants are more easily satisfied and its economic life is raised above the primitive condition; the "extra" labor of some for others begins.

If the rulers should remain content with the higher stage of economic life; if they could isolate their state from external influences, development would cease. But Lycurgian plans can never be realized; states can never be "isolated" even with Chinese walls about them.

Stagnation in development is prevented by the steady growth of the wants of both rulers and subjects, for the law that wants increase with the opportunity to satisfy them is universal, and the isolated state is also an object of desire to its neighbors near and remote, so that as they grow powerful it must increase its means of offence and defence. Even the least aggressive state will be drawn in spite of itself into the stream of "history;" evolution cannot stop. As wants increase, the state, which was called into being to satisfy them, is driven to further conquests of territory and power. But the same tendency which animates the state as a whole animates also each social division within it. The only difference is that its manifestation is confined by established political relations to a struggle for control by peaceful means; while outside the state it breaks out in bloody and destructive wars.

But, however unavoidable war may be, it cannot last always; for it produces physical and mental exhaustion;

* Spencer, "Principles of Sociology." Vol. i, sec. 228; Vol. ii, sec. 456.
† See "*Der Rassenkampf*," p. 40.

and if it becomes chronic the end for which it is undertaken is thereby defeated.

Peace is as necessary as occasional war, for both are the result of a natural law of strife; and so it was possible to establish states, since otherwise the more powerful must have had to exterminate the weaker. But peace is useless without the opportunity to satisfy the wants which war was undertaken to secure. However, only one party can be victor; one party secures the better satisfaction of its wants; and the other is circumscribed and oppressed. Some force is necessary to maintain the unequal condition in peace; suitable institutions must be set up and sedulously sustained. This the ruling and possessing class does while the other class accommodates itself to the law of the victors. But it jealously guards the established limits, now staking everything on preventing any further circumscription, now striving to enlarge them.

So apparent peace is only a continuous latent struggle. What is its object? What are the means employed? What is its essential characteristic? The immediate object of dispute is the body of reciprocal rights. The less privileged oppose every limitation whatever asserted in the interest of sovereignty: restricted connubial rights, exclusion from office and positions of honor, incapacity for holding landed property and others only relatively less important and less common. Sovereignty cannot be maintained without them, and the peaceful struggle of the unprivileged is directed to breaking them down and removing them eventually.

In the common interest, the subject class must be assigned some privileges and functions, for Spartan severity cannot be rigorously enforced. Even the superfluous Helot population was not always exterminated; neither do the Australian colonists hunt down the natives everywhere. In Sparta, to be sure, the contest of the Helots could not be conducted by peaceable means, but the sovereignty over them was not shortlived on that account; it succumbed to another course of development.

But wherever in the interest of the whole the least concession is made to the subject class it serves as a lever to enlarge their privileges. Two conditions, however, are necessary to success: well-being and enlightenment. When the ruling class is well off the condition of the subject class will necessarily rise too; otherwise the desires of the sovereign class cannot be fully satisfied. But appetite comes with eating and the first progress creates the desire for more.

Thoughts cannot be hermetically sealed, and as social facts even more than any other facts provoke reflection, the subject class, if relieved from external pressue and direct need, will experience mental growth. The ruling class is influenced less by the outside world and by the social relations; their life is easier and they are lulled to sleep mentally. But it is otherwise down in the seething mass of the "people." Huge numbers of them may succumb to the hard conditions of life and languish in ignorance and stupidity; but if the pressure ever relaxes, or if it falls on unusually strong natures, the mental reaction is all the more violent. On the whole the life of the subject classes is more fruitful in ideas.

Some degree of well-being and some ideas is the necessary leaven, as even Aristotle knew. It only needs a favorable opportunity, an external danger or defeat, a permitted popular gathering, a tumult of unusual dimensions, to make the first breach; further development in the market-place and on the forum is unavoidable. The same factors are active; the method is the same; the result is the same. Woe to the conquered, was the cry in the beginning and woe to the conquered is often the cry to the last.

DEVELOPMENT OF RANK AND POLITICAL ORGANIZATION.

But the social struggle is not so simple as it is here represented. Economic development and historical facts create a multitude of classes equally endowed with political tendencies and the result is a complexity of political rights. Intermediate classes intervene between the master and the slave which may hold the lower classes in dependence and be in subjection to the upper, or be superior to all in certain spheres of activity and dependent in others. They may be both rulers and ruled.

The simplest political organization consisting of lords and vassals, the simple *civitas* of the Romans, receives the first fatal shock from the foreign merchants. The effect of their visits upon the primitive political constitution is vividly portrayed by Cæsar in his "Commentaries." The Belgians were the bravest of all the Gallic tribes, he says, "because they are farthest removed from the civilization and culture of the Province and the merchants visit them least often bringing things which tend to effeminate.'' The merchants seeking gain penetrate the primitive political organization and disturb its monotonous course, for their ''fine articles'' charm the uncultivated man.

But these ''missionaries of commerce'' are the pioneers of culture. They visit the most inhospitable shores and impenetrable regions of unknown lands, staking both property and life; and the thousands who fall are followed by other thousands fearless of death—all for the sake of ''business.'' This is a universal fact, attested by classical witnesses, by the history of European colonization in all quarters of the globe, and, above all, by the living present. The clever Hansa-man, the trader with his wares seeking gain, is the first to enter the Congo and the Niger valleys, braving the difficulties of the dark continent and visiting tribes who receive the stranger as they would a wild beast; then, if his venture succeeds, come the '' chivalrous lords '' and ''patriotic statesmen.''

The merchant, coming as guest and offering his wares for sale, is personally free and knows how to maintain his freedom. Identified neither with the lords nor with their vassals, he soon becomes necessary to both, for the '' articles '' which he brings from a distance delight them and awaken new desires which must be satisfied. The one class labors more, the other saves more in order to get the new means of satisfying the new wants. They begin to grow '' effeminate;'' but it must be added that they also grow in '' civilization '' and '' culture.'' *

They learn to value and to tolerate the stranger, and he in turn discovers the virgin treasures of the land. Things are gladly given to him which before his time had no worth and without him would still have none. Occasional visits are followed by permanent settlements and the first settlers are followed by more numerous followers. A middle class forces itself in between lords and vassals; personally free and having no direct share in the government; instituting its own corporation in its own quarter—the later city; by compromise with the lords creating for itself rights within an assured sphere limited and defined both from above and

* Tacitus also understood that civilization is promoted by trade; and it is clear that he meant trade with foreigners. Thomas Aquinas speaks of the merchants as strangers in the state. He considered it desirable that the citizens should refrain from mercantile pursuits leaving them to "foreigners" lest "by the practice of trade" they "grow covetous." Thomas d'Aquin. "Opusculac Venitiis," 1587, p. 298. (" De Regemine Principum.")

below.* Thus a new factor arises in political evolution and social strife. Changes proceed more rapidly than before; foreign commerce makes domestic labor more productive and awakens handicraft and industry, while those who follow the new branches of economic labor are consolidated by their common interests into compact groups demanding their rights.

But such rights are only the realization, the unhindered exercise of acquired power, *i. e.*, supremacy within politically recognized limits, which, however various the means of acquiring it, consists essentially in the free and disposable possession of whatever will satisfy human wants.

Prominent in the list is the possession, or better, the disposal of human energy and labor. Without human services every other possession is valueless unless indeed by means of it human labor can be instantly secured, which reduces to the same thing. The power varies in greatness with the coefficient of disposable human energies and not with the amount of other possessions, though generally the former is proportional to the latter.

There is one method of utilizing human services directly, that is without the intervention of other possessions; it is the one by which the founders of political order assure themselves of the services of their vassals and slaves. They rely upon physical and mental superiority, strict military organization and discipline and innate tact in governing. Power thus acquired may be strengthened by various material and moral means; or it may fall into decay through weakness, lack of discipline and energetic opposition.

Other means of facilitating and assuring the uninterrupted application of human services is the possession of supplies and of institutions for promoting production. But the most powerful moral means is a purely natural factor, habit. Having elsewhere † emphasized its overwhelming power in political and legal relations, it is a great satisfaction to us to find our views confirmed in a recent work. ‡

"The power of habit is mysterious as witchery," it is said. "It sways the insignificant life of the individual and the great history of mankind. The dark impulse of all material things is in the midst of change to pause; in the midst of ceaseless motion to become stable for

---

* For historical evidence that the European merchant class began in this way, see "*Der Rassenkampf.*" p. 332.
† "*Das Philosophische Staatsrecht,*" sec. 23.
‡ "*Gegen die Freiheitsstrafen,*" by Mittelstaedt.

a moment; by the pendulum's uniform swing to give to constant vibration the appearance of regular motion; and essentially the same impulse gives equipoise to all the mental activities of our race.   First the natural inclination to repeat the same act, then the incorporation of the repetitions in regular habit: how much conscious thinking and willing thus gradually becomes the unconscious function of an unthinking machine ! .   .   .   .   Rule and order and custom and law transmitting civilization from generation to generation would be unintelligible without the incessant action of this mysterious force.''

Thus nature itself is the strongest ally of the rulers. Habit becomes an element of their power and its incessant action produces the other moral factors, order, custom, rights, and also the moral bonds that unite men of the same language and religion.   For however unlike the rulers and ruled in these respects the former have understood how to adapt themselves to the latter, at least outwardly, in both respects—an end to which, moreover, the force of circumstances directly tends.*

Thus do the founders of sovereignty sustain their power, but the power of the new middle class is built up differently. It starts from the possession of material goods and the more necessary they are the greater is the equivalent offered for the surrender of them whether in labor, services and goods or in the right to demand services.   In any case the equivalent can be reduced to terms of human labor; and so the middle class also acquires political power.   By labor, industry, inventiveness, speculation and thrift it can even attain to the balance of power in the state.

- That the possession of material goods can be a source of power only in the state is so self-evident as scarcely to need mentioning; for where club-law and anarchy prevailed they would fall to the physically superior; no power-producing energy is inherent in them.   Within the state however the purely economic power, as we may briefly call it, has secured recognition and has its part in sovereignty.

Let us consider how the middle class exercises its authority; who perform the services to which their authority, like every other, may eventually be reduced.   The rulers as a class do not perform them; they must be performed either by the subjects as a class or by wage-laborers drawn from other sources.   The rulers therefore cannot recompense the middle class directly by them.   They offer treasures of the land over which they exercise ''eminent domain,'' products of

* For the process of assimilation, see "*Der Rassenkampf,*'' p. 253.

the fauna which are also the "lord's property," agricultural products produced by the labor of the subject people, and finally the concession of rights to have the exclusive sale of articles of universal necessity, to hold markets, to claim certain services from the unfree, etc. In so far as the lords must acquiesce as a class and each can be compelled by law and right, it is proper to speak of the power of the middle class over the rulers, although up to a certain point in political evolution the balance of privileges, prerogatives and power is decidedly with the latter. The power of both can be expressed in services of the ruled class which, being superior in numbers, represents the greatest amount of human energy in the state and is the great reservoir from which the whole political apparatus is fed. In a word the whole state is supported by its lowest and most numerous stratum.

Later we shall inquire whether the burden becomes greater as the classes increase in number and variety; at present we must consider the course of political evolution. Though material wants created the middle class, even in the very beginning of social life wants of quite another character laid the foundation for another class which should some time mightily affect the evolution of the state.

We have elsewhere shown how the human temperament, worried by the riddle of its own existence, peremptorily demands pacification; how this is found in religious ideas; and how these lead to religious ceremonies.* We will not here enlarge upon the psycho-social process involved;† but it is a fact that universally these religious needs sooner or later produce a priestly caste inspired with the desire to sustain and increase its power.

Now its power also must consist in the ability to command men's services. The only difference is in the form of the power and the manner of securing it corresponding to its peculiar means of satisfying human wants.

While the nobility commands human services immediately by its superiority; while by establishing an organization it confers an undeniable benefit upon the whole; while further the merchant brings material goods to both the lords and the subject receiving an equivalent from both: the priestly caste conducts the religious ceremonies, thereby satisfying a peremptory need of human nature, and fortifies

* *"Der Rassenkampf."* p. 137 *et seq*
† *"Cf.* Lippert's *"Geschichte des Priesterthums."*

its position by acquiring material goods and human services.

The classes differ only in their functions; the equivalents received by all can be reduced to the same terms: a greater or less sum of human services rendered in kind or in goods or in the grant of privileges, rights and "royalties."

The rationalist might object that the services of the priest are imaginary and no real equivalent for what the recipient of them gives in the sweat of his brow. The same might also be said of the services of the ruling class. But what are these objections against the fact that men's religious wants are as peremptory as their material, and that the ruling class also fulfills its function in social economy and has no substitute!

Besides sociology must avoid criticising nature. It is interested only in facts and the laws of their behavior and it cannot raise the question whether the thing could not be accomplished differently or better. Social phenomena follow necessarily from and must be the requirements of the nature of men and their relations.

Sociology is coming to recognize that there would be no rulers if there were no servants; no priests if there were no believers; no traders if they could find no buyers. The phenomenon of class-building can be referred to a universal law: each want produces its own means of satisfaction. In so far as a class is able to satisfy a social want it first is indispensable, and, secondly, receives an equivalent which can be expressed in terms of human services, the instrument of power. But in exercising its acquired power it participates in government.

As new wants produce new professional classes and castes, the more progressive a state is and the higher its civilization the more numerous they are and the more complex must be the mutual dependence of the several social circles which jointly possess the elements of power.

Material and intellectual (moral) wants, it has been seen, are rooted and grounded in human nature; they might be called primary. But civilization keeps on developing others which may be called secondary, such as the uncivilized and those on lower stages of culture do not feel; such as men become sensible of only as a result of their higher culture.

On a low stage of culture, for instance, the priest is at

the same time medicine-man, and no need of a lay (*weltlich*) physician is felt. By a process which might be called a differentiation of wants, there arises out of the religious needs a demand for medical care and treatment which, on the higher stages of culture, is supplied by the medical profession which is organized, has social standing and enjoys legal protection.

The necessity of legal assistance has grown out of the intercourse and the legal relations of men in the civilized state. It is well known what great influence the legal profession wields in the modern state. But its power is no greater than the great and universal need it satisfies.

The necessity for an administrative department as the state becomes large, for distributing governmental duties among a number of functionaries and maintaining facility of communication between them and the people has produced the official class, which has its own interests, possesses power and exerts a controlling influence in its own sphere.

The trading and industrial class has been subdivided into very many different classes and callings, because a division of labor became necessary as the demand increased for many products which commerce brought to hand or trade and industry supplied.

In the modern civilized state large industries are opposed to the small, the laboring class to the capitalist and the undertaking classes, agriculture to manufactures, and so forth. Each has its own interest which it represents, its own power which it strives to increase, and each bears down upon the others according to its strength and their resistance. In other words each participates in sovereignty solely and exactly in proportion to its power. Wherein this power consists we have already seen.

Just as the middle class was subdivided to correspond with the division of labor and the development of specialties so also a military class was differentiated from the simple ruling class as the method of warfare changed. It assimilated portions of other classes and developed into the modern military profession, and though in deference to passing doctrines, some efforts have been made to sink this independent profession in the universal obligation of all citizens to bear arms it is a question whether they can succeed, whether nature will not prove stronger than doctrine, finally producing in spite of them a separate military class.

THE TWOFOLD ORIGIN OF CLASSES

We have seen that some classes, the ruling, the peasant and the merchant classes for instance, arose from the union [*Zusammentreffen*] of different [*heterogen*] ethnological elements; that their characteristic differences are original. Such classes antedate the state and are the more easily maintained in it because their differences are both anthropological and moral.

But there are others, as we have seen, the priesthood, large industry as contrasted with small, scholars, jurists, officials and so forth, which arise from the others by a process of differentiation. When they have become fully separated they in turn devote their whole conduct both active and passive to guarding their peculiar interests and take on the nature of the original classes.

These phenomena depend upon a universal law which we must explain before we can show its application in the social domain. Corollary to the distinction between original and derived classes is that between heredity and adaptation. Organic types seem to arise in two distinct ways and the solution of the whole anthropological problem depends upon setting aside the one or harmonizing the two. Is the principle of perpetual growth in organic bodies heredity, or adaptation, or what?

The wisdom of the ages which must not be despised answers heredity; radical modern materialism answers adaptation: "The man is what he eats;" Darwinism to reconcile the difference says: Both. Let us see which answer is nearest the truth. A superficial glance at organic structures is enough to show that heredity is the mightiest principle of their growth. It is clearly the rule that such structures are as their progenitors were. However there are some exceptions, for which the cleverest and at present the most widely accepted explanation is Darwin's theory of adaptation; what cannot be explained by heredity must be referred to the property of adaptation to external conditions, which organisms possess and to which the struggle for existence forces them to resort.

This theory would scarcely have found acceptance if Darwin's genius had not pointed out many cases which show that organisms do adapt themselves to external conditions in their growth and so change the hereditary type,

though he was less successful in showing that changes produced by adaptation would become hereditary.

So the law of adaptation is still an hypothesis in spite
of the particular instances cited in support of it, though
the law of heredity is established beyond a doubt, we
believe.

It is a fact however that natural structures arise in two
ways; they are either primary or secondary. There are two
universal and so to speak opposing tendencies in nature:
one we might call originality, the other imitation. That is
to say, what nature made originally in some unknown,.
"creative" way, is also frequently produced under the
influence of external circumstances which may be easily
comprehended. The latter origin is called by Darwin's
school evolutionary.*

Autogenesis and evolution always co-operate; and we are
often in doubt whether a particular organism is genetic or
evolutionary; while in many cases in fact it may be either.

Nature's processes are after all one and the same, like those
by which an artist produces an original and a replica. As it
is not impossible for a painter to produce an original because
he has made copies so it is a fallacy to conclude with the
Darwinians that the many instances of evolution prove all
organisms to have originated in that way.

Some human types originated in adaptation and evolution;
but not necessarily all. If the geographical character of the
habitat is sufficient still to modify a type of organism how
much greater must its influence have been upon the origin
of varieties, for once it produced, so to speak, genetic differences, but though still active the original genetic effect
proves to be more permanent. This might seem to justify
one argument used in support of evolution, viz., that if the
period be indefinitely extended the supposition of an original
method becomes superfluous. But this is only arithmeti-
cally correct, it is insufficient to refute the supposition of an
original genetic origin when so many other considerations
support it.

Both forms of origin, the primary and the secondary, the
genetic and the evolutionary, are common in social as well

* We are able to comprehend the secondary or evolutionary origin while that
which is original in the realm of organic nature is incomprehensible to our faculties. Accordingly we are always inclined to prefer the former process; as Darwin
and Haeckel do in the domain of organic and the sociologists in the domain of
social phenomena. But it does not follow that because this is the only way we can
explain there is no other.

as in organic phenomena. Social inequality arises originally from the union [*zusammentreffen*] of distinct [*heterogen*] ethnical elements of unlike power; and it also arises by
evolution, by the slow development of some elements at the
cost of others which sink in power owing to unfavorable
conditions.

Though the original method of forming states is by subjugation, it might happen (?) as an exception that a period
of peaceful development should result in the differentiation
of the population into classes, the stronger gradually separating themselves from those who were weaker and needed
protection. As a rule classes rise originally, *i. e.*, out of
different [*heterogen*] ethnical elements, or by the permanent
organization of such as are at different stages of development
at the time of their union. But there are instances of secondary origin also; since as we have seen some turn to this
calling, some to that, according to conditions and inclinations; and those of each calling congregate in a class.

But whether a social group arise in one way or the other,
its character as a group, as a factor in social development, is
not affected. It tends in the direction of its own interests,
it tries to protect and further them, to increase its power and
to acquire a corresponding influence in the state.

These efforts are always the same and all groups necessarily had to adopt the same policy respecting them. The
natural differences between the original classes and the
syngenetic coherence within them helped in maintaining and
extending their power; and the secondary groups in turn
must needs acquire like differences and coherences. Hence
comes the strong tendency to divide into classes and to
maintain the power of each by endogamy; or by celibacy to
sunder all connection with other social groups and prevent
the weakening of power by division.

SOCIETY.

The great number and variety of mutually related groups
within the state considered as a whole is called society in
contrast with the state. In this wider sense society is not
different from the state; it is the same thing viewed from
another point. But in the narrower and more accurate
sense of the word each group centering about some one or
more common interests is a society. This double meaning
often leads to confusion which is made worse because social

groups are not always separated by a hard and fast line. They overlap and intertwine so that the same men are bound to one group by one set of interests and to another by another set. Thus a government official may own a large estate, be a zealous adherent of a religious sect, and be a sugar manufacturer also. In the social struggles over material and moral questions his position will be finally determined by his relative interests.

On the other hand with the development of civilization, certain interests have become broader than the borders of a single state and some societies embrace the subjects of several states. Religious beliefs, the ties of kindred, social-ism, *e. g.*, have produced international groups.

Until these relations are thoroughly and scientifically analyzed the notion of a society will remain confused. Such unclear Hegelian definitions as von Ihering offers explain nothing.

"Society," he says, "may be defined as the actual organization of life on the plan of mutual assistance; and since the individual is at his best only through the others it is at once indispensable *per se* and in reality the universal form of human life." [*]

For society substitute state, political economy or anything else and the definition is equally good and equally bad; in fact the state has actually been called "the form" or "the organization of human life:" general phrases fitting any-thing and explaining nothing. Ihering's use of them is not surprising perhaps for instead of seriously studying the phenomena themselves he inquires, as Romanist, what the Roman jurists say about them and frames his definition to correspond. His meaningless definition of society is derived from *societas*. But others have failed without this excuse.

How helpful in contrast is Spencer's clear explanation of society considered as a unit.

"It is the permanence of the relations among component parts," he says, "which constitutes the individuality of a whole as dis-tinguished from the individualities of its parts." [†]

The "permanent relations" between men unite them into a society, and since there are different kinds of rela-tions there are different kinds of societies and a man may be bound to several at once, as we have seen.

[*] von Ihering. "*Zweck im Recht.*" Vol. i, p. 95.
[†] Spencer, "Principles of Sociology," Vol. i, sec. 212.

Much would be gained if we could use "society" simply to designate a concrete number of men united by "permanent relations," for it is perfectly clear. The broader use suggests nothing real; it is only another way of looking at folk-life. Schaeffle, who calls these narrower social circles "cohesive masses or tissue" (*Massenzusammenhænge oder Bindegewebe*), remarks that it is

"singular that social philosophy has as yet been unable to assign even the most insignificant place in its system to these elementary tissues which are neutral (?) as a rule, but at certain times extremely sensitive. They are thrown with much other rubbish into a heap called 'society,' which is alleged to lie midway between the state and the individual. In reality no such miscellaneous society exists." *

He fails to note that a "society," something less than the state and more than the individual, had necessarily to be assumed as the starting point of a social philosophy which began with Schloezer's and Hegel's "society of burghers," and later was powerfully influenced by the broader conceptions advanced by Mohl, Stein and Gneist.† But nowadays when people ought to know that there is no concrete reality behind the idea the use of the word in its broader signification has no further justification. If it should be objected that all the social groups in the state are united by "permanent relations," such as those of common territory, government, etc., and hence in turn form one "society," we reply that the word "folk" is a sufficient designation. There is no further use for this expression in its wider signification. ‖ It should only be applied to the simple social groups in the state or to those united by interests which transcend state limits.

SOCIETIES.

We cannot be expected to enumerate all the societies which occur in the state and still less to discuss the historical development of each. Lippert in his "History of the Priesthood" has described one successfully; to do as much for every other would take us far outside the limits of this sketch. We can only explain the social "relations" which bind the members of the several groups together and the general principles underlying their power in the state, for here

* Schaeffle, "*Bau und Leben*," Vol. i, p. 292, *3ter Hauptabschnitt, 2te Abtheilung,*
‖ "*Die formlosen Zusammenhænge oder Bindegewebe.*"
† "*Philosophisches Staatsrecht,*" sec. 12; "*Rechtsstaat und Socialismus,*" pp. 158 *et seq.*

also the description of what is individual must be reserved for history; sociology can only state the general modes of behavior, the laws of the phenomena. It is clear that the societies both in their origin and in their development are controlled by "laws" since human nature is the same everywhere and social differentiation corresponds to the growth and development of human wants as we have seen. Social structures thus arising from a common basis must be the same in essence; must have the same life-principle, make the same efforts and have the same aspirations. Whether they shall develop power and sovereignty depends simply on the greater or less resources they have at the beginning or acquire later. They differ in degree; they are alike in plan and tendency.

To discover what ties bind a number of men into a society we must start, as elsewhere in sociology, with an original or primary condition, one which we cannot analyze further, the origin of which we cannot observe. Such a bond is association in the horde .* It seems to be natural and, in contrast, all others are evolutionary arising with social development. Of course they are natural too in a sense; the difference is that we know their origin and do not know that of the former.† To those who feel this bond it suggests a contrast with the "stranger;" later reflection based on experience adds the aetiological explanation of common descent from some god or hero.

Analysis shows that the positive binding force is association and simple consanguinity with the resultant community of language, religious ideas, customs and mode of life, while the contrast with the stranger lies in his lack of participation in them.

In reality all the social binding forces are represented in the primitive horde: association and consanguinity, similar material and intellectual needs and similar interests in satisfying them; and there are no social contrasts which cannot be referred to dissimilarity in one or more of these respects.

Social development presupposes the junction of heterogeneous or the differentiation of homogeneous elements. In

---

* Spencer too has recognized the necessity of this point of departure in sociological studies; for he says that: "Social evolution begins with the small simple aggregates." "Principles of Sociology," Vol. i, sec. 257.
† For the distinction between "natural" and "artificial" social institutions, see "*Rechtsstaat und Socialismus*," p. 329.

the former case the combining elements are united by common interests and fall into social opposition for lack of them. In the latter the differentiating group develops certain common interests which hold it together and separate it from the rest. The first is the case when political relations are established between foreign elements or a middle class is gradually developed; the latter, when the various priestly, military and professional classes slowly appear.

The establishment of the first political relations calls two social classes into existence at once: the lords and the slaves or serfs. The social bonds which unified each group and created feelings of tribal loyalty will be strengthened by the common interest of rulers and the common lot of subjects respectively. Class feeling will be added to tribal; but it does not follow that mutual opposition will be intensified. The centrifugal factors will be offset by local association and all the ties which habit and adaptation develop under such circumstances. The psycho-social functions: language, customs, religious ideas and ceremonies will gradually become assimilated.

The subject class may even acquire a feeling of respect for the other; and all the factors together may be strong enough to make the two classes at times appear as one in contrast with outsiders. But the difference in rank, the separate consanguineous circles (while intermarriage is prohibited), and the difference in political interests will keep them permanently apart.

So when a foreign merchant class takes its place beside the others all are strangers at first in every respect. Language, customs, religion, descent, everything which binds the members of one group together separates it from the others. Some of the dissociating factors may disappear in time; local association may develop love of home and folk; and assimilation of language, customs and ideas may follow. But in spite of all and in addition to differences in descent, rank, customs, and class ethics, the interest of the traders will be permanently opposed to the interests of the other classes.

When classes are differentiated from a homogeneous element the course of events is different. There is simply some one interest which distinguishes the dissociating class from all the others and brings its members together. Besides, such classes are not composed of the members of one class exclusively but generally attract members from different sources. The sacerdotal, military, official and learned classes are recruited from the older classes indiscriminately for the inclination, fitness and capacity for such callings is not distributed with regularity.

Though the peculiar interest of one calling distinguishes all who follow it from all others, still the individuals stand in the greatest variety of relations to the classes whence they sprang. Hence new complications arise and social classes become curiously involved, crossing or coinciding in part, or becoming wholly exclusive. These conditions often exert a decisive influence upon their position and power in the state; upon the results of the social struggle.

THE GROUP-MAKING FACTORS.

Let us now attempt a scheme of the forces or " relations " which classify and unite men in societies. On a former occasion* I distinguished " three natural " bonds: consanguinity, local association and common interests. They are very comprehensive, especially the last; but I now think a double classification according to fundamental principles and permanency is plainer and more to the point.

According to fundamental principles they may be divided into material, economic and moral. The material factors are common place of residence, sociableness or common social life, consanguinity and relationship. The economic factors are similar and equal possessions and like callings: agriculture on large or on small estates, tenancy, manufacturing, skilled trades, commerce and so forth. The grouping into nobility, burghers, priests, artists, scholars, writers, etc., is partly economic and partly moral; that according to language, religion, political allegiance, nativity, citizenship and nationality wholly moral. Accidentally sharing the same fate, as in a common migration, is a moral factor also.

But most of these factors are of varying duration and their permanency must be considered. The influence of a common place of residence may continue from generation to generation or no longer than a visit at a watering-place and its effects vary accordingly. The effect of common religious views is different according as they have been

* "Das Philosophische Staatsrecht."

inherited generation after generation or are the result of recent proselyting.

The following table illustrates the double classification showing that each relation enumerated may endure for a longer or shorter period:

	Generation after Generation.	For Life.	Temporarily.
MATERIAL.	¡Common place of residence (in immediate or remote neighborhood). Common social life. Consanguinity. Relationship.		
ECONOMIC.	Rank—Nobility. Burghers. Peasantry. Priesthood, etc. Possessions—In the country. In the city. Occupation—Landowners, Tenants. Manufacturers. Merchants. Artisans, etc.		
MORAL.	Language. Religion. Science. Art. Accidental fate (emigrants, etc.).		

The greater the number of group-making factors binding men together the more intimate is the social bond and the greater its cohesive force and power of resistance. Strongest of all is a community united by permanent material, economic and moral forces. It is a unitary race, and in the struggle for existence is superior to all lesser social combinations in endurance if not in power.

In the primitive horde, in the " small simple aggregates " with which, according to Spencer, social evolution begins, we find all three classes of factors permanently acting: common place of residence, common blood, common means of subsistence, common language, religion, and customs

generation after generation.   When such social groups are
politically organized they retain their compactness and
cohesion.   But the union grows weaker as language,
religion and other factors became common to several social
groups.   Membership in the same political system is sure to
produce this result in the course of time.

Without doubt consanguinity is the strongest group-
making factor.   The consanguineous social group always
retains something of the elemental power of primitive
hordes, treating all strangers as hostile beings.   The division of European nations into lords, middle class and
peasants would not have produced such rigid social distinctions if the three classes had not, generally speaking,
represented distinct consanguineous groups, for economic
differences would have been counteracted by the assimilation
of language and religion.   However it is also the tendency
of each economic group to become a consanguineous unit.

THE SOCIAL CIRCLES IN THE SOCIAL STRUGGLE.

It has already been pointed out that it is not the size of
the social group which determines its power.   The lords were
always in a minority, and in modern states with millions
of inhabitants the power rests with the "upper ten thousand."
The intimacy of the union and the resultant organization
and discipline together with mental superiority complement
numerical inferiority giving the minority the preponderancy.
The minority applies the strategical maxim: march as individuals, strike as one.   The masses always lack unity and
organization as the result partly of their great bulk, partly
of indolence.   Since the result of the social struggle depends
on discipline the minority has the advantage because it is
small.   Besides there will be greater intimacy and more
common interests; the group-making factors will be more
numerous, more intense and more permanent.

The more indolent a man is the less appreciation he has
for the ideal goods of life.   As he has fewer wants he has
fewer interests in common with other men and is less energetic in defending them.

The power of a social group increases with the number of
common interests among its members irrespective of its size.
When success depends on numbers it relies on uniting with
other social groups.   This is very important; it is the key

to social politics. The number of common interests necessarily varies inversely with the number of individuals in the social group. For though the number of interests increases as conditions improve, it is the condition of the minority especially that improves since the majority must labor and serve to produce it.

Prosperity is the natural lot of the minority; with improved conditions the number of interests increases; with these the intensity of social cohesion; and this gives more social power.

In the final analysis the intensity of the union depends upon the personal character of the individuals. But as their mutual intercourse is made easier by custom, and as good customs grow with common welfare and culture the union is strengthened too.

The highest and smallest aristocratic circles are mightier than all the other social groups in the state though a thousand times larger. The masters united in a guild are stronger than the journeymen and laborers.

In times of revolution everything may depend on numerical strength and then the small groups are at a disadvantage. Their power can be realized only under normal conditions of political organization. But this must be considered the normal condition of civilized man.

Each group exerts whatever power it normally possesses and tries to have its relative position recognized in the state in the form of rights. But every right is made the basis of renewed efforts. Human desires are constantly growing and no social group ever rested content with what it had obtained; on the contrary present attainments are used to increase power and satisfy new desires.

From this fundamental law the conduct of each social group can be definitely predicted in every case. It will strive, like the state, to increase its power. But the result of the struggle does not depend on the individual. Though there are always individuals who deviate first one way and then the other, they, like meteoric stones which are loosened from their planet and fly off in all directions, are abnormal, and do not influence the behavior of the group as a whole.

In its political actions each social group is a perfect unit. It opposes other social groups in behalf of its own interest solely and knows no standard of conduct but success.

The struggle between social groups, the component parts of the state, is as inexorable as that between hordes or states. The only motive is self-interest. In "*Der Rassenkampf*" we described the conflict as a "race-war" for such is its inexorable animosity that each group that is able tends to become exclusive like a caste, to form a consanguineous circle, in short to become a race.

What is the character of the struggle between the social groups? What are the methods and the means? No general answer can be given; for they differ with the position which the groups occupy in the state, with the amount of power and the instruments which they possess.

The refusal to perform religious rites is an instrument in the hands of the priesthood. The higher nobility can make certain lucrative and influential offices exclusive. The guild-masters require "proof of competency." Attorneys restrict the privileges of practicing law. Manufacturers insist on free trade in grain. Laborers strike, etc., etc. The social struggle consists in establishing appropriate institutions for increasing the power of one social group at the expense of the others. However it may be with the individual the society never errs in seizing and applying the right means; its instincts are always right.

If this seems to be a contradiction consider the actual experience of history. At every step it shows the mistakes of even the cleverest individuals and the demoniacal cleverness of society infallible as natural law.* Theories and passions often confuse the individual; but society never fails for it never reflects and never chooses but naturally follows the powerful attraction of its own interests.

THE FIELD OF COMBAT.

It is a peculiarity of the social struggle that it must be conducted by a collective whole. Previous organization into assemblages is necessary, and every society must secure some suitable organ for conducting the social struggle. Thus the ruling classes through their parliaments exercise the legislative power and are able by legal institutions to further their own interests at the cost of others.

In the cities the middle class very early resorted to the use

* See below. Part iv, sec. ix, " Individual Efforts and Social Necessity."

of guilds and representatives. The priesthood also organized into hierarchies and created synods and councils, consultative and representative bodies. The fact that the great mass of the people in the very nature of the case could not thus organize made the conduct of the struggle in their interest more difficult. It is in consequence of having entered upon this struggle that laborers now organize and wily agitators even found peasant unions; the procedure is logical.

Yet the difference must not be overlooked. The prosperous and property-holding classes perfect their organization more easily because the greater number and intensity of their common interests make it easier to unite and act as a body or by representatives. The weaker social connection of the masses prevents a sound and strong organization. Such as occurs is generally the ephemeral artificial work of selfish leaders seeking selfish ends. But this much is certain: without organization, without united collective action the social struggle is impossible.

The proximate end of organization is to establish a legal norm for the mutual relations of the groups, to confirm by right the commanding position which has been acquired or is striven for. Hence it is clear that the society which has already acquired the right of legislation in the state occupies the most powerful position, and that it is the aim of every other society to participate in the same right.

It is well known that the history of European politics generally turns upon the struggle of the lower classes for participation in legislation; that it has been partly successful, and that it is still in progress. Indeed, it can never end, for after the third estate comes the fourth. The real object is to be able to conduct the social struggle with equal weapons.

THE MORAL CHARACTER OF THE STRUGGLE.

Nothing impresses thinking men so seriously as the contemplation of the social struggle, for its immorality offends their moral feelings deeply. Individuals can consider ethical requirements, they have consciences, but societies have none. They overfall their victims like avalanches with irresistible destroying power. All societies, large and small, retain the character of wild hordes in considering every means good which succeeds. Who would look for

fidelity, veracity and conscience in the intercourse of the
" most civilized " states of the world? Lying and deceit,
breach of confidence and betrayal is on every page of their
history; and saddest of all, no one can foresee whether it
will ever be different, though the noblest men may stand at
the head of affairs, with the highest intentions. What self-
deception it is to believe that monarchs rule the social world!
They are not responsible for all the moral lapses that occur
daily in politics.

How trivial are royal assurances that the friendliest relations exist with all the neighboring states! Often they have
scarcely been uttered before bloody war breaks out. They
were not really perfidious. The current of history, the
rivalry of states, is not under the arbitrary control of
rulers.

However cordial the personal relations of the monarchs
not one will cease arming. It is felt instinctively that with
the first favorable opportunity any state will pounce like a
wild beast upon a defenceless victim. Indeed, it is generally recognized that states oppose each other like savage
hordes; that they follow the blind laws of nature; that no
ethical law or moral obligation, only the fear of the stronger,
holds them in check; and that neither right nor law, treaty
nor league, can restrain the stronger from seeking its own
interests when the opportunity is offered.

The same is true of the struggle of the social groups in
general. It is conducted not by individuals but by societies and communities.

The lack of moral principle is nowhere more conspicuous
than in the leagues into which societies unite for the sake
of assuring success. The overmatched horde makes terms
with its recent enemy in order to fall with superior force
upon the present foe; civilized states consider only their own
advantage in making alliances. No consideration of principles, intimacy of relations or community of ideas avails;
republican France and America ally themselves with Russia
without scruple; constitutional and liberty-loving England
upholds Turkish rule and aids American slaveholders, and
social units behave in the same way. The extreme conservatives fight side by side with the social democrats to-day
for the sake of defeating the middle classes, and to-morrow
perhaps will join their defeated foe to overcome their
quondam ally.

But these "perfidious" struggles do not show the individuals to be utterly base. They only prove that in the struggle of the wholes individual opinions play no part, that here social groups struggle inexorably to satisfy their own interests, to demonstrate their own power. Blind natural law controls the actions of savage hordes, of states and of societies.

THE STRUGGLE FOR EMANCIPATION.

Though the exercise of legislative power, as we have said, is indispensable in conducting the social struggle those who do not possess it are not condemned to perpetual passivity. The unique method which they employ against the ruling classes is aptly called the struggle for emancipation. The might of ideas is on their side, a significant statement which needs careful explanation.

The superior classes, as we have seen, cannot rest content with the fact of superiority; political relations need to be confirmed; might must be turned into right. It seemed simple enough for them to say: Let this be right. But every right has its obverse obligation; however comprehensive, it has its limits at which obligations begin, the rights of those who hitherto have had none. So the rights of the rulers produced the rights of the ruled. The germ was there and it must develop.

But more than this; the human mind probes to the foundation of things seeking the principle of causation and analyzing the changing phenomena to find their eternal unchanging essence. Now in the changing phases of right the enduring principle is the idea. Thus rights not only led to obligations but also to the idea of right.

If the obligation could be called the consequence of right in space, the idea was its consequence in time. Whoever asserts his rights can not escape their consequences. Thus the rulers themselves forge weapons with which the ruled and powerless classes successfully attack them and complete the natural process. The egoism of the powerful prepares the way for the uprising of the weak.

The idea of right is not a purely fanciful conception. It has power to influence men and can be practically applied. Men grow accustomed year by year to submit to rights; they use legal forms constantly and learn to respect rightful limitations, until finally the conception, the very idea, of

rights pervades and controls them.   In this way the idea
of right becomes the fit weapon for those who have no
other.
   But its application is not simple.   The legal bulwarks of
the powerful will not yield to a simple appeal to ideas as
Jericho's walls fell at the blast of trumpets; and, besides, the
propertyless and powerless are unable to use such mental
weapons immediately.   Again we see the egoism of one
class promoting the social evolution of the whole.   The
bourgeoisie in the struggle with the other property classes is
the first to appeal to universal human rights, to freedom and
equality.   It claims to be contending not for itself alone
but for the good of the whole folk.   And it succeeds not
without the support of the masses whom it flatters and
to whom it discloses the resplendent goal of freedom and
equality.   Its might like that of the higher class is now
based on right, and though for the moment what it has won
seems to be clear gain, it has found the yoke of legal logic
about its neck and must submit to its ideas.
   For the lowest classes participation in the struggle was a
profitable experience.   Even the slight amelioration of their
condition was an advantage.   It taught them many a lesson.
But it is hard for them relying simply on ideas to undertake
the social struggle, for political regulations are firmly based
on the possession of material goods and are defended by the
middle class also, and moreover as time goes on some of
their ideas prove false and indefensible.   But in spite of
exaggerations they are logical consequences of principles
which the ruling class asserted in its own interest and from
which the middle class profited declaring them at the
time to be universal.   They cannot be wholly eradicated;
they aid the struggle for the emancipation of the fourth class
powerfully.   They inspire the masses with fanaticism and
the struggle for emancipation succeeds.
   Meanwhile, however, an unsocial compound of societies
has taken the place of the primitive horde.   The principles
suited to one condition are unsuited to another and cannot
be permanent.   The false consequences must be corrected
step by step back to the point where might of its "own
right" as spontaneous factor of public life undertakes the
control of a society tired of revolution.   This completes the
period of evolution in the social struggle: from the freedom
and equality of the anarchic horde through might and

inequality, right and law to the freedom and equality of
revolution and state-destroying anarchy; and from this
unbearable condition to the despotic might of reaction and
the beginning of a new period of evolution.

THE GROWTH OF STATES.

Semper Augustus, always augmenting the empire, the
characteristic title of honor borne by the Roman and German emperors, is a naive recognition of the nature of the
state; for its most natural tendency (here predicated of the
ruler) is incessant increase of power and territory.

It is inherited from the horde and characterizes every
social community. A roving horde subjects strangers and
uses as many of them as possible for servants and slaves.
After permanent settlements have been made and states
founded the object of the raids must be either to levy contributions and exact tribute or to annex territory. As the
latter is the most successful way of augmenting the state it
is the most frequent and desirable; it is the general rule of
history, and all great states have attained most of their
greatness in this way. So long as inherent strength and
external circumstances allow the process is continued; but
there must be some natural limit to the tendency, otherwise
the whole inhabited world would long since have become
one state.

The first condition precedent to external growth is relative stability of political authority within If the political
authority is not firmly established; if there are no firm
bonds of reciprocal interest between rulers and ruled, or of
common interest in the state the rulers cannot undertake
foreign conquest without risking their position, as many
historical examples show.

A state can undertake foreign conquest with prospect of
success only when by shrewd and strong political organization or through community of interests it has succeeded
outwardly at least in giving its constituent parts the nature
of a social element. It must come into action as a unit.
Hence follows the social law that a state's ability to undertake foreign activity grows as the process of unification
proceeds within it. Since every new conquest adds a new
element no conquest can be undertaken successfully until
the spoils of the former have to some degree been assimilated
and social unity is re-established.

It is a simple consequence of this social law that statesmen have always looked upon internal divisions in neighboring states as security against attack upon their own.   For
as soon as the state is strong internally it must utilize its
power externally, though in some cases an enterprise which
promises advantage to all will even relieve considerable internal friction. So necessary and so strong is the tendency to
foreign conquest that no state can escape it what ever may
be the feeling of the ruler at the time.   The method will
vary with the circumstances; and unfavorable circumstances
will be circumvented or overcome.

So long as a compact and powerful body politic finds
itself in the midst of weaker states it will continue its
policy of conquest and annexation to the last possible limit,
as Rome did in Italy and as Russia is doing in the East
where its neighbors are weak and loosely organized.

If all are equally powerful so that no one can hope to
overthrow any other one then two or more will form
alliances in order to conquer the selected object of attack.
If a weaker state happens to be neighbor to several more
powerful it must supplement its strength by alliances or
they will not fail to partition it among themselves.   No
code of private morals can successfully oppose; even the
men who are individually the most exemplary are forced to
act in harmony with their surroundings.   The scruples of
individual feeling and sentiment are unknown in politics; as
Emperor Francis said: '' The state has no daughter.''
Political conditions are peremptory. Natural law prevails though the will of the individual seems to be ''free.''
Those who suffer speak of ''crimes.''   As well call an earth-
quake by which thousands have perished a crime, for the
only difference is that in the one case we think we see the
responsible agents while in the other we can find none.

But the conditions of the party attacked may present serious obstacles to the policy of conquest.   For a folk, which
is the product of a long period of development, is such an
exclusive unit that the attempt to incorporate it must tax
the strength of the conquering state and leave it for a long
time incapable of future external activity.   That is to say,
it is not easy neither does it promote humanity nor good
morals to subject a foreign folk by violence.   Though
simple conquest and annexation cannot be treated as
''crimes'' without characterizing the whole history of

mankind as one long crime, yet every violent attempt to
destroy a folk, which is a product of history, is after all
immoral and inhuman.)

To profit by the conquest of a neighboring folk a state
must sometimes resort to war indemnities. Plundering
expeditions, conquest, annexation, incorporation and war indemnities: these are the various forms in which the natural
tendency of the state to augment its power and extend its
authority is manifested.*

It would not be hard to set a limit to the increasing size
of a state. But in fact the tendency is ceaseless and may
lead on to destruction as history proves. Every great state
has striven to increase its authority and the greatest have
striven to·rule the world; the end has come only in their
sudden downfall, in an historical catastrophe.

The social law thus illustrated is not peculiar to the
growth of states but is manifested in all other social
domains. The periodical crises of economic production, for
instance, are due to it. Each lucrative process of production is repeated until the limits of present need have been
far exceeded and business breaks down for lack of demand.
The experiment though often tried is constantly repeated.
Admonitions avail nothing and "wise moderation" will at
most influence a few individuals; the tendency of social
communities knows no limit but the "crash." | In trade
and commerce, everywhere, social strife for power or for
wealth and property lasts until all energy is exhausted.
Disruption, crisis, panic are then unavoidable.   \

So long as the state has aggressive power it strives to
augment, to increase its territory, to conquer, to colonize,

---

* To illustrate the whole range from the most primitive to the most modern
manifestations of this tendency I compared ("*Der Rassenkampf*," p. 166) the
Apaches and the Kirghese, who are content to capture a few horses or asses
or a herd of cattle, with the modern "European victor" who knows how straight-
way to force the payment of several milliards. This passage offended some of
my honored German reviewers, though it is plain that no exception could be
taken save on the supposition that Bismarck was referred to. But he is neither
the first nor the only "European victor" who has won his milliards. But if he
were the only one still the insinuation is unjustifiable considering my contention
that historical events are subject to natural laws and independent of individuals.
But they should not have applied to the German war, of which I said nothing,
what should be applied to false idealism which I have always attacked. I confess
that in politics I fully accept the realistic standpoint of Prince Bismarck. He
has never spoken of the great indemnity with false pathos, and in his report to
Herr von Manteuffel, from Frankfort in July, 1853, he said: "The other German
states have the same interests that we have, to be left in peace where there is
nothing to be gained," and weighing the chance of war he added: "If we can
profit by it then the case is different." If those who to-day write upon politics
would study the works of Prince Bismarck there would be much less pathos,
fewer Chauvinistic phrases and fewer political quarrels.

etc. This continues until strength fails from internal or external causes; or until it is surpassed by other states and crippled. Only when strength fails does strife cease.

STATE AND FOLK.

Since each political organization creates a civilization and each localized civilization is with the aid of such spontaneous moral agencies as language, religion, custom and rights* transformed into a folk, it follows that with the development of a number of states side by side a number of folk must arise also. If the mere fact of common allegiance is sufficient to bind the subjects into a social unit it is clear that as the number of mutual relations between the subjects increases the unity will be more pronounced. In this way the folk-state acquires greater offensive and defensive power. But in the course of time the folk-states will fall into opposition; the original contest will be repeated in higher form; and as the perpetual strife for power animates them also it cannot fail to happen that some are disrupted and others grow.

As the impulse to increase power is not checked by the establishment of any political or national relations whatever, a great variety of social and political combinations are bound to arise in the course of history and it cannot fail to happen that there will be political organizations consisting of different folk and parts of folk.

The greater difficulties which the conquering state must encounter and the scruples it may entertain at annexing foreign folk in whole or in part we have already discussed. But if the margin of superiority is not too narrow the foreign folk-elements will eventually be assimilated by the conquering race and blended into a social unit, a new folk. There have always been composite folk-states; they are the necessary result of the historical process which is constantly breaking down the old and establishing the new. To deny their right to exist or to justify them less fully than folk-states would display crass ignorance of history. Social relations tend to develop; and as surely as history produces only what is reasonable this higher order of political organization will overcome the internal struggle of the composite folk and justify itself.

* For an explanation of this process, see "*Der Rassenkampf*," pp. 23 *et seq.* and 253 *et seq.*

The struggles are severe; they are, so to speak, higher powers of the simple social struggles. To the social contrasts of the unitary folk-state the contrasts between the different folk are added. As the most conspicuous difference is in language the contest centres about the right of one or the equal right of several in official business. But the essential point is the struggle for authority; the contest over the language is only an excuse to make the tendency seem plausible.

The question at issue is whether the authority shall be monopolized by a privileged folk speaking a privileged mother-tongue. The struggle becomes justified when the unprivileged folk-elements possess sufficient social and political power and have acquired sufficient mastery of the official language to oppose the ruling folk successfully. Other things being equal the folk which can use more than one of the competing languages will win, the polyglots will overcome the ruling class which remains monoglot.

But when the victory has once been secured the unpractical idea of the equality of tongues must yield to the real needs of the state. Either there must be one official language or the whole people, or at least the ruling classes, must speak several. In a composite folk-state there can be no serious question which should be the official language. As it is simply the means for promoting general intercourse throughout the state plainly the most available one must be chosen, and this must be the one most generally used or rather the one most widely diffused among the educated classes of all the different folk-elements. Generally this will be the language of the older civilization. Only living tongues of course can be considered. But its rank will be questioned so long as its natural representatives enjoy any political advantage or other folk-elements suffer political prejudice. In a word the struggle which begins with the battle-cry " no discrimination on account of language " will continue until the actual relations are so altered that the complete equality before the law of all the elements is no longer imperiled by the official preference accorded to the language of the oldest civilization; or a general polyglottous condition of all the folk-elements may end the struggle.

IV. THE PSYCHO-SOCIAL PHENOMENA AND THE INDIVIDUAL.

INDIVIDUALISM AND COLLECTIVISM.

The point of view from which social phenomena are considered has oscillated between two opposite principles—individualism and collectivism. Not only the attempts at explaining "the social world," but also all propositions that aimed at shaping it in virtue of its accepted nature, and all the differences and disputes in the domain of social science turn upon the antithesis between "mankind" and the individual. There was no third standpoint, no middle way known to the theorists.

While Smithianism and materialistic philosophy considered egoism and self-interest the source of social development and the sole motive of human behavior; others pointed to the self-sacrifice of the individual and contrasted egoism and self-interest with "charity" and "altruism." While some sought to explain social phenomena by the egoistical nature of the individual, the statisticians pointed to the "community," "society," "mankind" and its nature and "development according to law" for explanation. The real truth was overlooked. Neither one alone and neither to the degree supposed is the cause and motive of social development. If we prefix to each the adjective "social," giving it the meaning not of the abstract whole but of the limited social circle, like the syngenetic group, we shall have found the middle way which social philosophy has hitherto missed.

Not personal but social egoism is the motive of social development; not devotion to the world at large, nor "charity" in the broad universal sense of Christian theory, not fellow feeling with mankind; but social sympathy, self-sacrificing, loving devotion to the natural social community. Man is not so bad as crass materialism pictures him; neither is he so large hearted as Christian philosophy in vain requires him to be. He is neither devil nor angel, simply human. Fettered to the community by natural ties of blood, habit and mode of thought, his egoism is social, his sympathies are social; to demand more than social sympathy is to demand something unnatural and superhuman and to credit him with less than social egoism is to do him wrong. But social egoism includes social sympathy, social sympathy is social egoism. Let us call their union syngenism and we have identified the motive of all social development and the key to its solution.

Those who conceive the whole social world from the individualistic standpoint, who explain all development by reference to the individual and look upon his development as the highest goal and simple object of all that transpires in society, want to heal all the hurts and ills of the social world by freeing the individual and proclaiming his rights.*

Doctrinaire liberalism and abstract constitutionalism both occupy this position. Every individual as such must have every possible right and enjoy every privilege of the "most favored" individual—that it may be well upon the earth. The plan has been tried in Europe repeatedly and has failed, for the individual profited nothing from all these rights; relying upon them alone he hurled himself against the unyielding barriers of social institutions which no proclamation of individual liberty can force.

At the opposite pole is socialism, communism and every other form of collectivism. The collective whole, preferably the largest at hand, must labor for and protect the individual; the worry and the care fall upon it; the labor must be performed in common; the individual must be directed and utilized: but also supported.

Unfortunately the legislative conditions have never been adequate for an experiment or it would appear that a collective whole caring for the individual so providently is as Utopistic as a self-determining individual.

In truth, everywhere and from the very beginning the social world has moved, acted, fought and striven only by groups. Legislation to be wise and true must take account of the actual conditions, neither being blind to them like the "constitutionalist" nor imagining with the collectivist that it can change them. The only possible solution of the social question lies in the harmonious co-operation of the social groups so far as that is possible.

THE INDIVIDUAL AND HIS SOCIAL GROUP.

The great error of individualistic psychology is the supposition that man thinks. It leads to the continual search for the source of thought in the individual and for the reason

* Marx was quite right when he said: "The real insignificance of the individual is in strong contrast with the importance conceded to him in scientific speculations. His insignificance is apparent; not only in political affairs but in economic."—"Capital" pp. 235, 236.

why the individual thinks so and not otherwise; and prompts naïve theologians and philosophers to consider and even to advise how man ought to think. A chain of errors; for it is not man himself who thinks but his social community; the source of his thoughts is in the social medium in which he lives, the social atmosphere which he breathes,* and he cannot think ought else than what the influences of his social environment concentrating upon his brain necessitate. There is a law of mechanics and optics by which we compute the angle of refraction from the angle of incidence and in the realm of mind there is a similar law though we cannot observe it so exactly. Every ray of thought falling in on the mind is reflected in our views. What we think is the necessary result of the mental influences to which we have been subjected since childhood.

The individual simply plays the part of the prism which receives the rays, dissolves them according to fixed laws and lets them pass out again in a predetermined direction and with a predetermined color.

The influence of environment upon the human mind has always been recognized by psychologists and philosophers; but it has been considered a secondary factor. On the contrary the social medium which the child enters at birth, in which he lives, moves and has his being, is fundamental. Toward this environment the individual from childhood to ripest old age is more or less receptive; rarely can the maturest minds so far succeed in emancipating themselves from this medium as to undertake independent reflection while complete emancipation is impossible, for all the organs and modes of thought, all the organs for constructing thoughts, have been moulded or at least thoroughly imbued by it. Granted that very mature and independent thinkers have passed the age of receptivity, still it is questionable whether the most eminent and original philosopher in the world can so far dissociate himself from the acquired modes and organs as to substitute independent creations in their place.

Consider the mental make-up of the ordinary or "average" man. The child gets his first impressions from his earliest surroundings. His earliest ethical ideas come from the conduct of his nurses and early tutors! Praise and blame,

* " To think is to be conscious of the growth of psychological activity. . . . " Bastian, " *Ethnologie*," xii.

reward and punishment, the hopes and fears that are raised, the frights which he is given, all go to make up his first impressions and educate his mind.   Before it is noticed the little world-citizen has become the exact mental image of his "family," giving the word its broadest Roman meaning. His childish mind corresponds exactly to the many-sided mould in which it was cast; it bears the impress on every hand stamped upon it.

Thus prepared the youngster comes in contact with the "world" in the shape of a troop of playmates and companions for the most part cast in the same mould.   Their impressions are much the same; all have been inspired with the same admiration for certain things and persons, and filled involuntarily with the same hate and abhorrence for others which prevailed about them.   Even for food and drink they have received the same tastes and distastes. They are mere clockwork, which runs as it is regulated. Who is it who feels, thinks, tastes; not the individual but the social group.   Its thoughts, feelings, tastes, impressions, hence also its plans and purposes, its objects and its conduct re-live again; as the elders sung so chirrup the young.

Who can comprehend all that has been accumulated in the mind of this new individual?   The mental precipitate of generations long gone is condensed in the mind of one person.   There are experiences thousands of years old which have been inherited for generations as completed intuitions; destinies historic, and prehistoric, with their effects upon mental character and inclination, with their forms of thought and mode of reasoning; sympathies, prejudices and prepossessions deeply seated and concentrated in the mind of the "free" individual like countless rays in a focus.   They live in him as thought, though the crowd imagines that he thinks freely; and as feeling, though the crowd imagines that whether right or wrong, praiseworthy or blameworthy, it is he that cherishes them.

For the great majority of men intellectual development, strictly so-called, ends with this; the educative impressions of childhood and youth suffice for the whole life.   Only an insignificant minority continue their education by receiving mental impressions and influences from without their social group as they have opportunity.   How much we overrate the efficacy of classical antiquity and the accumulated culture of other nations in this particular!   How insignificant it is in

comparison with the inherited and inculcated culture in
which the spirit of the social group is manifest!

Unprejudiced consideration will convince us that all the
"education," especially that of our schools, is scarcely
sufficient to varnish over the mental heritage which each has
received. None of it ever penetrates into the depths of the
soul unless the pre-existing conditions are favorable.

What do the so-called educated men, doctors, teachers,
officials, etc., generally get from their education, whether
acquired in school or not, save a little knowledge? But
knowledge is not thought, neither is it feeling. What does
knowledge profit if it cannot alter thought or influence
temperament? and it can do neither. Hence the sad
sight of people who with a little knowledge so much the
more easily conceal from the world the vulgarity of their
ideas and their inborn baseness; who varnish over rudeness
by pretending special knowledge and vainly cloak a coarse
nature in "education."

Even if it were as Buckle contends in his great work that
mankind is improved by knowledge and by that alone; it
must first improve the mass or at least the group which in
turn would ennoble the individual.

Though paradoxical it is true that the knowledge of the
mass, of the social environment, benefits the individual,
while the knowledge which he acquires comes too late to
affect him. Like a piece of coin he is complete when he
steps out into the world.

A mature young man is bound to his family, class, or
social group by ties of common interest. He is treated by
the world, that is by the other social groups, simply as a
member of his syngenetic circle and so feels that his identity
with it is involuntary and often a misfortune. However
much he may know he is only what his social medium
makes out of him, subject however to modification by the
heterogeneous social elements that confront him. Though
there are rare and exceptional cases where individuals,
whether living in isolation or separated from their own circle
by force, have been thoroughly absorbed by a strange group
or have of purpose submerged their identity in it, a complete transformation of character taking place, they simply
confirm the rule.

The fate of the youth determines the destiny of the man
in his broader sphere. Hard conflicts of interests arise and

struggles with powerful currents which the individual can neither cause nor control, but by which he is tossed to and fro, with which he must swim lest he sink. Does he choose?

The current beats him back; of what avail is his knowledge? He must struggle, but if he would not sink he must swim with the favoring tide; and his freedom consists only in holding himself as much above it as possible and warding off the opposing flood as best he may. To get into an entirely different current, or to change his course is a matter of accident, not of choice.

The struggle of life brings the individual to self-consciousness indeed and he obtains an unobstructed view of the field of conflict; he has acquired personal knowledge, not simply adapted another's. But it cannot transform him for he is at the end of his career and cannot begin life anew. Like the youth of Sais he has drawn the veil, and knows the secret; he knows what he was and must make his exit. His own knowledge is his only comfort—or disappointment.

Between the cradle and the grave one thread is spun which breaks not and cannot be reunited; a chain is extended whose every link is wrought into the preceding. Man may choose to break it by violence, but not to re-weld it. He may die by his own hand, but can never be born again, though even the self-determination to die must be conditioned in the whole preceding life.

The whole belief in the freedom of human action is rooted in the idea that man's conduct is the fruit of his thoughts and that his thoughts are exclusively his own. This is an error. He is not self-made mentally any more than he is physically. His mind and thoughts are the product of his social medium, of the social element whence he arose, in which he lives.

Those who doubt whether the influence of the social medium can be so powerful must consider what is more remarkable, that the social element in which a man moves exercises an undeniable influence upon his physical features. The fact is well known to physiognomists and is too apparent to be seriously contradicted. Who does not recognize an Englishman, a Frenchman, an Italian, a north or a south German among a hundred different nationalities? It is difficult to say exactly how we recognize them; only the artist's crayon can express it; but we recognize John Bull, the "honest Swabian," the Frenchman polite and tractable and even the Parisian, the Italian somewhat uncanny and Mephistophelian, and so on.

Who has not observed how living for years among a people of a pronounced type of culture conforms a foreigner's whole external appearance and bearing to theirs?

Does not the German become a perfect John Bull after living a decade or two in England? Who has not observed the remarkable orientalizing effect of life in the East upon the European? We have known Poles, offspring of old Polish families, who after a long residence in Turkey have assumed the oriental type completely. But it is useless to cite further instances. Those who have no experience can neither comprehend nor believe it; but those who have will certainly corroborate us.

To these alone we turn with a logical demonstration. That which works the greater may also work the less; if the social element changes a man's physical features surely it has already changed his mind, has more easily transformed his thoughts and opinions and exerted upon his feelings and disposition an influence which betrays itself in his whole outward bearing; for this is nothing but the expression of the mental man, the mirror in which his soul is reflected.

Human speech may never be sufficiently discriminating nor our thoughts clear enough to express what we recognize as characteristic in the different types, though the artist's crayon already does it in the illustrated comic papers. Still we must confirm the fact that there is something by which we recognize the members of various nations, peoples and social groups, etc., that it is transferable to the individual by means of the social influence regardless of descent or relationship; that this influence seizes upon and transforms the human mind quicker and easier than the body, but that after a while it seizes this also and transforms it by its power.

While we are considering the action of the social factor on the individual whom it surrounds, we must not fail to notice that the character of a social group is developed by the continuous assimilating action of the whole on its parts. We distinguish different nationalities not so much by physiognomy, figure, complexion or proportions, for our eye is not sensitive enough to perceive all this without practice and without the aid of scientific apparatus. But what strikes us is the type—something inexpressible and indefinable—which is the effect of social influence, *i. e.*, of the influence of the social factor.

It is of the utmost importance that this should be fairly appreciated for it shows us that the character of the social group depends more on its mental than on its physical constitution. In a word the type or physiognomical character of a folk or social group is not anthropological but social. On the one hand this explains how it is possible for a foreigner to assume the type of the group into which he has fallen; while on the other the transformation of the individual by the group proves that we are dealing with purely social and sociological facts; for if the type were anthropological the transformation and assimilation of the individual through the group would be inconceivable.

After the influence of the social medium upon the individual has been established it only remains to investigate the nature of the factor which exercises it. If it is not anthropological what is its character?

After what has been already said no one will expect a precise answer. The most that can be said is this: Between each thought or desire and the accompanying act intervenes man's φύσις. We know that violent thoughts and efforts are expressed externally in the φύσις, because we see it daily and hourly in cases of sudden anger, joy, pain or despair; the effect follows the cause immediately. But a natural result which is real and true where we can observe it is no less so where our eye is too weak to notice it. If an internal emotion, thought or effort exercises an influence upon our body, upon our deportment and bearing, it may exercise it in such infinitesimal degrees that our sense is too weak to perceive the separate and distinct effects. Our perception does not begin until, after a long series of effects, the completed type confronts us.

But can we designate the effective agents more exactly? Thoughts and desires produce the type, we said. Life in turn, social life, produces them. As it differs from zone to zone and land to land among men of different races and different ethnical composition so their thoughts, their entire conceptions and their efforts, are different and difference of type follows necessarily. As a people's conceptions and thoughts stand also in the perpetual stream of evolution and alter from time to time, there arises the well-known variety of type among members of the same folk in successive generations.

INFLUENCE OF ECONOMIC STATUS ON THE INDIVIDUAL.

Our assertion that thoughts and opinions are created by the social life can be made still more specific. A man's behavior is determined immediately by his economic status, which constrains him to follow a certain mode of life and awakens the corresponding mental conditions within him. In all freely organized states amid the multitude of divisions and subdivisions there are, as we have seen, three grand social circles distinguished by economic status: the ruling class, the middle class including merchants and tradesmen, and the peasantry. They bring up their members differently by accustoming them to their respective opinions, customs, legal usages and principles and, by offering them and even imposing upon them a particular calling, compel them through self-interest to continue in the path traversed by the whole circle.

Thus the nobleman is accustomed to rule and command and to have his life made comfortable for him by others in the hereditary way. Higher appreciation of personality arises naturally, and self-assurance, depreciation of others and the thousand and one traits which, independent of land, folk, nation, religion, race or individual peculiarity, characterize aristocracy universally.

The peasants and slaves of every land and people cherish deep, suppressed ill-will towards the lords. It is inherited from generation to generation, and is held in check by the consciousness of mental inferiority and economic weakness; but when opportunity offers it bursts into flame with the wildness of a barbaric horde.

Neither persuasion, kindness nor advances can uproot it. In stolid resignation the peasant closes his social circle to the higher classes—which however do not open theirs to him,—hears the consolations of religion as a matter of habit without the least reflection, and throws the blame for all the misery of his life upon the lords. Yet habit and inherited notions have taught him to bear his hard lot calmly, and acquired feelings of respect make it easier for him to do so; though all together they would be insufficient to maintain the political organization were it not protected by the strong arm of the state's power.

The member of the middle class is educated in "business" traditions. Trade, commerce and business profits are his ideals from childhood on and he sees many examples of accumulated riches. Fortune-hunting, an idea that the peasant never knows and which seldom incites the nobleman, is the great object which attracts the middle class. They soon learn that skillful labor and inventiveness lead to success and every thought turns in that direction.

Seldom can the peasant, bound to the soil by law or by the force of circumstances, think of leaving his hereditary pursuit. As a rule he is unable to conceive of such a thing. So overwhelming are the legal and political regulations that it does not even occur to him to oppose them. As a result of his inertia his horizon grows narrower and narrower, not extending beyond the neighboring village; he must either give up and labor and adapt himself to the circumstances or pine away and die in misery—or in prison; there is no alternative.

It is otherwise with the townsman. Trade extends his horizon; the world lies open before him; his plans are ambitious; but the narrow limits of political regulation hold him in check. What is more natural in such circumstances than the attempt to break through or circumvent them! This it is which causes the social fermentation and starts the social struggle. In such an atmosphere as this the quick-witted townsman's thoughts and opinions germinate and grow; and his eternal discontent opposes the contented conservatism of the ruling classes. He it is also who first stirs up the resigned conservatism of the "masses."

Lord, townsman, peasant: these would be the three types of individuals if the state had not progressed beyond the primitive stratification of society. But we know how complex the social structure has become and how the different types have multiplied.

It is impossible for the scientist to distinguish them all; art alone can present the typical and the sociologist must yield to the delineator. We will only add that as civilization advances and the sphere of the state enlarges the ruling class subdivides into the civil class, the military class and the large landholders and transfers its various functions to particular organs.

Each of these smaller circles has its particular interests, its peculiar calling and its corresponding views and manner of life. The subdivision into classes determines also the method of participating in the government of the state. Compare the general who remains a soldier and stakes his professional honor on fulfilling the royal orders even against his own convictions; the minister who feels in honor bound to hand in his resignation on account of some difference of opinion with his monarch, or incident which does not please him; and the "great lord" who will accept a royal invitation to hunt but will politely decline a minister's portfolio in order not to sacrifice his freedom. How different the views of life's duties and principles! What different ideas in one and the same ruling class through the social differentiation of pursuits!

With the middle class it is the same. How different is the artisan's line of thought from that of the merchant or ship-owner! How different the type of mind among merchants themselves according as one stays in a shop, another is engaged in foreign trade, and a third trades on the exchange! Yet these are not individual fortunes, but social destinies, social fates.

What must be the mental character of the workman's child, accustomed to uninterrupted labor in the family, meagre earnings and the monotony of the small tradesman's life; and how different in the circle of the traders on exchange with the abrupt alternations of wealth and misery and the continual excitement of speculation where success depends on the turn of events the world over.

How many educated professions are differentiated in the middle class: doctors, attorneys, judges, teachers, officials, master mechanics, engineers. Each circle creates its own peculiar spirit, so to say, a moral atmosphere of principles, ideas, views and conceptions, in which its members live and in which their posterity is born and educated.

The number of types is endless. But it must be pointed out that in every case the individual's thought and conduct, feeling and effort is not created in him but in his social circle. Least of all is it created by him freely and independently; it is laid upon him without his knowing it; and sociology must emphasize some of the fundamental factors in the process.

It follows from what has been already said that it is the

moral force alone which transforms the individual. The group affects him through his moral nature, his thoughts and views; he is only a part of it, growing up in its moral atmosphere, drawing his intellectual life from it. In this process bodily descent and long lineage is not the decisive factor. Whatever the anthropological material, if it comes early enough into a group however strange, if it is uninfluenced by any other and is treated like the other members it will be as completely assimilated as though it had been born there. Hence it is that while anthropologists assure us that no race in the world is pure; and while experience daily shows us the greatest variety of anthropological types in one and the same society, the members of each group show a unitary moral type. Anthropological variety and moral unity is characteristic of every social community, not simply in Europe, but of the whole world. Yet so predominant is the impression made upon us by the latter that the impression of the former disappears in comparison. As we are in general more impressed by what is human in man, i. e., by his intellectual and moral faculties, than by what is animal, so we are most impressed with a man's social type and the anthropological escapes our observation. Thus when an individual has certain outward marks denoting membership in a group, such as costume, head-dress and the like, the moral type of the group is still more striking in him and we do not notice his anthropological type or deceive ourselves about it unless it is very conspicuously unusual.

The notorious fact that all Chinese seem alike to us is due to the fact that, being struck with the well-known outward characteristics, queue, clean-shaven crown and the like, we observe nothing else except the moral type, although there are as different anthropological types among them as in any other folk. Similarly, to a negro all the soldiers in a regiment of European grenadiers will look exactly alike because in addition to the similarity of costume, head-dress, etc., he notices only the moral type, the expression, mien and bearing. Nevertheless an anthropologist or craniologist would certainly find in such a regiment sufficient data for a classification into many races and anthropological types.

But some social circles, as we have seen, are very firmly bound together, compact and cohesive, while others are loosely connected and less cohesive. The degree of cohesion depends, as we have further seen, on the number of group-making factors, on the interests holding the group together and on their permanency; for some are inherited and will endure while others are temporary, ephemeral and momentary.

The difference in the degree of social cohesion has great influence upon the creation and the endurance of moral types, and we do not hesitate to formulate a sociological law that the tenacity and endurance of a moral type is directly related to the degree of cohesion and firmness of social structure, and so to the number of group-making factors.

It is as if their greater number put the individual under better control; for highly cohesive social circles are well adapted to create firm characters. The individual members seem to be cast from one mould, to be flesh of its flesh and blood of its blood; nothing more nor less than pieces of it. Hence the elemental moral power of men contending for their class, their rank—their folk, to which every group-making factor and every heartstring binds them.

Contrast with this the vacillation and unsteadfastness when one of the forces binding a man to his own is dissolved; and the unnaturalness and artificiality of the individual who presumes to represent a group with which he has only a loose, ephemeral connection, the most of the group-making factors being absent. Therein lies the perpetual ridiculousness of the parvenu, which meets us not only where the "upstart without family connections" puts on airs on account of his intimate relations with counts and princes (who is not familiar with this type) but also where the townsman among peasants would demean himself like a peasant or the aristocratic candidate explains his political and industrial program to his agricultural constituents. The ridiculous effect in every case lies in the absence of every natural bond of union between the individual and the group which he would have it appear he belongs to or represents, for unnaturalness is always ridiculous. With such comical figures compare the man who represents his own social group. His appearance commands respect everywhere; its very naturalness is imposing. Even an individual of little importance must be taken seriously for his coming is natural and in good character.

But social life is not confined within the exclusive social circles. In the very nature of political and social development there is an incessant movement of individuals back and forth, up and down, so that the social circles lap and overlap in the greatest confusion and individuals stand in the greatest variety of relations to their own and to foreign groups.

Thus life is richly provided with every degree of variation from cheerful pleasantry to bitter earnest, from delightful comedy to shocking tragedy. But it is a barren task for science to distinguish the countless shades of individual form and situation, though not for history and art.

MORALS.

We have tried to explain how the moral type of the individual is produced by the group and have already pointed out that the social group not only creates the individual's thoughts and opinions, sentiments and feelings but builds up what we call morals also. For morals is nothing but the conviction implanted by the social group in the minds of its members of the propriety (*Statthaftigkeit*) of the manner of life imposed by it on them. This conviction, the individual's innermost thought concerning his whole conduct and that of others, is the second factor in the development of morals. The first is the acquired and customary habits, the manner of life and conduct. There are certain rules and principles which the individual receives from his group applicable to all spheres of life and to all possible situations.

Consider a man who is firmly rooted in his group. In no situation which is accessible to it considering its nature and position is he in doubt how he should proceed. He has acquired a standard of conduct and possesses a moral code which guides him everywhere.

While the simple unitary group (Spencer's "small and simple aggregate") constitutes the individual's whole world, in the primitive horde and wild natural stock, he knows what is right, proper and permissible toward his fellows and toward strangers.

But as soon as two or more groups have been united and sovereignty has been organized the different moral views begin to contend in the larger social circle. The primitive moral codes are useless and a new one must be formed if the union is to continue. Not only do the relations of sovereign and subject peremptorily demand this, but they provide it for themselves. The members of the new union become habituated to the new institutions which become necessary to sustain sovereignty; and new conceptions of what is right, proper, allowable and good grow up; and as the new political organization grows and is perfected the new moral code gives forth rights, *i. e.*, statutes promulgated by the state the transgression of which is punishable by the state.

Hence there is a fundamental difference between rights and morals. The former is a product of the union [*Zusammentreffen*] of different social elements, the latter is the product of the relations between the simple social group and the individual. Rights never arise except in a union of societies however simple it may be; organized sovereignty is always presupposed. Morals arise in the most primitive social element, in the simple aggregate or horde.

Every complex community, consisting of parts which are united by certain group-making bonds, constitutes in so far a social unit aside from the social circles comprised within it. Necessarily the very fact of the existence of this social community will create a common moral code binding on all its members. But on account of the weaker cohesion of the whole it will of course not have the effective power and intensity of the moral codes of the several social elements and will frequently come in conflict with them and sometimes be broken down by them. It may be confidently asserted that probably the greater part of the crimes and offences occurring in the state arise from the conflict between the general and the particular moral codes. Thus the poacher does not offend against the morals of his group when he hunts game in the mountains although in so doing he violates not only the rights but also the moral code of the political whole.

Many infractions of right in the mercantile world, such as usury and the like, result from the antagonism between its moral code and that of the political whole and prove that the higher unity, the state, has not succeeded in reducing the social elements to a homogeneous community and imbuing every individual with that higher morality which is as needful for the welfare of the whole as the primitive morality of the horde is for its welfare.

It is the state's supreme object to do this. Consciously or unconsciously it strives toward it and though it should never be quite accomplished, no higher sanction or more complete justification of the state can be given than the determination to educate mankind to a higher moral plane. But the ideal moral code must never be limited to national sentiment which is nothing more than a potentialized love of the horde. It should at least embrace mankind so far as it is civilized or capable of civilization. The way to its realization has been entered upon by the construction of political systems like the European, which will in time reduce Europe to a social unit, however loose; the process may then be extended to other portions of the world. Although its realization may lie in the unseen future, civilization must hold fast to it if it would be anything more than a blind natural process; and it is certainly the noblest function of social science to point out the wearisome way along which mankind, dripping with blood yet pants for the distant goal.

MORALS AND TRUTH PERCEPTION.

It has undoubtedly already become clear that morals are not the result of human reflection, the conscious product of the human will and understanding; but are, like all social institutions, the result of natural development, a product of the natural and necessary feelings and thoughts of man in connection with the active impelling forces of life, the resultant as it were of the mutual action and reaction of nature and human life.

Hence we can distinguish two elements in the result, the natural and the human. The former is everlasting and unchangeable and is constantly and universally repeated. The latter is perpetually changing because it represents the ways in which individuals react upon natural realities and forces.

Hence it is that in the morals of all ages and peoples we find something similar and typical and also something changing and individual, for while the social process that produces morals is always the same, its various contingencies make the psycho-social result different.

Placed by nature in a sequence of necessities which he cannot alter, man strives naturally to adapt himself to them as best he can and to make life as pleasant as possible; habit helps him over the worst difficulties by deadening his sensibilities. He gets accustomed to the rack on which he is stretched and ceases to feel it. He attributes his sufferings

to a higher necessity and, knowing the uselessness of pro-
test, gives up the futile fight and looks instinctively for
means to alleviate his hard lot.

In following this natural tendency, or rather in being
driven to do whatever his nature and conditions compel, he
reflects (which again is a part of his nature) and believes
that he acts freely, finding a proof of his freedom in the
individual shading of his acts, though this happens simply
because reflection, in essence the same, is individualistic in
form.

If, acting as he must though reflecting as he acts, he hits
upon a mode of behavior which long experience proves to be
the most suitable and appropriate to his conditions, he takes
this to be the right, the only good and the moral way; the
contrary is to him immoral.

Thus the man acquires moral ideas which correspond
to the larger or smaller extent of his needs and experiences, the higher or lower stage of his civilization, the more
or less complex relations of his life, growing, broadening
and developing with them.

But, as we have seen, an individual's moral feelings all
develop within the sphere of his social group through its
influence upon him.

Take a primitive savage, a gregarious human being; what
are his moral ideas? He is bound to his fellows by the
natural feeling of connection. They help him in his need;
to hold to them, help them and stand by them loyally
is one of his moral ideas. But strangers from another horde
waylay them, try to get their property, invade their hunting
ground, slay them occasionally and steal them; therefore to
kill these strangers and rob them is another of his moral
ideas.

Now the element in these ideas which is natural and
eternal inheres in the mind of man, surviving savagery and
appearing in changing garb and more refined form throughout the whole period of human existence. To-day as thousands of years ago there is the struggle with the foreigner
for lordship. Between strange social groups to-day as always
there are only two possible relations: conflict or alliance
against a third. After century upon century of development, in the midst of high civilization, the primitive moral
idea of the savage meets us in the form of patriotism, heroism and bravery.

The savage feels more keenly than the civilized man that he is only a part of the community; for without his own horde his life is every moment exposed to the superior force of hostile beasts and alien hordes.

It cannot appear to the savage immoral to satisfy hunger and thirst; and to feed the helpless children of his own horde must seem to him good, profitable and a moral duty.

Between young and old, helpless and strong, arises a mutual relation of protection and gratitude which with the changes of years becomes reversed; protection of children and the infirm creates a moral idea. But if times and circumstances and also individual dispositions cause a horde to put an end to the misery of old age by violent death, this practice also becomes, locally and temporarily, a moral act; and the same is true, locally and temporarily, of fostering or exposing children. The essence of the moral idea is the same: practices springing from natural tendencies take on one form or another; whichever one lasts and proves to be suitable comes to be considered moral.

The relation of the sexes and the division of industrial labor between them is regulated by time and circumstances, the temperament of the particular horde, and its physical and mental constitution. Whether the result is promiscuity, polygamy or polyandry, whatever practice persists and is recognized as suitable becomes a moral duty and command, a part of morals.

When one horde establishes lordship over another, when two make offensive or defensive alliance against a third, or finally when captured aliens are reduced to servitude and slavery, the circle of life's relations broadens, a new series of practices begins and a new sphere of moral ideas arises.

The best method of handling captives, slaves and servants, and the best conduct toward allies offer new grounds for moral opinions; and the most reasonable and appropriate government of subjects becomes the only moral one. Fidelity towards allies produces a new moral idea. The different treatment of members of different social circles makes in time moral principles, conforming to the usage, which eventually settle into rights.

As a different treatment seems wise and appropriate for each condition of life, so different moral standards grow up according to the different social position of the younger or older generation, of able-bodied or infirm men, of women in different periods of life, of masters and dependents, of the rich and the propertyless. Unconditional obedience is recognized as moral in servants and slaves; inflexible energy and strict discipline in masters. The killing of a master is recognized as immoral conduct in a slave, the killing of a slave is by no means immoral in a master.

Now men are never satisfied with actual occurrences simply; it is a peculiarity of the reflecting human mind to ascribe them to causes which have no relation whatever to the natural causes and to give the most far-fetched explanation possible. A myth-maker and poet by nature, man ascribes poetical and generally anthropomorphic significations and derivations to natural phenomena and he treats social occurrences in the same way.

As man at first ascribes his own existence to the creation of a supersensual being so he traces all social differences to different creative acts of the same being. Social organizations which the force of circumstances has produced he prefers to ascribe to an original arrangement of the creator of the world, being led by an unconscious desire to give a higher sanction to his various moral ideas. Thus when social relations have been so far developed that murder is interdicted and to spare a fellow-being's life is a moral commandment, the myth-making mind has a god appear in flames and deliver to the law-giver in the midst of thunderings and lightnings a table on which stand the words: Thou shalt not kill.

Every code of human morals from the earliest times to the present day has this thoroughly characteristic peculiarity; the product of actual occurrences and real relations is everywhere explained by and derived from imaginary circumstances, and men cannot comprehend a moral idea otherwise.

Whether theologians base morals upon divine commandments, or philosophers derive them from ideas inherent in man, fact and fancy are blended together until one seems incapable of existing without the other. As moral ideas take root in men's hearts, get control of their dispositions and become a part of their mental ego, the myths which support them take root there also; until it appears as if morals could not be maintained without myths and every attack on the latter must cause the former to fall.

Socrates was accused of undermining virtue and morality,

the real forces of life, because he questioned the existence of those creatures of the imagination, the Olympian gods. And so to-day, whoever ventures to criticise and doubt one of the myths which have been put forward as the explanation and foundation of our morals, whoever denies the "universal and eternal truth of inherent, moral ideas," and seeks to represent them as the product of actual social relations changing with them and taking manifold forms and shapes, is considered a dangerous enemy to them.

This fight of naïve ignorance against truth in the name of morality is observable in very many spheres still.

Advanced moral sentiment seeking to explain and support the idea and the feeling of brotherly love produced the monogenetic myth of the descent of all men from one pair of parents; and so polygenism, which is thought to menace the myth, is immoral, though brotherly love might just as plausibly be founded upon the unity of species in a polygenetic mankind. Its real explanation, however, is quite different: the development of human society.

The history of sectarianism presents the same spectacle under countless different forms. The simplest religious ceremonies are connected directly with certain moral ideas and an attack on the former is denounced as an attack on the latter, when in truth they do not need to stand in any connection whatever. Every new system of philosophy, every hard-won scientific acquisition has the same contest against the alleged "guardians of morals."

When the intellectual revolution and the materialistic philosophy of the eighteenth century overthrew some of the prevailing prejudices the jesuitical alarm cry was everywhere raised that morals were being undermined. Because in a certain age the stock of moral ideas corresponded to a certain degree of scientific knowledge; because at a given time the opinion was universal that the soul is a temporary occupant of the human body and after its decay will rise straight to heaven and begin a new life there: the whole moral and ethical code was thought to depend upon the maintenance of this belief. Whoever dared to doubt the immortality of the soul was thought to have sinned against morality and virtue as though immortality and the dualism of soul and body were the only conditions on which they could thrive. Many a time indeed have men sought to uphold the existing moral order by this fable; and when no one knew better the effort was praiseworthy. But every such prop is ready to fall the moment advanced knowledge lays bare its untruthfulness; though it by no means follows that morality is undermined and threatened by the removal of the alleged prop; for the basis of morals is truth and not fiction and all these pious fictions have not prevented the grossest immoralities, the horrors of the inquisition and trials for witchcraft, the greatest crimes mankind has ever committed.

The alleged descent of man from lower animals is denounced by the church as undermining the whole ethical and moral code; as if this had some connection with the alleged creation of man by a god or was indeed the result of it.

Following natural and necessary tendencies the human state has grown up and has become in civilized regions what it is to-day, the guardian of right and custom, the promoter of welfare and culture. Corresponding to this fact a moral theory of the state has been produced in the human mind, a pretty myth, according to which the state sprang from a social contract which the citizens once made for protecting rights and securing justice; and it gives adequate expression to the ideas which the actual evolution of the state has produced.

But when it is announced as the result of modern objective investigation that the state arose by violence and owes its existence to the superiority of some over others, the "moral" heresy-hunters (*Angstmeier*) and hypocrites raise the alarm that the moral idea of the state is undermined, right is uprooted and public morals corrupted. It is the policy of stupid parents, who expect to inculcate morals and a sense of obligation in a child by telling him all sorts of ghost stories. Science should not be misled by such ungenerous and narrow views. Morals is the ripened fruit of the actual development of civilization and cannot be harmed by the scientific investigation of its real foundation; on the contrary the truth will certainly be much more wholesome for its promotion than the stupid lie upon which it has been sought hitherto with little success to base it.

As the origin of moral ideas is a very difficult problem and a dark region in human knowledge, it has always been easier to explain it in poems and fairy tales. Nevertheless it is not difficult to see that every progress in the perception of truth, and especially of nature, must promote morals.

For as nature's sway and the acts of man go to make up the events of life, human acts are reasonable when they correspond to natural tendencies and complement them; and unreasonable if they mistake these tendencies and oppose them.

There can be but one principle of human rationality and of human morals and ethics: to be governed by the import and tendency of nature's sway. Hence knowledge of nature, natural science in its full scope, embracing every department of human life, is the only and the necessary basis of the science of morals and ethics.

Without natural science no moral science. Hence the low state of morals where natural science is neglected, and the higher and purer morality with greater progress in the knowledge of nature's sway.

The explanation is simple. Nature has all the characteristics which oriental monotheism ascribes to its god: omnipresence and omnipotence; everything everywhere happens as nature wills, according to nature. Indeed at bottom the idea of god is only a symbol of nature, perhaps unconscious and poetical at first, later misunderstood and misinterpreted.

As man himself is subject to nature, is constrained by her demands, must satisfy his natural needs, lives according to the measure of the strength and capacity she has given him, and following her commands must close it, so his mind is deeply impressed by her omnipotence and the resulting course of events. He can scarcely conceive another mode of existence; and this one seems right and just, reasonable and moral (*sittlich*). He has no other standard for the events of life than the assumed will, *i. e.*, the visible tendency, of nature; while "unnatural" is synonymous with unreasonable and immoral. Man's ethical sense has been engrafted upon nature's sway. Her norms even in social life have been transformed and condensed in his mind into moral ideas. By nature the parents and elders assume direction of the rising generation—and the honor and respect which the younger pay the elder accords with our moral ideas. Whatever is natural is moral. Therein lies the eternal, fixed and unchangeable basis of all ethics and morals.

Hence there is really but one code of ethics and morals which has been and always will be as fixed and unchangeable as the forces of nature. But if nevertheless there have been temporary and local differences in ethical views it is, first, because knowledge of nature has not everywhere reached the same stage of advancement and men often yield to the grossest self-deceptions in respect of it; secondly, because there are whole spheres of human life, like the social sphere, which on account of meagre knowledge are not considered natural, in which the sway of nature is not conjectured or presupposed, in which therefore a correction of inherited moral conceptions in accord with the recognized "will of nature," or a concession to nature's tendencies is entirely out of the question.

By searching for truth, therefore, and by investigating nature and her sway, in the social sphere as well as elsewhere, science labors in the service of morals and breaks the way for its progress, although incidentally old and cherished idols may be overthrown and the wail of the "moralists" aroused.

RIGHTS.

Heretofore rights have always been treated from the standpoint either of individualism or of a very indefinite collectivism. As these two extremes contended against each other, progress swayed from one to the other in literature. But since neither was true, it ought not to be surprising that neither the philosophy of rights nor the prevailing scientific treatment of them is satisfactory, and that the schools of the philosophers have produced nothing but disgust and rancor after centuries of labor.

Let us briefly review the dreary maze. The original rules of human conduct receive their sanction in part from precedent and custom and in part by reference to the will of the gods. Belief and custom are the earliest sources of right, of that which is the standard of conduct. As reflection awakens it distinguishes between these precepts of religion and morals and the laws which the rulers set up, and hence the earliest jurisprudence could consider political law alone to be the source of right. Upon further scientific investigation this naïve conception was found unsatisfactory; and then began the argumentation in a circle. Some sought the source of right in man immediately, in his nature, in his social instincts or in similar characteristics which were ascribed to him. Others believed that they had found the source in the community, the folk, in society and its "common will." *

The truth lies between the two, as we have shown.† Rights are not the product of the individual and his nature and constitution, nor are they the creation of the folk or of a common will or national spirit invented *ad hoc*. Rights are a social creation, a form of communal life produced by the conflict (*Zusammenstoss*) of unlike social groups of unequal power; such unlikeness and inequality is the necessary precondition of all rights. In the primitive horde, a homogeneous, simple, undifferentiated group, there are no rights, nor are they necessary. Complete equality prevails; it is not the soil in which rights are wont to grow. There are neither family rights (promiscuity prevails) nor property rights—hence no rights of inheritance; nor any sort of rights in personalty where there is no trade and commerce. Life is not regulated by published ordinances; whatever is is holy. The forms of life produced in the course of time to satisfy wants, which we call custom, are fully sufficient to regulate the life of the primitive horde. No one marks their gradual rise and they are generally ascribed to the will of the gods. Custom and a few religious precepts suffice for men in such a state.

But when unlike groups come together and different ethnical elements have to live side by side the custom of neither is sufficient, for it is not recognized by the other. One subjects the other, sovereignty is organized, and the superior power of the stronger makes existence side by side possible by regulating the manner of life. The regulations thus built up for the existence of unlike elements side by side are reduced by practice to rules and principles which create rights.

Thus, as we have seen, by the rape of women from another tribe arose the first family right, the right of the man over his wife; thus also by reducing the foreign element to servitude arose the right of the lord over his slave; and from the resulting distinction between the lord to whom the fruits of the soil belong and the slave who cultivates the soil for his master arose the right of property. The soil together with the acquired sovereignty passed from father to son in

---

* *Cf.* " *Philosophisches Staatsrecht,*" secs. 4 and 21; " *Rechtsstaat und Socialismus,*" I, sec. 4 *et seq.*

† See Part IV, sec. 1 above.

the father-family—hence the right of inheritance arose. If an alien trading element invaded this primitive sovereign organization the exchange of goods produced other property rights, first of all the rights of debtor and creditor with all the complications to which the development of trade and commerce give rise.

Rights are always due to the contact of unlike social elements and every right bears evidence of such an origin. There is not one which does not express inequality, for each is the mediation between unlike social elements, the reconciliation of conflicting interests which was originally enforced by compulsion but has by usage and familiarity acquired the sanction of a new custom.

Thus family right subjects the wife and children to the control of the father and compels the reconciliation of opposing interests until in time usage and familiarity substitute new customs and new morals for the original constraint. Property rights regulate the inequality between owner and non-owner in respect of the thing owned; the rights of inheritance regulate the inequality between the heir and the non-heir in respect of the inheritance; the rights of debtor and creditor regulate the inequality between them in respect of the object of the obligation. In short every right arises from an inequality and aims to maintain and establish it through the sovereignty of the stronger over the weaker. In this respect every right is a true reflection of the state to which it owes its existence, and which also aims only at the maintenance and regulation of the life of unlike elements side by side through the sovereignty of one over the other. And since the maintenance of inequality is the soul and real principle of every right, corresponding to each there is a duty; corresponding to each one entitled to receive there are one or more obligated to give; just as in the state by its nature there are rulers and ruled.

RIGHTS AND THE STATE.

Thus it is plain that rights can arise only in the state and nowhere else for they are eminently political institutions, flesh of the state's flesh and blood of its blood, containing as it were a particle of political sovereignty. For whence comes the grain of sovereignty in every right if not from the great reservoir of sovereignty which we call the state's power? From this great reservoir political sovereignty flows like water through an aqueduct into a network of rights. It is only necessary to turn the cock of execution, and political sovereignty, the state's power, is there. In civilized states a small fee is paid, generally in the form of a stamp tax, for the privilege of drawing upon political sovereignty. Rights can no more be conceived without the state than an aqueduct without a reservoir and pipes and cocks.

Nevertheless scholasticism succeeded in building up countless systems of "natural rights" which were alleged to exist without the state, beyond its borders and superior to its authority. Fortunately they are all overthrown, dead and buried. But their spirit hovers over the sea of jurisprudence where "innate" human rights are still spoken of; in addition to those "proclaimed by the French revolution," such as freedom and equality, other "inalienable rights" also, such as the right "to live," "to work" and so on. They are deduced either from the "conception of man" as a "free, sentient and reasonable" being or more generally from the "conception of justice." We have elsewhere shown the arbitrariness and insipidity of these deductions.* They are simply deductions from natural rights though every premise is false and the whole system is buried in its grave. That man is a "free" being is pure imagination, still less is he a "reasonable" being, if by "reason" we mean the peculiarity that a person is led in his action by reason and not by blind impulse.

The premises of "inalienable human rights" rest upon the most unreasonable self-deification of man and overestimation of the value of human life, and upon complete misconception of the only possible basis of the existence of the state.

This fancied freedom and equality is incompatible with the state and is a direct negation of it. But the only choice for men here below is between the state with its necessary servitude and inequality, and—anarchy.

There is much unavoidable evil in the former; but on the other hand it promotes and protects the greatest good that man can experience on earth. Anarchy raises to infinity the evil which is unavoidable in the state without affording

* "*Philosophisches Staatsrecht*," sec. 21-23;" "*Rechtsstaat und Socialismus*," sec. 33 *et seq.*

even the least of its advantages, for the greatest human evil here below is human stupidity and baseness. Scarcely can the state hold it in check; in a condition of anarchy it rages without restraint heaping horror on horror. There is no third choice, for it is impossible to return to the primitive horde;* and between these two modes of social existence: the state and anarchy, it is not hard to choose.

It is no less an error to deduce rights from "justice" or a "feeling of justice," to place them above the state and to propose their realization in the state. This procedure rests on an optical illusion. For what is justice? Whence do we get our conception of it? It is created only by the actual rights as they exist in the state. Our conception of justice attaches itself to political rights; our receptivity, our sense and feeling of it have no other source. It is no contradiction that occasionally we have reason to acknowledge that a political right is wrong and violates justice; for the development of our sense of justice, which takes place under the influence of political rights, may apparently outrun their development in that all institutional rights exist only in virtue of written law or deep-rooted usage and tradition while political relations together with our sense of justice go right on developing. In such a case our yearning for justice is only the forerunner of a new statutory right which has been previously grounded in the conditions and in the degree of the state's development and which it might be said is already recognized though as yet unwritten. In a word we must distinguish between justifiable reform movements based in the nature of the state and mere Utopias. The former spring of themselves from its whole previous development; the latter are separated in thought from the state and stand upon ground upon which no political institution has ever stood such as freedom, equality and absolute justice, apart from the state and based on "natural rights."

What "justice" in this sense is and how it is found we do not and cannot know. To us justice is the simple abstraction of political rights and it stands and falls with them. If we imagine our past apart from political development and political rights the conception of justice vanishes utterly from our mind. Plato recognized this, and as he was about

* Engels, in his "*Ursprung der Familie, des Privateigenthums und des Staates,*" and Marx too, has in mind such a return to the "gentile constitution." It takes a large amount of naivete to conceive of the return of forms of social existence long since surmounted. It is as though an old man would become a youth again.

to explain in the "Republic" what a "just man" and what "justice" were he began by describing the founding of the state out of heterogeneous unequal elements. Presupposing that each part would assume the most fitting rôle that befell it in the state he called this organization of the state and of political sovereignty just; hence this normal condition of the state in which each accommodates himself to the rôle that befalls him is his type of justice. By this shift, starting from the state, which is really the only possible way, Plato reaches his conception of justice which he then applies as a standard to the individual.*

The words of Thrasymachus in the same dialogue: "My doctrine is that justice is the interest of the stronger," (338) might be applied to justice in the state, for in fact the weaker must accommodate himself to the stronger; the state can be regulated by no other rights than such as are most agreeable to the stronger. Indeed this is relatively best for the weaker, and in this sense political order presents the only conceivable idea of justice, the only source from which we can draw conceptions of the just and justice. But it is universally the very contrary of freedom and equality and indeed naturally must be. In fact justice has universally been the real expression of the relative power of the social elements in the state. With changing conditions and especially with progressive development of the state in agriculture and industry, in science and art the relations gradually became more humane and lenient. Rights and legal regulations are humanized and the idea of justice in the abstract grows more perfect. But to-day no less than in Plato's time the state is the only standard of justice. The necessary conditions of its perpetuation determine the concept. What the state must do is right and that can never be "justice" which the state cannot do.

RIGHTS AND MORALS.

We have seen that rights arise at the point where the new whole composed of unlike social elements cannot longer be held together merely by customs and morals since the customs and morals of one party are not the same as those of

*Let us complete the investigation which we undertook in the belief that, if we first endeavored to contemplate justice in some larger object which contains it, we should find it easier to discern its nature in the individual man." Plato, "Republic," Bk. iv, p. 434, Jowett's Translation.
This greater object was wisely chosen. Only by starting from the state was it possible to arrive at a conception of justice.

the other. Into this discord in moral views, with which social unity is incompatible, rights first entered in the form of the commands of the rulers; but in time, as we said, they are transformed into customs and morals so that, being rights, they become the substance of new moral ideas. The apparent contradiction between morals that precede rights and morals that in turn are produced by them needs some elucidation.

The customs and morals of the primitive horde come from the necessities of life and the common wants of the primitive social unity; but needs change in the new social whole composed of two or more unlike elements. At first indeed because there are no common customs and morals, force, compulsion and political rights must bind the new whole together; but usage, habit and all the forces which conduced to fixed customs and morals in the primitive horde will not fail of their effect in the new social unity also.

The new rights only indicated the line along which the forms of life necessary in the new social unit must be developed. In time they will enter into the moral consciousness, for plainly the new social unity will consolidate. In one way or another certain modes of peaceable communal existence will be discovered; people will adapt themselves to their necessities and by recognizing and accepting them create new customs and morals to which rights gave the first impulse.

The old morals of the respective social elements must necessarily be subordinated to the new morals of the complex whole, for while the former insures the existence of the simple group only the latter preserves the complex community.

For example, to a primitive horde and an unmixed stock alien and enemy are synonymous terms; its morals command the sparing of fellow members and the ruthless destruction of aliens. But as soon as any foreigners become a part of the community, whether received as slaves or allies or to serve some other interest of the new whole (the relation will be determined by a treaty from which rights will arise), instantly the interest of the new community which produces the new right begins to set aside the old morals which made "alien and enemy" equal and prepares the way for new ones which give the slave, the ally and whoever else has been taken into the social union a claim to protection and respect. However long rudiments of the old morals may persist in opinions and sentiments the new interest of the new whole has framed new morals which prove victorious over the old.

Wherever there are rights the process is the same. Although in primitive times, or even in the feudal state of Mediæval Europe, the wealth of tolerated classes such as the traveling merchants may have been good booty to the ruling classes and robber knights, the theft of which did not offend against the old morals or detract from knightly honor, yet the new rights which protected the property of the burghers in the interest of all prepared the way gradually for the new morals which to-day forbid the nobility to seize the property of other classes. With difficulty and after centuries of trial, but with final success, political rights have provided new morals concerning property and it is now inconceivable that in the Middle Ages knights and noblemen, who made so much of honor, did not scruple to surprise a city and rob its citizens of their hard-earned goods.

The displacement of the old morals by new rights due to the wants and interests of the new whole is seen most plainly in the development of patriotism. The original tribal consciousness of the respective social elements of the state is changed in time into a folk or national consciousness. While the old morals recognized only the duty of the individual to sacrifice himself for the narrowest syngenetic group the common interests of the new whole have created new morals which demand his unconditional sacrifice for a whole which is ethnically and socially complex.

If we must cite examples at least we shall not need to go far afield for them. What was the nature of that patriotism to which every German was morally bound not many decades ago? If we characterize it in one word as "particularism" we shall at the same time have indicated the powerful change through which morals have passed in this respect as the result of events and new rights. The Rhenish Union was commensurate with the older morals, though the same thing to-day by the same people in the same land would be called the height of immorality, treason and infamy. These moral changes have taken place since the events of Jena and the war for freedom, since the rights of the German Union and the new German Empire. The former morals of the parts must yield to the new morals of the new whole to the making of which the new rights gave the impulse. As the new rights paved the way for the new morals and made them, so now the new morals will continue to be the strongest prop of the new rights—until in the perpetual change of earthly things new events and circumstances make new rights again to which existing morals must be sacrificed.

The objections that can be made to our presentation of the relation between rights and morals are easily foreseen, for frequently the relation is apparently reversed. Even in the present century how often have we seen decayed rights swept away by the powerful current of " public morals;" and yet it was only apparently so, for in fact every such right was merely a screen behind which other conditions came into existence peremptorily demanding recognition as rights, and although existing written rights seemed to prevent the realization of the demand nevertheless moral ideas were created which, exerting a powerful influence and taking possession of the consciousness of the masses, suddenly rose like a tornado overthrowing the old rights as though they were paper; whereupon the rights which the conditions had long since demanded and which had already entered the moral consciousness procured legal expression and validity.

If I might use a somewhat questionable metaphor to illustrate I should say that behind the regular rights legitimately wedded to the nation and known as such there appeared secretly, from the force of circumstances, illegitimate rights which shunned the light and in illicit intercourse with the nation begat morals; and as these, still illegitimate, came into the world and grew up they helped to set the betrayed old rights, which had lost their force and justification, violently aside; whereupon the legitimation of the new morals followed by subsequent marriage, *per subsequens matrimonium.*

"So there was an unwritten natural right based in reason," cries some supporter of natural rights triumphantly. Not so fast. It is true that in such moments of development rights rise through hard birth pains from the dark womb of actual conditions into the light of existence. But they are not natural rights, based on reason and independent of time and conditions. On the contrary they are always conditioned in the actual circumstances. In the sense that they correspond to the conditions from which they spring they are natural and reasonable, but not in the sense that their source is in a natural consciousness of right or in reason and that they always remain the same. The requirements which arise from actual conditions according to time and place, which correspond to them and are therefore natural and reasonable, being formulated into laws, become rights after having struck deep root, as has been said, in moral consciousness.

Thus the objection that the source of rights is moral is based on a misconception of the actual forces. Equally unfounded also is the doctrine of natural rights. But there is another objection which seems to be supported by the facts. Political rights do not always enter into the moral consciousness of the community. However long they may endure they have public morals against them and eventually must succumb. This frequently occurs and though it seems to establish the moral source of rights, in truth it does not.

We often see valid political rights stand like dead machines in spite of the application of the state's whole power, never operating without the display of the political force, disliked and repudiated by public morals, unable to create new morals and finally ending their burdensome existence somehow unregretted. Upon closely examining what sort of rights these are which cannot produce a moral ground into which they may strike firm root, we observe that there was no pressing need for them, that they arose from the momentary caprice of one party, from false ideas and theories, from misconceptions of the actual conditions, etc. Such rights always hang in the air without footing and are powerless, valid only through external support and protection, without internal living force, a stranger and an enemy to public morals, unable to create new morals and hence from the start ordained to perish. Such rights are not rights at all. They have no vital force, they are still-born.

All that has been said of the mutual relation of rights and morals applies to private as well as to public rights and morals. The former generate their own moral atmosphere as well as the latter and are equally dependent on it for existence.

For example, take the changes in interest (usury laws) during the last three decades in certain states of Europe, especially Austria. First, the severe old usury laws according to the intent of the canonical law (*Recht*), dating from the period of industrial servitude and guilds. Overstepping the minimum rate of five or six per cent was not only made punishable by the state, but was also contrary to public morals. The industrial conditions, the restraints upon trade, commerce and agriculture fully justified the laws of usury. The severe right was the outcome of actual conditions and produced in public opinion a moral consciousness of the objectionable character of usury. Meanwhile industrial development went ceaselessly forward, economic barriers fell; trade, commerce and land became free; productive industry felt an expansion hitherto unknown; productivity far exceeded former limits, and the old interest right was felt to be oppressively narrow. Behind the screen of this written right the need for a new one more commensurate with the conditions made itself felt and began to undermine the morals based on the old. The latter lost its footing and was overthrown and a new right—complete freedom—was proclaimed, which soon made way with the old morals and created new which saw nothing immoral in the free contract of the parties about the rate so long as no other immoral factor was involved such as taking advantage of youth, inexperience, necessitous predicament and the like. Then the state permitted and even incited the erection of institutions of credit which, even when lawfully managed, brought such rates of interest as two decades before had been repudiated and denounced by both rights and morals, while prominent men of spotless character who esteemed honor and morals highly competed for their management.

Meanwhile the industrial boom wore itself out for according to economic laws a relapse must come. Trade, commerce, industry, agriculture again declined and their productivity fell off. Again safety was sought in erecting old barriers and returning to the former restraints and unfreedom. But above all else the new right of unlimited freedom in interest rates contrasted with the industrial decline and lost footing in the actual conditions which demanded something else. The need of change became manifest; the new morals wavered; the new rights had to fall and the old restrictions on the rate of interest became statutory rights again. At first the newly resurrected rights struggled with the vanishing remnants of the morals which were based on the fallen rights. But they were victorious, "for only the living is right," and soon morals will be completely transformed, especially as political power and criminal courts pave the way for the new rights in public morals.

In every department of private rights examples may be multiplied at will of rights arising from actual conditions and shaping morals. Permit us further to point to the many changes in the law (*Recht*) of marriage and the resulting change in morals. Wherever for centuries the marriage tie has been indissoluble by statutory right a taint of immorality is attached to divorce; and if the law is compelled by actual conditions and the freer development of modern society to sanction the dissolution of marriage, as recently in France, the new rights have still to struggle a long while with the old morals. A recent article in the Paris *Figaro* occasioned by the new law read somewhat as follows: "Divorce—well; but remarriage? Public morals will not endure that in France (!)" The *Figaro* need not worry. In Europe and even in France public morals have at times endured worse things than that in marriage rights; for example the *jus primæ noctis*. They will soon, if they have not already, come to terms with the new rights, divorce and remarriage, which, supposing them to last, are reasonable because they take account of existing needs and conditions.

One more question in conclusion. If morals are constantly changing and follow almost slavishly the rights which originate in actual conditions, why do men always conceive of them as changeless in the midst of change, the unvarying source of rights and the eternal idea throned high above all transitory things of earth? Why do they thus appeal to them and regard them as the standard of rights and political institutions?

The explanation is very simple. The changeableness of rights and political institutions is visible and appreciable; they cannot possibly pass as changeless. Official announcements annul to-day the rights of yesterday. A ministerial ordinance suspends an existing political institution and substitutes another. But the change in morals is slow and unmarked as the progress of the hour hand of a clock. A generation is often but a minute on the moral dial—who can detect such a slight progression! Generations later the historian and the philosopher notice that the pointer has moved. The average man " hears it told indeed but lacks believing faith." Naturally so, for in the flowing stream of events man must lay hold on something fixed and unchanging or lose his bearings. Until Copernicus, the earth at least stood fast under his feet; since then it moves in a circle and not even the sun stands still. What wonder that men grow dizzy and look hither and thither for some fixed point by which to direct their unsteady course in the ocean of life ! It is an absolute necessity of human temperament to have such fixed points like stars on the horizon. To it all the "eternal powers" which man worships owe their existence, nor will they pass away while man lives on earth. Among them are found the moral ideas; for in them man seeks and hopes to find a firm point of support for all his actions, a guiding star by which to regulate all his acts and undertakings, a fixed standard by which to judge between good and bad, noble and ignoble; and indeed he finds in the moral idea what he seeks. It is really a basal point and a guiding star for the whole life. The error lies in each one believing his moral ideas are the only ones, changeless and the same for all times and peoples. It is no more true than that the earth is a fixed point in the universe. But just as the earth in spite of its ceaseless revolutions affords a firm enough ground for human efforts, so the individual's moral ideas afford him a solid support upon which to base his character, his efforts and his will. What cares the landlord or the houseowner that the soil he tills or the ground on which he builds revolves with the whole globe ! It is just as little concern to the individual that his morals will seem immoral to future generations; to him it is the one possible fixed ground which he can cultivate and build upon.

For the individual, however transient he himself is, ultimately finds in himself the firm support to which he can cling in the wild tumult of life for protection—and woe to him if he does not find it ! It is only shortsightedness and pardonable weakness in man to believe that it is external to himself, for he seeks it there in vain. "It is not from without that it comes, thine inner self creates it." Thus whether it be purely personal feelings like real love and friendship which accompany man through life, or true faith to which pious temperaments devote themselves, or higher ideas like enthusiasm for folk and fatherland, for truth and science, to which the individual unselfishly sacrifices himself, every feeling and every idea is a "fixed pole-star in the flood of events" which shines before him, consoles and comforts him and ennobles him, too, though after all it is purely subjective and passes away with him.   So it is with morals.

Thus though philosopher and sociologist inquire how morals arose, what changes they have undergone, whether they are justified or not, the individual finds it sufficient for his life that he has them.   But whether he has any and what they are depends upon the degree of development of his social group, upon the family in which he was born and brought up, upon his environments, upon the impressions received in tender years, upon the experiences he has passed through, perhaps also upon the knowledge he has gathered, but certainly to a high degree upon the rights which the state has maintained and to which he has had to conform.

INDIVIDUAL EFFORTS AND SOCIAL NECESSITIES.

Thus by observing the social world and its phenomena we come to perceive that there is a necessity immanent in the condition of things according to which they move, by which they act and which sooner or later reaches fulfillment.

It is not in man's power to suspend or check it.   He is himself a part of that world and an element in those phenomena and all his actions are subject to this all-embracing and universally immanent necessity.   His alleged and apparent freedom cannot alter or prevent its fulfillment.

The common understanding recognizes indeed that the so-called " natural laws " are fulfilled on a grand scale. But in the fine, microscopical details of individual action it is not so easily apparent.

Concede for a moment the beautiful illusion that the individual acts ''freely,'' and consider what significance it has in view of the fulfillment of natural necessity in individual life and human society.   All of man's " free acts " may be reduced to a universal concept and a common denominator: preservation.   Likewise all the processes in nature and human life which take place of immanent necessity may be reduced to a universal concept and common denominator: change and decay.   In the realm of nature all is perishable.   Man would preserve everything.

. This fundamental antithesis lies like a curse on all of man's " free acts,'' which are condemned to be exhausted in fruitless struggle against nature's necessities.   Human " freedom " is but the freedom of the captive lion, to run to and fro in his cage and to follow the menagerie, cage and all, hither and thither through city and country.

But the general perception that human freedom accomplishes nothing against natural necessity, that it dashes like waves against a rock-bound coast only to be broken and scattered in spray, is of little worth. It is more important from the universal relation between human freedom and natural necessity to gain some insight into the essence and character of human actions. This we will now attempt.

We said that the whole tendency of man's so-called free activity was to preserve what is by nature perishable and must pass away to make room for the new. We try to preserve our health while nature works quietly and incessantly for its decline. We try to prolong our life as long as possible even when nature has made its destruction necessary; and as it is with these "personal" goods so it is with all the rest of life's goods. Men try to preserve economic goods beyond the end of their lives for their descendants, and under favorable circumstances their efforts are successful for generations. Nevertheless the wealth of the Crœsuses of antiquity has fallen a victim to the all-powerful law of natural decay and perpetual change and the Rothschilds of our century will leave as little trace in the future.

Man tries also with his whole thought to preserve "forever" all the social institutions which he, the blind instrument and means of natural impulses and inclinations, creates and all the mental products for making life tolerable, beautiful and noble, while natural and necessary decay labors to overthrow them, undermines them, gnaws at and devours them. We would preserve the social community in which we are well off; but it must end as surely as the life of the individual. We would preserve our language, religion, customs, nationality and do not notice how they daily waste away like rocks under dripping water.

Self-sacrifice to preserve what is inevitably destined to fall is considered noble and heroic; but it is cowardly and ignoble to submit to natural necessity. To oppose natural impulses is asceticism, which men do not refuse to admire. To follow natural impulses and necessities is generally considered low "materialism." Fanatics who have neither eye nor mind for the omnipotence of natural conditions are our heroes in art in whom we delight. The more fanatical the "greater" they are. The founders of univeral empires, the Cyruses, Alexanders, Cæsars and Napoleons won our admiration because they perished trying to accomplish the impossible and unnatural. The simple man who adapts himself to the natural and necessary conditions of his environment is not worth consideration.

Our freedom of action and heroism may make the inevitable fulfillment more painful for us, but it cannot prevent it or delay it a single moment. The necessity immanent in things and natural conditions is fulfilled however much we oppose it; and it is quite proper to picture human life as a perpetual struggle against nature though it is false to believe that man could ever at any point be victorious. What is fulfilled is always and exclusively natural necessity, never man's "free will." Man's efforts vacillate from side to side until finally they fall into the line of necessity—that is decisive for fulfillment. If we may be allowed to use a trivial illustration, let us suppose that from a number of stoppers of different sizes we have to select one for an open bottle. The relation between the open bottle and the pile of stoppers is controlled by an immanent natural necessity in consequence of which only one stopper, of suitable size, will fit it. This necessity will be fulfilled if we cork the bottle from the supply of stoppers at hand, and it will be fulfilled in spite of our "free acts," which consist in applying a number of stoppers, some too small, some too large, to the mouth of the bottle and convincing ourselves that they do not fit. Eventually one will fit, the one of proper size, and when we find it we cork the bottle with satisfaction, proud of our "free action." A trivial illustration to be sure, in which other openings might be found besides the one in the bottle. But let us pass to a more serious example, better fitted for scientific investigation.

Probably human freedom seems under less restraint in the sphere of scientific and philosophical thought than anywhere else. "Thoughts are free" and the field not subject to censorship nor made unsafe by the state's attorney is large enough. Free man may gambol there at will and enjoy his freedom, and he has always done so to the fullest extent. But the object of intellectual labor is the discovery of truth or knowledge; and what has been the result of these "free" efforts for thousands of years? It is the old story of the bottle and the stoppers. After thousands of

failures somebody makes a lucky grab and seizes the right
stopper for the philosophical hole.   But is that the work of
a free mind or of meritorious intellectual labor?   The necessity immanent in things and conditions was simply fulfilled.
Groping in the dark we hit upon a truth.

Scientific and philosophical investigation, that noblest
occupation of "free minds," is a pure game of chance.
Philosophical and scientific truths stand like rare prizes
among thousands of blanks in a wheel of fortune revolving
about us.   We "free thinkers," so proud of our "intellectual labors," grab awkwardly like innocent children and lo!
among a million blanks somebody gets a prize.   This makes
him a thinker of great renown whose "merits" are praised.
Yet he is not at all accountable for the result of his intellectual labor.   He is no more and no less meritorious than the
"dunces," scorned and ridiculed, who had the misfortune
to draw nothing but scientific and philosophical errors.   No
more meritorious, we say!   Indeed "the great philosopher"
who appears once in "thousands of years" is less meritorious
than the crowd of little philosophers who by drawing countless blanks made it possible for him to win the great prize.

Let us go to another field of "free" human actions, legislation, and see what relation human freedom there bears to
the necessity immanent in things and conditions.   How
proud and self-conscious the gentlemen of the majority are,
whether of the parliamentary right or left.   They make the
laws for the state to-day.   They stake their best knowledge,
they would apply all their wisdom, they appoint their best
minds on the committees and entrust their shrewdest jurists
with the drafting of the bills; and then the amendments by
sections!   Every one bestirs himself to furnish the greatest
acuteness his cranium can supply—and what is the result
of all this application of "mind" and "free" thought?

For the most part a miserable botch which the real conditions of life and the necessity immanent in them must
correct in order to meet the wants of the case and be endur-
able.   Savigny denominated it inaptitude (*Mangel an Beruf*)
for legislation and ascribed it to "our times."   As to the
inaptitude he was right; but no period has been or ever will
be better than our own in this respect.   Only by adapting
themselves to immediate wants and taking account of real
interests, in short by bending to social necessities, can law-
givers make useful laws—and it has always been so.   But

as soon as they mount the high horse of theory, set up ideal principles and deduce laws to bring about ideal right and justice; when instead of submitting to social necessity they enter the sphere of free intellectual activity in order to make laws in accordance with ideas and not in accordance with real needs and interests, the inaptitude is clearly demonstrated.

This inaptitude for " free " origination is manifested in a still higher degree in politics.   Every institution " freely " made is a wretched experiment which must be thoroughly transformed by the powerful currents of real interests and needs in order to answer to social necessities and gain any permanence at all.   Human   freedom   (diplomatic)   is   the worst sort of bungler and must be forced into the right course by social necessity.

What makes the institutions of human freedom especially frail in the sphere of politics is the fact that the fundamental tendency of all free human action, preservation and acquisition, is most pronounced right here where the natural necessity of eternal change and decay holds most inexorable sway.

The aspirations of statesmen are directed toward political and national preservation and expansion.   The natural necessity to perish and decay can go on only by violently overthrowing every free human institution.   Hence no new political institution can come to light without force and destruction, struggle and bloodshed.   Here human freedom, bent on preservation and acquisition, plays a most lamentable part; and social necessity, tending to change and decay, is revealed in its most awful sublimity.

There is still another important question to be decided. What is the relation of this pernicious human freedom to man's happiness in life? and can a better insight into its nothingness and vanity help him in avoiding evil and being happier?   Let us see.

Certainly if men always recognized inevitable necessity in advance they might escape much evil fortune by quietly resigning to it.   But this is impossible, first because such knowledge is never vouchsafed to mankind as a whole, at most to exceptional individuals, and again because human freedom, that oscillation back and forth on both sides of the line of necessity, is based in human nature and is therefore a necessity.

Although it is thus impossible for mankind as a whole to avoid the disappointments and escape the evil results of the opposition of individual freedom and social necessity still it is worth while to inquire whether a more correct knowledge of necessity does not in many relations of life and spheres of human activity lessen the sum of evil allotted to man here below, or better expressed, whether through such knowledge much superfluous evil due to human freedom might not be avoided. Let us see how far this is possible.

It has already been pointed out that we can never conceive of man as an isolated being; for he never has existed and never can exist in isolation. If then we conceive of him as having always been a member of a swarm or horde—and we cannot reasonably do otherwise—his life and well-being depend upon his environment and is conditioned by it. Now the impulse of self-preservation, the source of the most powerful motive of human efforts and "free" activities, is by origin not simply individual but social. It finds expression in attachment for one's own and desire to subdue others.

This social impulse of self-preservation, the reverse side of which is the necessary desire to subdue and exploit the alien, opens new fields for human desires and activities, for example the economic and the political, the technical, the scientific and even the artistic. In most of them individual desires come in conflict with social necessities and since, as is self-evident, the latter assert themselves over the former there is a preponderance of "misfortune" and "evil" in human life. If now man could know the necessities immanent in things and conditions and had strength to reduce his desires to their measure his life would surely be much happier. Generally this is impossible for reasons both subjective and objective. However let us consider in what spheres it is possible to subordinate individual desires to social necessities, to adapt and accommodate one's self to the circumstances.

Now the sphere of human efforts best adapted for this will be the one in which knowledge of natural necessity is farthest advanced, the sphere of personal life. Here men are least deceived and have long since learned to subordinate their efforts. Every half-way reasonable man suppresses the desire to preserve his life beyond the limits set by nature and submits to the natural necessity of death.

One thing, however, many people have not yet learned, or perhaps an artificially cultivated trend of thought has made them forget: the low value of life.   Its overvaluation is the source of great personal ill, especially is it an unfortunate conceit of the " civilized " nations to place too high value upon the " good " of life.

Yet if man would measure the " natural " worth of human life by nature's forbearance and by the productiveness which she allows play to in this realm, how low the value would be set.   A subterranean quake and thousands of human lives are sent to destruction.   Thousands perish in every storm at sea.   A plague here to-day and there to-morrow and hundreds of thousands fall victims.   A bad summer, the failure of harvest and hunger frequently snatch off millions in overpopulated regions.

But on the other hand nature can indulge in lighter play with human life—millions of children see the light daily and nature has shrewdly provided that this productivity should not cease.

Considering these natural conditions is there any sense or justification in overestimating the worth of an individual life as civilized nations do?   How much misfortune and evil men might be spared if all the social, political and juridical institutions which follow from such an exaggerated estimation of human life should fall away.

Next to the preservation of life the satisfaction of natural wants is the most important content of human endeavors. Here too the wants produced by man's freedom are directly opposed to natural necessities and fill the life of civilized man especially with useless torment and strife. Nature directs man to an unhampered satisfaction of these material wants according to his physical powers.   An unnatural trend of thought produced forms of life which increase the sum of evils incident to life and run counter to natural necessity without being able to check it.

The impulse to satisfy wants forces man into the economic field.   How hard his struggle with nature is needs no lengthy explanation.   Natural necessities press him hard and close. He endeavors to make head against the embarrassments. Apparently he succeeds frequently, but at last succumbs. His efforts are expended in two chief directions.   He strives greedily for possessions which he must ultimately leave behind, and he endeavors to get still more in order to be equal with the more opulent, whereas economic inequality is a natural necessity.

The economic wants lead men into the political sphere; for the state is expected to furnish to some the means of satisfying their higher economic and cultural wants at the expense, though not to the harm, of others. But the state, like all human institutions, is perishable, and the older, already in decline, must give place to the new, developing in power; and yet how much energy will be devoted to checking the uncheckable, to preserving alive what is doomed to perish.

In the internal organization of states also human freedom overshoots the limit of natural necessity either to force the natural development of social relations prematurely or to suppress it unduly and cause stagnation. Hence comes that perpetual oscillation in the inner life of a state which Comte supposed to be the result of two opposing principles, the theological and the metaphysical, and which he expected would disappear with the dawn of positive political science, but we consider it simply the natural process of "human freedom."

But human freedom celebrates its greatest triumphs in the sphere of technics, science and art. For the simple reason that it is only a question of discovering what are the natural necessities, the actual facts and the laws of nature or (in art) of reproducing her productions. Men need only to sniff about in technics or science until they discover how; or to experiment in art until they strike it right; and this they do with great patience and with assurance of ultimate success.

Technics and science have no higher task than to discover nature and learn her laws. Since she is always the same and the stream of mankind flows ceaselessly and man's thirst for knowledge is always the same, he must eventually succeed in learning her secrets from her. But the whole of man's freedom here consists in submitting to nature's necessity—his great success is in recognizing what it is; in adapting himself to it in technics and learning it in science. Thus human endeavors are in no wise opposed to natural necessities here; hence their greatest success and man's greatest good lie in this sphere. Likewise in art. Free reproduction is the highest aim. The impulse thereto lies in human nature and hence its satisfaction, like that of every other impulse, yields human pleasure. But the better he succeeds in reproducing, the more faithfully he clings to nature and her necessities, the truer the expression, so much the greater his triumph and his good fortune. He meets with success all the oftener because he does not act contrary to nature but rather takes her for his chief example and teacher.

The result of our investigations is indeed not very commendatory of mankind in general. For since the sum of human ill increases in the degree that "free" human endeavors are shattered fruitlessly on natural necessities it follows from what precedes that real success and good fortune can be found only in the domains of technics, science and art, which is accessible to only a small minority of mankind; whereas in the sphere of economic and political life, where these endeavors run powerlessly to waste against natural necessities, very little real happiness is to be obtained, and in the sphere of personal life only discreet resignation can ameliorate the necessary evil at all.

V. THE HISTORY OF MANKIND AS LIFE OF THE SPECIES.

SOCIOLOGY AND THE PHILOSOPHY OF HISTORY.

The relation between sociology and the philosophy of history is similar to that between statistics and history. The former has been called a cross-section of the latter. That is to say, statistics is occupied with a given condition, while history would embrace the entire course of human destiny (*die Geschicke*) as a whole. But it is very plain that this is an impossible task; so far as its accomplishment is concerned, statistics has a great advantage in the temporal and local limitations which it assumes.

So with sociology and the philosophy of history. The latter would give us the idea of human history in its entirety, would set forth the theory of the whole course; and hence it must fail through inability to survey it all, for the idea of a part conceived to be the whole always falsifies the idea of the whole.

On the other hand, the task of sociology is more capable of solution because of the limitations which it assumes. It disclaims embracing the history of mankind as a whole. It is content with investigating the process of human group-making, the constant repetition of which makes up the content of all history. Without inquiring the import of the whole course of history, which it does not know, it is content to show its conformity to law, to investigate the manner of social evolution, in a word to describe the processes which regularly arise from a certain contact of human societies and the mutual effects displayed. We would treat the principal questions of sociology: conformity to law in the course of political history, the way societies develop, and the problem whether in historical periods of considerable length we meet with certain ideas, general tendencies (like progress, improvement, and so on), or even general forms of social process.

CONFORMITY TO LAW IN DEVELOPMENT.

Conformity to law in the events and developments of political history has been often suspected and much discussed, and even positively asserted. But, as we have pointed out elsewhere,* no one has succeeded, so far as we know, in demonstrating it concretely and clearly; while, on the contrary, the shallow objections of antagonists who denied its existence and spoke of free will and the guidance of Providence seemed to be growing more formidable.

But it is a very interesting fact that in spheres which are very near to political and social life and which, though not identical, are connected with it by an intimate bond of causal relation, such conformity is so plain and apparent that it cannot be questioned by even the most zealous adherents of free will and of the guidance of Divine Providence; and yet they have never realized that by conceding development according to law, independent of the will of the individual, in art and science for example, they concede it *eo ipso* in these deeper, fundamental domains.

Let us therefore consider those spheres in which conformity to law is doubted by no one, in order next to show the intimate connection between this conformity to law and that in the social and political sphere upon which this depends.

Is it not a scientific commonplace to speak of the evolution of a people's art, science and philosophy? What do the modern historians do but demonstrate their development in conformity to law in each several nation; an evolution in which plainly the individual must, and unconsciously and involuntarily does, accommodate himself to the law of the whole and the movements of the community? What does it signify that for example the connoisseur can tell almost exactly when a work of art was created, the school to which it belonged and almost the place whence it must have come, without knowing the artist? What but that it is not the individual fashioning according to his own arbitrary will but the community and its evolution, whose slave he is born to be, as whose slave he works and creates? The individual does not compose; it is the poetic mood of his age and social group. The individual does not think; it is the spirit of his age and social group. Otherwise the connoisseur could not tell whether the picture exhibited belonged to the school of Tintoretto or Rubens; whether a rediscovered Latin poem is classic or post-classic; whether a philosophical fragment belongs to the Aristotelian or Alexandrian age. That the connoisseur can tell is the best proof that the individual's

* See "*Rassenkampf*," p. 6 *et seq.*

thoughts, feelings and actions are influenced and determined
by his age and social environment.

Thus we recognize these facts generally and without contradiction, while refusing to draw the necessary conclusions
from them elsewhere. But we have seen that the mode of
a man's feeling, thought and action simply result from the
stage of social and political development upon which he
happens at the time to be.* Can it still be doubted that the
social and political situation exercises a determining, con-
structive influence on the mental constitution and endowments of men which are on the whole always equal?

The peasant boy with artistic talents will draw rude figures
in the sand or carve in wood with a pocket knife all his life
long. Raised upon a higher social plane, educated in an art
school in a cultivated community, he will become a representative of his time and people, that is, of the educated
classes that stand at the top of the historical development of
the nation. What he has become is due not only to his
natural endowments but especially to the social environment
in which he was educated and its degree of development.
But he cannot arbitrarily be anything; he can be only one
stone more in the mental structure which the community
and its grade of development necessarily determine, a stone
whose place is assigned to it by the development of the
whole.

There is therefore no doubt and it will be generally conceded that the joint mental development, or, as it is also
called, the development of the human mind, or of the mind
of mankind, follows fixed laws and that the individual so far
as he participates in it, actively or passively, must patiently
endure, doing nothing, thinking nothing which does not of
necessity follow from the given historical premises of the
evolution. There is therefore no individual freedom of will
here; only all-controlling law.

But how is this mental evolution related to evolution in
the social sphere? That the former is not possible or even
conceivable without the latter conclusively follows from the
close causal connection between mental development and
social, political and economic conditions which we have elsewhere demonstrated.†

Man's mental character, his mental evolution and so also

*Cf. Part IV, sec. 2.
†"Rassenkampf," p. 23 et seq.

his mental activity is conditioned upon the stage of his political and social evolution. The nomad wandering about with his horde has one set of thoughts; the hunter pursuing game in the forests has another; the subjected slave has another; the townsman living by trade and commerce another; the member of the ruling caste another; and the priest whose power is in the mysterious charm of religion another. Their thinking is determined by the place which they occupy in society and by the degree of its evolution.

But though we can comprehend how collective mental life and activity is connected in a general way with the stage of social evolution, we lack the microscopical insight to see how each individual is connected with it and how his thought, feelings and behavior are influenced by it.

Similarly the physicist is able to explain the appearing of the rainbow from the position of the sun and the stratification of the clouds; but he has not the means to show how each atom of steam and water acts in relation to each ray of sunlight, nor how the refraction of the prismatic colors arises from the action of each ray of sunlight on each atom and drop. Nevertheless after the general demonstration of the necessity of the phenomenon who would doubt that the same necessity which sways the collective whole constrains each little part to take its appropriate place!

We see and know the whole mental evolution to be, like the rainbow in the heavens, a matter of necessity; we know that a condition of society, like a particular position of the sun, must deflect culture and civilization just so and not otherwise, and that with a given degree of social evolution we must meet with one set of mental colors in art and science and not another, although we lack the means to show microscopically, so to speak, the necessary influence and effect of the passing social conditions upon each individual's acts, thoughts and feelings. Who can consider the necessary total effect and doubt that it is the sum of necessary individual influences and effects which no man can escape?

Intermediate between the individuals and the general mental effect are social structures whose necessary evolution in conformity to law must be concluded from the necessity and the conformity to law of the total effects though there were no more direct or immediate indications of it.

Thus whoever concedes conformity to law in the evolution

of art and literature, science and philosophy (and who will deny it?) must grant the same conformity to law in the evolution of social structures and the consequent restraints upon the individual.

THE EVOLUTION OF MANKIND.

We have learned that social evolution is always partial, local and limited in time; and it has been especially emphasized that we can form no conception of the evolution of mankind as a unitary whole because we have no comprehensive conception of mankind as a whole. But, let us ask, can we not form a conception, broader than the evolution of individual groups and social communities, of mankind so far as known to us; and if so how should we have to conceive this relative whole (relative, *i. e.*, to our knowledge)?

For we know that Biblical *naïvete*, corresponding to a "theological way of looking at things," to quote Comte, likened the evolution of man to a genealogical tree springing from Adam and Eve; and it has been repeatedly pointed out that the same view still prevails in the domain of social science, in which Comte rightly recognizes the persistence of the theological phase down to the present.

The polygenetic view which prevails quite generally at present necessarily does away with the conception of a unitary genealogical evolution. But the change only involves assuming several or innumerable starting points; precisely speaking it is a change of form only, or rather of number, that is, there is the evolution of several genealogical trees instead of one. There is assumed to be a steady progress, as before, along a line of evolution from simple to complex, from rudimentary leaf to full grown tree, from primitive to refined and, what is decisive in evolution, from some given original point of incipiency to our time "of great progress, the summit and climax" of all.

It is plain that such a conception is irreconcilable with a duration of life upon the earth that surpasses comprehension. Starting from the idea which the results of the modern investigation of nature make clearer and clearer we dare not liken the social evolution described above to any such single or even multiple genealogical scheme. For such a scheme proceeds only from our inclination to investigate beginnings above all else, while in the nature of the case we are only capable of knowing the *becoming*.

True science, or, again to quote Comte, "positivism" begins only when we overcome the desire to know the beginning of things and are content with a knowledge of their becoming. If we keep in mind the two ideas of the eternality of life upon the earth and our inability to know the origin of things, we shall obtain an entirely different scheme of social evolution. We have a conception of its becoming formed upon the basis of facts; if now we banish all thought of the unity and the commencement of evolution, we have left, as concrete remnant, a process of evolution going on at different times and in different places but always according to the same laws. Thus those transitions which we described above, from what is to us the primitive horde with promiscuity and the mother-family to woman-stealing and marriage by capture, and then to a simple organization of sovereignty, to property, state and "society," must not be conceived to be processes which befall mankind developing, as it were, from a certain point of beginning onward whether along single or multiple lines, but processes which are always being completed and renewed wherever the requisite antecedents occur. With such a conception only, and in no wise with the contrary one named, can we reconcile the fact that the primitive stages of this process are still observable in distant parts of the world as fresh and original as they must once have been in our own past.

Evolution as we have presented it is no chronological or local verity and applies to no particular subject; it is a typical truth—in so far as it presents a process which is always true of human species wherever groups of men are found in the proper social condition.

It is erroneous and entirely false to speak of the "evolution of mankind" ("*le développement de l'humanité*") as Comte does. For we can speak only of social evolution within the compass of the human species. It always begins wherever and so soon as suitable social conditions are at hand and it runs in conformity to law to a conclusion, dying out and disappearing because there is no further manifestation of necessary social energy. It is impossible to doubt that evolution really dies out and becomes extinct in view of the countless sites of whilom culture and mighty social evolution which now lie waste and barren. There are many examples in Asia, America and Africa of extensive regions from which all life has now disappeared, yet upon which social development once brought forth the most magnificent results of civilization.

These facts are calculated to support the idea of a cyclical course of social development in general, an idea which gains a foothold just from the cyclical development of states. I have discussed this point often and must here return to it again.

THE CYCLE OF DEVELOPMENT.

It sounds like Hegel or Schaeffle to assert that the life of every people runs in a cycle, that once it has arrived at its highest stage of development it hastens to its decay; and that the first best barbarians will make ready its extinction. Sober minds are not inclined to take it seriously.

Nevertheless it is not difficult to show the causes of this cyclical motion in the natural, economic and social conditions of folk-life. The causes are so plain, their operation so very powerful and general and at the same time so obvious and indisputable that the knowledge of them ought to convince that their effects will fitly and necessarily follow; for they are economic and demographic and thus lie in the region where man's unfreedom and his dependence on physical wants are wholly undeniable; where irrefutably men must be reckoned with as blind natural forces pursuing their courses in conformity to law.

Men's wants and desires, as we have seen, cause them to raise themselves by groups and societies from a primitive condition to a condition of culture and civilization; and, having once attained it, so to conduct themselves that their fall necessarily follows through other groups and societies in a progressive state.

In a primitive political body, which is economically poor, men have only one want beyond the desire of self-preservation, the reproduction of the species. On this stage many children are begotten and population grows with great rapidity. The wish, which emerges on a higher plain of culture, so far as possible to insure a better material existence for the descendants is not effective to check the increase of births for the reason that future members will be no worse off than the present so far as property goes while every living human being represents one more unit of labor, which of itself may conduce to betterment of condition.

For this reason political bodies in the lower stages of culture and welfare increase rapidly and so make a great relative gain in numerical strength which can be sustained by increasing productivity and economic prosperity at home. A population in such a state of progressive development is very likely to lay the foundation for a body politic over which a highly civilized and cultivated minority will rule.

But if, with the development of the body politic, the lowest classes also rise to a higher degree of civilization and become prosperous, and it cannot be otherwise, anxiety for the future welfare of posterity begins to exert a restraint upon the natural increase of the people. The former heedlessness, companion of poverty, gives way to a ''wise care'' and population begins to stagnate and finally to decline. Thus the collective body becomes numerically weaker than those which have not yet reached this degree of ''refinement,'' and this further conduces to economic weakness and political decline; while the community that still stands lower in development, that still has a poor proletariat in process of sound development, carries off the victory through its numerical strength.

These are the real, ever active causes which bring about the cyclic movement in the life of folk and state and which explain why it is always the highly cultivated state that is destroyed by '' barbarian hordes.''

But such hordes are not necessarily external, and if they were they alone would not be able utterly to destroy powerful civilized states. But unfortunately every state conceals in its own bosom, and the higher it rises in the scale of civilization so much the more, barbarian hordes enough who only await the given signal, the critical moment of civil or foreign war, to begin the work of destruction. The fall of many a powerful civilized state under the assault of rather small barbarian hordes could not be comprehended if it were not known that domestic social enemies of the existing order let the secretly glimmering hatred of the property and ruling classes burst into bright flame in the moment of danger; and this alone is often sufficient to turn the toilsome labor of centuries into dust and ashes. This inner enemy necessarily increases with the development of civilization so that every centre of civilization, apart from the danger threatening it from without, fosters the seeds of destruction within itself.

PROGRESS AND INNOVATION.

But the fact of cyclical development in state and folk is also decisive of the question of "progress" in the sphere of human activity. Two assertions which I made in "*Rassenkampf*" have given considerable offence and provoked lively contradiction, viz., that there is no progress and that there can be nothing essentially new in the realm of mental knowledge.

That I of course recognize progress in the development of an isolated centre of civilization, each time beginning and running to its end, has been brought out conspicuously by the briefest of my reviewers in the English periodical "Mind." "The general conclusion to which he finally comes," it reads, "is that there is no such thing as either progress or regress in the course of history taken as a whole, but only in the particular periods of a process that is going on forever in a circle—in particular countries where the social process is forever recommencing." It is indeed remarkable that the English critic who reviewed my book in fourteen lines caught my thought correctly while so many German critics who made extended reviews of it are of the opinion that I deny all progress whatsoever.* However I see from this

---

*On the other hand Maurice Block, in the *"Journal des Economistes"* was inclined to accept the complete negation of progress (though I do not go so far) if I had made a reservation in respect of science and its technical application. The passage is so remarkable that I quote it. " One of the author's views," says M. Block in concluding his discussion of the " *Rassenkampf;* " " will meet with many objections: it is the negation of progress. Things change apparently but not in reality. The vesture changes, so to speak, but not the body nor the spirit; and yet there is some truth in the proposition and if the author had taken the oratorical precaution to except science and its industrial applications I should have been persuaded that he was right, for I have asked myself more than once whether it could be proven that there were in Memphis, Babylon and Nineveh less good men in proportion to the whole population than in Paris, London or Berlin." I readily assent to the reservation in favor of science and art which M. Block requests, only however with the counter reservation set forth in the text above respecting the uninterrupted development of human civilization. Who will guarantee that its thread, and even the thread of mental development, will not be completely sundered from time to time so that for later generations trying to rise again nothing will remain of all the former achievements? What profit did the entire European Middle Ages draw from the astronomical knowledge of the Chaldeans and old Egyptians, thorough as it doubtless was? Was not the thread completely sundered? and if we compare the grotesque sculpture of Christian Europe in the Middle Ages with the works of Greek art must we not confirm the fact that the stream of development of human civilization from time to time disappears in the earth without trace only to reappear after a long while in some far distant place, working its way laboriously up through rifts and fissures? Or is the opinion justified perhaps that such catastrophes, suddenly destroying results of civilization hundreds of years old and causing them to disappear utterly were only possible in " earlier times " but that we, armed with the printing press and the steam engine, are entirely free from them and that our mental labor will not perish? We would gladly share this opinion if only the authorities will set us at rest upon one point, the cosmic stability of our planet. For to judge from some very recent indications the forces seething under our feet in the interior of our planet seem to have very little respect for our mental and our artistic productions and to care as little for laws of the development of human civilization. Indeed human civilization is threatened by two distinct anarchistic forces: social and cosmic. The former we may indeed resist—may gracious destiny long preserve us from the latter. Then would we be assured of endless progress in science, art and technics.

circumstance that I could not have expressed myself clearly enough on this point and therefore feel bound to carry out my views further or rather to express myself more clearly.

As I consider man to be a permanent type not only physically, with Kollman,* but mentally, I am of the opinion that there is a fixed upper limit to his mental activity also, to which individual natures fortunately endowed have always been able to attain, but which no man can ever pass.

Man's physical strength in the nature of the case can never exceed a certain maximum, which of course certain individuals have at all times attained to. In morals there have always been good and noble natures everywhere; and low and bestial ones too in the greatest variety of gradations; and it is recognized that a real improvement in men is scarcely to be noticed here and that an apparent improvement is brought about locally and temporarily only by conditions, institutions and measures introduced from the outside. It is quite the same in intellectual matters.

Man's intellect is ever the same—it moves in a sphere having a fixed and inexpansible upper limit which has been reached from time to time by individual geniuses. But there is an apparent progress arising from the fact that from place to place and time to time an intellect of equal power finds footing upon the total accomplishments of his predecessors and uses them as the starting point for further successes; not that later generations work with higher or more complete intellects but with larger means accumulated by earlier generations, with better instruments, so to speak, and so obtain greater results.† So it is of course impossible to deny progress in the field of invention and discovery—but it would be a mistake to explain it from the greater perfection, or the progress of the human intellect. An inventive Greek of ancient times, if he had followed Watt, would have invented the locomotive—and if he could have known the arrangement of the electrical telegraph, it certainly might have occurred to him to construct a telephone.

Between human intellect four thousand years ago and

---

* See above, Part II, sec. 4.

† Quetelet, vol. ii, p. 393. "Newton deprived of all the resources of science would still have had the same intellectual strength and would still have been the type of many eminent qualities, in particular, correctness of judgment and imagination ; if only a part of science, greater or less, had been put within his reach he would have been a Pythagoras. an Archimedes or a Kepler; but with all the resources which his century presented to him he was, and he had to be, a Newton."

to-day there is no qualitative difference nor any greater development or perfection—only the completed labor of all intervening generations inures to the advantage of the modern intellect, which with this accumulated supply to-day accomplishes apparently greater "miracles" than the like intellect four thousand years ago did without it. But in fact, laying aside the advantages of the former, the latter accomplished no less wonderful things.

Fortified with this, one could object to my assertion that progress is relative and appears only in separate periods of development by saying that it only needs such a continuity of mental labor to lead mankind into unsuspected and indefinitely prolonged progress.

The conclusion would be impregnable if the premise, the uninterrupted development of human civilization in general, were equally certain; but it is to be doubted, for, first, we find proof in well-known history of the continual recurrence of catastrophes which send centres of civilization precipitately to destruction. What happened in India, Babylon, Egypt, Greece and Rome may sometime happen in modern Europe. European civilization may perish, overflooded by barbaric tribes.

But if any one believes that we are safe from such catastrophes he is perhaps yielding to an all too optimistic delusion. There are no barbaric tribes in our neighborhood to be sure—but let no one be deceived, their instincts lie latent in the populace of European states. The deeds of anarchists are only scattered flashes of lightning—who will guarantee that the storm will not some time break? The barbarians do not live so far from Europe as appears to be generally assumed and the insurance of Europe against these infernal powers would not be entirely free from risk.

Thus the proposition that the development of civilization is perpetual and uninterrupted, as premise to the conclusion that progress may be indefinitely prolonged, could have only a potential value.

But it must also be considered a proof of the stability of the human intellect that in spheres which have no connection with invention and the discovery of natural forces, in moral and social philosophy, not only is there no indication of progress but nothing new whatever has been said for thousands of years. "There is nothing new under the sun" and nothing new can be "invented." Our cognitions respecting virtue and custom, human happiness and social relations are no more mature than those of the oldest peoples of antiquity; on the contrary we often become aware that we are behind them in many things.   Though brotherly love has been taught at different times to very different peoples by individual law-givers and founders of religions, our attitude toward relatives and kinsfolk is just as different from our attitude toward strangers as ever.   To make war upon strangers and overpower them is a virtue; to betray one's fellow citizens is a crime.   Respecting the value of life, the mutual relation of the sexes, the institution of marriage and the like the individual centres of civilization continue to revolve in the same vicious circle, from every particular point of which the point opposite seems the lower.   Whatever strikes us as new and original is only a new combination of very old thoughts and opinions—a combination springing of course from a new individual conception, for in nature only individuality is endlessly varied.

Individuality is always producing new combinations from the ancient store of human thought, and if it were possible for a man to know all the thoughts of past ages, if he could even know all the philosophers and thinkers of olden times and peoples, he could easily reproduce his own most original systems and his most characteristic conceptions of the world merely by citing from his predecessors.   In fact Bastian does something similar; we often find his phenomenal mind working out entirely original ideas with simple citations from other authors.   The whole is the most original product of his individuality; but his remarkably comprehensive memory enabled him to gather up the ready cut stones for his system from the works of thinkers of all ages and peoples.

The individual conception is new, but the material is exclusively old.   Consciously or unconsciously it is constantly repeated, never newly created.   For here where no invention or discovery in the field of natural forces is involved the human intellect has from the first traversed the whole sphere of perception possible in the nature of its organization and can never rise beyond.

The conceptions of the human mind in this sphere are just like kaleidoscopic views.   Philosophers and thinkers have been turning the kaleidoscope for ages, and it is impossible but that particular portions have often been exactly repeated though probably the whole picture never will be, since the combinations are infinite. The difference in the picture we ascribe to the difference in individuals, and perhaps correctly.

JUSTICE IN HISTORY.

Nothing so shakes the conception of a " just providence " in simple devout souls as the perception of the " world's " " injustice " obtruding itself at every step in human life. In spite of toilsome theological explanations and justifications simple faith in God is disturbed and pious hearts are stung by the doubt whether all the injustice with which human life overflows can be the work of a good and just God? It is the necessary and inevitable consequence of an anthropomorphism which conceives of God in the likeness of man and hence ascribes to him human " justice." But that which comes to pass in the world and in life, or properly, in life and history is in no sense human justice, rather it is historical justice which to man's mind must seem to be harsh injustice; though here again the fault is due to that false individual standard which man applies to the events of life—whereas they come to pass according to an entirely different, so to say, a great social standard by which they must be judged. If we measure them with individual human measure we suffer.

What is commonly meant by justice? A certain standard in the distribution of material and moral goods—in fact there are two conceptions of justice. One starts from the complete equality of all men and hence requires an equal measure of rights and possessions for each individual. The other takes into consideration the unequal value of individuals and their powers and doings and is content with a proportional distribution. Both take the individual as the object and standard in exercising justice and in every transaction having man for its object ask whether it is commensurate with the value of the object. If so it is pronounced just; if not, unjust. There is no opportunity for variety of judgment save as difference of opinion prevails concerning the value of the object or the proper conception of justice.

These conceptions of justice start from the consideration of man's conduct toward man to construct their criteria of judgment, which have a certain justification in themselves. But men are not content to apply them to human conduct alone, but transfer them to historical events also and even to natural events in general.

In the case of historical events the transference is due to the false hypothesis that they are brought about by men through their free will; and in the case of natural events it is due to an anthropomorphism which represents God as acting after the manner of men and bringing them about.

No elaborate proof is necessary to show how incongruous such an idea is. Historical events are not brought about by men any more than natural events by God; and if they have no author whose conduct can be regulated according to the value of the objects affected nothing can be said about justice or injustice in connection with them.

In a somewhat different sense, however, without regard to the subject acting, the question could be raised whether the course of history and of natural events strikes individuals according to their merits, i. e., whether the good are spared or rewarded, the bad fallen upon and punished; hence whether there be justice or not in history and nature. But even in this form such a question is inadmissible because the individual is never the object of history or nature; with them nothing depends upon him, and we have no criteria of his worth even if we should conceive him to be the subject of the historical and the natural process.

History and nature are visible and recognizable only through their effects on masses—indeed they may be said to occupy themselves only with certain natural groups and quantities consisting of a number of individuals—that is with folk, stems or families existing either together or in the relation of successive generations. But the only possible relation which is perceivable between the effects and the existence of the objects is that of causality, the connection between their natural constitution and the fate that falls to their lot.

In other words, these natural human groups under the action of history and nature play precisely the part of any other natural objects exposed to the workings of natural forces. Natural forces will produce effects upon them according to their character—rotten limestone will yield to the process of weathering quicker than hard granite; rain will change a treeless declivity into a bare rock, while a wooded slope will gain fresh strength and luxuriance from it. In this interplay of cause and effect, of occasion in the objects and action by the natural forces can we speak of justice and injustice ?   No more can we in the destinies of a folk or an individual.   They are the results of causes lying partly in the object, partly in the natural forces of history and nature. Hence there is no justice in history unless we wish to apply this category to the conformity of results to causes.   Such justice as this we always find everywhere realized with inexorable rigor.

In life and in history every man suffers whatever fate is conditioned by his natural constitution.   Yet his natural constitution depends not on him, but, as we have seen, upon the social medium from which he emerges.   This is to blame if individual fates are so seldom proportional to individual merits.   For fate strikes the individual in proportion to the merits of the species, so to speak.   His own merits may be different.   Historical development cares nothing for that.

Hence the individual often suffers wrongs which he does not deserve, but which are the natural results of causes lying in the past of his social medium, as when the children atone for the " sins " of their ancestors, of which there are so frequent examples in history.   It is quite natural; for the development of the natural forces of history depends upon the character and the conditions of its subjects.   But the subjects are, as we have seen, not the individuals, but the social media in which the individuals are included as results.

The course and the events of history are commensurate with the character and conditions of the social media; and this we must recognize as historical justice.   There is none other in history or even in nature.

Hence the alpha and omega of sociology, its highest perception and final word, is: human history a natural process; and even though, shortsighted and captivated by traditional views of human freedom and self-determination, one should believe that this knowledge derogates from morals and undermines them yet it is on the contrary the crown of all human morals because it preaches most impressively man's renunciatory subordination to the laws of nature which alone rule history.   By contributing to the knowledge of these laws sociology lays the foundation for the morals of reasonable resignation, higher than those resting on imaginary freedom and self-determination and resulting in the inordinate overestimation of the individual and those unreasonable aspirations which find expression in horrible crimes against the natural law of order.

SUPPLEMENT.

Addendum to Part I. History of Sociology.

GUSTAVE LE BON.

The rise of sociology in our day from anthropology, ethnography, the study of prehistoric times, and the history of civilization, is easily explainable. First anthropology treated physical man simply, and the chief races of mankind. Ethnography constantly added new material from the living human world and raised the number of varieties almost to infinity. Then prehistoric man was studied in order, from his condition, to explain the phenomena of historic man. Making the phenomena of prehistoric civilization the subject of their investigation, scholars passed unexpectedly from this introduction into the history of civilization as a whole, treating also the later period of the same subject. But at last it appeared that all four disciplines were merely descriptive, furnishing material for a science of man which, if it would be a science, must for the reasons above laid down be occupied not with the individual, but with social groups and societies. In this way it becomes sociology. But the principal difference between these four disciplines and sociology is that the latter is in no sense descriptive; but, supported upon material from the former, undertakes scientific investigation in order to establish scientific laws.

While various authors have severally set forth the disciplines named with more or less significant digressions into neighboring spheres, Gustave Le Bon, in a noteworthy book, " *L'Homme et les Sociétés, leurs Origines et leur Histoire,*"* gives the chief features of them all, together with a thoughtful presentation of sociology (in Part II) based upon them, so that his work presents to view the entire course of scientific development beginning with anthropology and ending with sociology.

In the first part Le Bon simply gives short sketches of the sciences preliminary to sociology. After an " Introduction " upon the changes in our knowledge and opinions, in which the author shows that he is at once monist and positivist in

* Paris, 1881.

the best sense of the word, he subjects the "Universe," in Book I, to a rigid realistic examination.   In Book II "The Origin and Evolution of Living Creatures " is portrayed according to the theory of Darwin and Haeckel.   Book III, entitled "The Physical Evolution of Man," gives a description of anthropology and prehistory.   It treats of primitive man, the formation of races and the several prehistoric ages according to the usual divisions.   Book IV, "The Mental Evolution of Man," gives a sketch of psychology on a physiological basis.   Upon the broad foundation of such disquisitions upon these broad sciences which have to do with the universal and the individual, Le Bon constructs his sociology which occupies the second part of his work.

Aside from Book I of Part II, which simply contains a special introduction to sociology ("Sociology and its Limits, Uses and Methods "), the substance of what he has to say falls into two books: " Factors of Social Evolution," Book III, and "The Development of Societies," Book IV. However excellent all that Le Bon offers us in these two books, however willing we are to subscribe to the most of the sociological views and considerations which he advances, still we must say that in spite of the broad foundation which he has given to his sociology, there is a very serious mistake in the superstructure.   He has missed the real subject-matter of sociology and has not really found a single sociological law although he set out with that purpose.   A detailed examination will confirm our judgment.

Le Bon first treats "The Factors of Evolution."   What he understands them to be appears from the titles to the several chapters on the influence of *milieu*, of intelligence and feelings, of the acquisition of language, of commercial relations, of the progress of industry, of literature and art, of the struggle for existence, of the development of military institutions, of the knowledge of agriculture and the growth of population, of stability and variation, of race, of the past and heredity, of illusions and religious ideas, of politics and administration, of education and instruction.   Without doubt these are very important questions touching the sphere of sociology.   But these " influences " are in no sense " factors of social evolution."   They are all simply "influences" acting on them.   The factors of social evolution, as has been shown above, are the social groups themselves, and they are influenced by the physical and moral agencies surrounding them, which Le Bon, as shown, enumerates correctly. But it is a mistake to confuse these conditions, these influences and agencies, with the real factors or subjects. So Le Bon in the chapter on "Factors of Evolution" really says nothing that he had not already said in Part I where, speaking of the development of the individual, he showed the influence of all these same agents and circumstances upon it. Hence the repetitions which the author cannot escape in spite of his great literary skill and his evident pains to present the same thing in different lights and to illustrate it by a great variety of examples, because they follow necessarily from the false plan of his sociology, false because too limited and scanty. Thus for example, he treats, in Part I, page 190, of "The Physical Condition of the First Human Beings." In Part II, Book II, on "The Factors of Social Evolution," he is forced to return to the same theme and treats of the "Existence of the First Human Beings" again in connection with the "Influence of *Milieu* upon Social Evolution." To be sure he strives here in Part II to relate other details about primitive man; but the subject is the same and what is said in Part II could have been said pertinently at the appropriate place in Part I.

Again another illustration: In Part II Le Bon treats the "Past and Heredity" as a factor of social evolution. But he treated the same thing in Part I in connection with the "development of instinct" in the individual, where he speaks of "habits gradually modified and preserved by heredity." In short Le Bon knows no "factors of social evolution" to present other than the same agents and forces which influence the individual.

In the second half he does not fare much better. Here too the contents do not correspond with what the title promises. The latter reads, as has been mentioned: "Development of Societies;" and what do the several chapters offer us instead? First comes "development of language." Is language a society? No doubt language has great influence upon the development of society. But can the development of language for that reason be regarded as the development of society?

The same is true of the chapters on the development of religion (chapter iv), morals (chapter v), rights (chapter vi) industry and agriculture (chapter vii). The last is an economic phenomenon; the others are simply psycho-social.

THE OUTLINES OF SOCIOLOGY.

Their development is conditioned upon that of societies; their development presupposes social development and in turn exerts a certain influence upon it.   Yet the development of religion, morals, rights, etc., is not the development of societies.   So Le Bon has not offered us here what he wished to offer and what sociology ought to offer.   He undoubtedly came nearer solving the real problem in the two chapters on the development of the family and of property (chapters ii and iii).   For as we shall see both these institutions are eminently social and immediately connected with social development, rising directly from it, forming indeed an essential part of it; only he should have presented them in this connection as we shall demonstrate and insist below.   He has indeed done so in part but not entirely. For though he does not present each phase in the development of these institutions as the direct result of the contact and reciprocal effect of unlike social groups, yet he makes a beginning of seeking the cause of changes in these institutions in such transformations as alterations in the relations of the social ingredients to each other.   For example he inquires (pt. ii, p. 294) how maternal kinship passed into paternal kinship? how the father became the head of the family? and answers the question correctly on the whole. " It seems to me," he says, " that it (this transformation) must have come to pass at the time when man began the pastoral and agricultural life and had need of slaves to aid him at his work.   Instead of killing his prisoners he kept them to aid him and became the sole proprietor of those he had conquered, of the women especially."   Here Le Bon's acumen led him aright, even though he did not take for his starting point the reciprocal action of unlike [*heterogen*] social groups as the only impelling factor in all social development as we shall.   Indeed had he done so too, he would not only have struck that transformation in the form of the family correctly, but he would also have had in hand the right key to solve the not less difficult problem of the changes in property. But as it is he stands helpless and at a loss before it, for this time the lucky idea did not occur to him.   He knows that " property has not always existed in the form in which we know it to-day.   The idea that soil, air or light could belong to any one could not have been comprehended by our first ancestors and mankind had to run the greater (?) part of its cycle before this notion could arise."   But in what way, from what impelling causes the change in property, or better the establishment of private property, took place Le Bon cannot explain. He is confronted with a conception that arose in the human brain one fine day, an idea that sprang up suddenly. "When agriculture had become known and mankind already had an immense past behind it, a very long time had still to elapse before the idea of personal property appeared. The ground, like the women, belonged at first to all the members of a community. Only very slowly did it become the property, at first temporarily and then permanently, of a family and then of an individual." Thus we see that without any attempt whatever to explain the causes of these changes in property, he here simply takes refuge in that phrase with which we have become acquainted * that it "arose gradually." Doubtless everything arose gradually, but how? in what way? It is the task of sociology to explain.

The fundamental failure in the construction of his sociology of which we spoke is to blame for his failure to give us the explanation. If he had comprehended that the first and most important sociological task was to investigate the mutual relations and reciprocal effects of unlike social groups, he would himself necessarily have found out that changes in the family and in property are nothing but the result of these reciprocal relations and effects. He would have reached another result also which in the beginning of his undertaking he confessedly strives for but completely fails of in consequence of the entirely wrong path into which he struck. We mean the discovery of those "invariable laws knowing no exceptions," those "fixed and inexorable laws" (Part I, chapter viii), which, as he quite correctly assumes, control historical events as well as the evaporation of a drop of water or the movement of a grain of sand. We find indeed the recital of events and developments conforming to law in the psycho-social sphere (language, religion, rights, morals, political economy and so forth), but of real social laws, of such laws as control the relations and reciprocal connections of social elements, we find no trace with him.

In view of this it is certainly characteristic of Le Bon that he treats all the secondary social phenomena, like language, religion, rights, etc., at great length; but has not

*Cf. p. 63 note.

devoted a single chapter of his " social science " to the most important and primary social phenomenon, the state. This is indeed a gross and obvious omission, but it is also merely a consequence of the entirely mistaken plan of his sociology.

Nevertheless it must be recognized that Le Bon's sociology is one of the most valuable achievements of scientific labor in this field. He is distinguished for thorough knowledge of all pertinent disciplines, comprehensive view and above all for a sober unprejudiced mind. His work unquestionably forms an important landmark in the development of sociology; and we greatly regret that in the foregoing discussions we have not been able to appeal to his coinciding views frequently. He would have afforded us welcome support on many a hazarded point.

ADDENDUM TO PART IV. MIGHT AND RIGHT.

There are several omissions in the " Outlines " before us. For example I have not treated the psycho-social phenomena of language and religion because I discussed them at length in my " *Rassenkampf*," to which I must refer the reader, especially as I should like to have the " sociological investigations " appearing under that title considered preliminary in part, and in part also supplementary to these " Outlines." For a similar reason I have given no space in the statement before us to the special question concerning the relation of might and right, because in the first place I treated it at great length in my " *Rechtsstaat und Socialismus* " and so would have to repeat here, and moreover the criticisms made on many sides failed to make me change my views. Further, my position on the question is sufficiently characterized in the present " Outlines " in the thorough treatment of the origin and development of rights as also in the examination of the essence of the state and the social struggle.

Nevertheless I should consider it a serious omission if I failed at this point to consider the criticism made upon my position in this question by a highly esteemed scholar and juristic philosopher, Professor Merkel, of Strassburg, who did me the honor to review my book in Schmoller's *Jahrbuch*.*

This review refers me to an article by my honored critic on " Right and Might " in the preceding number of the

* 1881, *Heft* iv, p. 301.

same magazine, and I am probably not mistaken in believing that that article was written after he knew the contents of my book, "*Rechtsstaat und Socialismus*" and with reference to it; and that I am justified in considering it an integral part of the review.* In fact Merkel has so divided his critical material as to enumerate concisely in the short notice in *Heft* IV his doubts about my position, but to put the solid reasons for them in the previous article on "Right and Might." This appropriate division of the material greatly facilitates my reply to the objections made.

First of all I notice with satisfaction that Merkel's position is in fact not so far from mine as it might seem from his "notice," for between my discussions and his "article" I can discover no essential difference. I shall therefore confine myself to showing that the objections which are made in the "notice" are considerably weakened if not entirely removed by the concessions made in the previous article.

The first objection is that I assert an "essential" difference between political and private rights whereby "the differences really existing between these subdivisions of rights are in part expressed correctly, though generally with exaggerations;" but that I do not recognize "what they have in common."

The objection is correct in so far as the entire plan and economy of my work aimed at proving the essential difference, *toto genere*, between public and private rights; to which end I was in that place only interested in emphasizing the prevailing differences. I have not denied "what they have in common" and it would be hard "not to recognize" it after the whole juridical literature had based the identity of the two "rights" on it. But it could not fall into the plan of my work to enumerate it for the hundredth time, because it would be superfluous. However, that the really essential

* "*Rechtsstaat und Socialismus*" appeared in the summer of 1880 and shortly after a copy was sent to Schmoller's *Jahrbuch* for review. A year later, in the summer of 1881, appeared a double number (2 and 3) of the *Jahrbuch* with Merkel's article on "Right and Might" at the head. At the same time my book was mentioned among the "books received" with the remark that the "next number would contain a notice of it from the pen of Professor Merkel." Thus, plainly, he had knowledge of the contents of my book at that time. Besides I think that I find in the article unambiguous allusions to it: e. g., p. 16, where it reads: "Scholars of former and of quite recent times have thought that they could prove that the sovereign power in the state could not be surrounded with effectual barriers and restraints," etc.; and again. p. 18: " The arguments just recently urged with especial emphasis against the possibility of such progress (in the sphere of international law)," and so forth. The attempts and the arguments mentioned are in fact contained in "*Rechtsstaat und Socialismus*" which Professor Merkel should have had in hand some time before this number appeared.

differences which I asserted exist, in spite of what there is in common between these two subdivisions of rights, can be proven from Merkel's article on "Right and Might" by showing, in particular, that the statements and assertions concerning rights therein contained are inexact and incorrect just because the author does not make the distinction which I demand; but rather formulates his propositions upon "rights" in general. In consequence it happens that he asserts something false about the one subdivision every time that he states something true about the other. Thus, for example, at the very beginning of the article cited, Merkel says: "Rights in their origin, their stability and their changes, as witnessed by history, appear to be dependent upon might in many respects and questions of right not infrequently find their solution in the guise of decisions by might which combine the effects of the proof of the better right with the proof of the greater strength. Events of that sort are difficult to harmonize with the prevalent ideas of right." What Merkel says here is only true of public rights, for whenever anywhere "private rights" are settled by the "decision of might," we speak not of "rights" but of caprice and wrong. Public rights alone may be settled in this way without sacrificing their character.

In view of such an assertion as this, intended to hold of both "subdivisions of rights," but really true of only one, shall I withdraw my proposition that the difference between private and public rights is fundamental? I think not. So much the less as I see my honored reviewer, in consequence of falsely grouping two fundamentally different things under one concept, ensnared in a net of doubts and contradictions from which he tries very hard to escape without success; though in my humble opinion they disappear upon holding fast to the essential distinction between public and private rights as I formulated it in "*Rechtsstaat und Socialismus*," possibly with somewhat too much bias but correctly in the main. Thus, let us hear Merkel's lament over the impossibility of reconciling the concept of "rights" with the solution of questions of right by appeals to might.

"It is hard to bring such events into consonance with the prevailing ideas of right. Right is here determined by factors which seem foreign and even contradictory to our ideas of its nature, since according to them questions of right are not questions concerning the relative power of the contending parties but rather concerning the truth and merits of their assertions and the value of their claims before a higher forum.''

What Merkel here says of '' rights '' applies only to private rights. For only questions of private rights concern '' the truth and merits of the assertions of the contending parties and the value of their claims before a higher forum '' and not rather '' their relative power.''

But questions of public right are different, even though they are often put in this form. One example among many : Shall the Duke of Cumberland succeed his uncle in the government of Brunswick ? Is that a question '' of the truth and merits of the assertions of the contending parties and the value of their claims before a higher forum ?''

By no means, because it is not a question of private rights; because it therefore does not depend upon the '' truth and merits of the assertions ;'' because there is here in fact no '' higher forum,'' for the German Empire is at once party and judge. Thus it is in fact a question of public rights, a question which will undoubtedly be determined by factors which are foreign to the nature of '' rights '' (political interests); a question undoubtedly '' of the relative power of the contending parties,'' one of whom, the German Empire, does not need to recognize a higher forum over it, because within the sphere of its operations it is itself the highest forum. Whoever insists upon grouping public and private rights together under one general concept will never escape from doubts and obscurities and is necessarily forced into the delicate situation of setting himself, for the sake of '' rights,'' in opposition to the most vital interests of his folk and state in questions of public rights. Now I consider this false doctrinarianism, and perceive the occasion of the error in the incomplete distinction between public rights and private rights. Though they have much in common it is only in form; in principle they are fundamentally different. But Merkel's whole argument rests on their identity and he procures the appearance of confirmation for his view only by alluding to private rights, which of course do not stand under the criterion of might, to prove the inadmissibility of that criterion, and then appealing from the arbitrary vacillation of the decisions of might to the higher idea of right— which unfortunately avails nothing in questions of public right.

The consistent disregard of this essential difference runs through the entire article and even leads to absolutely incorrect statements of fact. When, for example, it is said that "statesmen have always shown an inclination, seldom unreservedly confessed however, to treat questions of right as questions of might . . .," the statement is incorrect when referred to private rights. It is correct only when applied to public and international rights.

They would be strange "statesmen" who threw the weight of their influence and power on the side of private rights. I should not be able to name a single one, and they would certainly not deserve the title. But even Merkel is not thinking of such a meddling with private rights here for he immediately adds as example that these statesmen "generally stand in the position of the Athenians of old whom Thucydides makes to say in a dispute with the Medians: ' As to the Gods we believe and as to men we know that of necessity every one lords it over whomsoever he has power. . . .' "

Thus "rights" in the broader sense, including private rights, are not brought in question here, only public rights. Sovereignty (*Herrschen*) alone is spoken of, not doing justice or acting the judge. But if, as Merkel says later on, "theory in the greater number of its advocates affirms the independence of rights and the essential difference between right and might," in the first place theory has been largely and chiefly occupied with private rights, a field in which the state has left it full authority (juristic rights, *responsa prudentum*, etc.), and if there are isolated cases in which it has drawn public rights into the scope of its discussion it was still only theory—and we know what that signifies in relation to public rights, for whose advocates, the statesmen, no reproach can be more bitter than "doctrinarianism."

Thus after all there has never been any contradiction within the several subdivisions of right; for the statesmen never troubled themselves about private rights; and their assertions, like those of the Athenians of Thucydides, applied only to public rights. But the jurists have always been up to the ears in the latter and still have the most narrow views of the state; so that their opinions and assertions are serviceable only for private rights; for public rights they have never given anything but "theory," "precious material for the waste-basket." In fact there is no real contradiction because people did not have the same thing in mind.

Just so I find that there is no real contradiction after all between what I said in " *Rechtsstaat und Socialismus* " upon public rights and what Merkel says in his article on the same subject. Though, where he speaks of "rights" in general without distinguishing public and private rights, our assertions appear indeed to contradict but only in so far as they do not apply to the same thing.

So if Merkel makes the essential distinction between public and private rights a reproach against me, it would be easy for me to show that his discussion would have gained much in clearness and verity had he maintained the same distinction throughout. He would not have been forced to limit every proposition upon "rights" in general as soon as it was expressed and to restrict it in respect first of public and then of private rights.

For example when he says:

" Where this might [of objective right] is appealed to in the struggle over subjective right, it is presupposed that its activity will issue from a position lying outside the conflicting claims and interests and appearing to hold a neutral relation to them. . . ." (p. 5),

the statement holds good of private, but not at all of public rights. For of the latter he himself concedes that

" the conditions for establishing and extending the sovereignty of the neutral factor [that ' neutral position '] are less favorable. . . . in public rights. . . ." (p. 16). " That factor [objective right as neutral might] ," he says further on, " finds itself confronted with more powerful forces in the struggle for sovereignty in the state and for limiting or extending it while the sources of its own might flow more sparingly and far greater hindrances are opposed to the development of its organs than in the sphere just considered. The question here is to surround the supporters of sovereign power, whom right itself furnishes with superior weapons, with barriers and hinder the misuse of its weapons. To many this appears a self-contradictory problem, which must therefore simply be abandoned. Scholars formerly and in quite recent times have thought they could show that the supreme power in the state could not be surrounded with barriers because, as they say, there can be but one supreme power within one and the same sphere."

The last expression seems to imply that Merkel does not share their view.

Is it really so? We would not venture to affirm it; if there is any difference between his view and theirs it is

certainly not fundamental. We will show from his article
presently that he is not so very far from those "scholars"
and that there is only a slight shade not so much of opinion
as of scientific tendency separating him from their position
and ours.

Merkel is wrong in charging the opposite view with overlooking the fact

"that the force of the neutral factor itself, rooted in common and
deep-seated convictions and usages, as for example in the form of
traditional constitutional law supported by a feeling of right and a
lively sense of need in all classes, may conceivably be the highest
force within a community."

Without overlooking this and other considerations enumerated by him, it is possible to maintain that all these substitutes for the "neutral factor" will not suffice in a given case
of public rights to take the place of that higher might
which stands neutral above party.   For even Merkel himself who overlooks none of these factors speaks of a "remnant
which no progress [in the development of rights] can overpower"—and more than that I have not asserted; only I
located it unequivocally where it always has and always
must appear, that is, in the highest sphere of public and
national rights.   But it is plain from more than one statement in his article that even he, though reluctantly and
with evident regret, makes the unconditional sovereignty of
rights cease in that sphere where we, without circumlocu-
tion and with well-founded resignation, substituted might
for it.   He freely concedes that

"in the field of international rights, down to the present, the original
connection between subjective rights and subjective might" has been
retained "in respect not only of the acquisition but also of the
enforcement of the former in its broadest scope."   "In this field," it
is said again, "in consequence of the weakness and slight development of the neutral factor the competition for more favorable conditions of life still maintains in part its primitive form.   Still the
existence of the former is manifested even here in many ways that
will be referred to later, among others, in the mutual recognition of
rights between civilized nations.   But this is frequently associated
with plain decisions of might made in the most primitive way and
does not prevent the contest for rights from finding its solution, in
the most important 'cases even, in the form or upon the basis of
elementary decisions by might."

"Acquisition through power here takes the form of acquisition by
rights, in so far as this is affirmed, without the necessity for a direct
genealogical line between him who 'has taken possession' [playing on
Goethe's words: "Whence did grandpapa get them? He took

them!''] and him who establishes right to possession. . . . War here proves to be a continual and abundant source of new rights, the rule for whose creation is not to be sought in some higher principle but in the result of the test of strength which war imposes upon the struggling parties.''

Thus there is no disagreement between our position and Merkel's in reference to international rights. With reference to national (state) rights, likewise, he concedes, as stated above, that ''the conditions for founding and developing the sovereignty of the neutral factor are little favorable;'' and he does not allow himself to be led astray by the favorite formula of public rights which speaks of ''sovereignty in virtue of one's own right.''
He says explicitly:

''Whenever sovereignty over another or any right of decision in public affairs is exercised 'in virtue of one's own right' we have to do in truth with the principle of might.''

But thereby he too strikes '' rights '' from the supreme position in the state. We expressed the same thought by saying that between public and private rights there is an essential difference. He objects to the form of expression but plainly agrees to the fact. For however much he points to progress in the idea of rights, with which the neutral factor acquires an ever higher and more dominating position in the state, which we do not deny, he has to concede at last that '' the problem of saving right from its dependence on might through progressive development will continually present itself anew as still unsolved in spite of all progress.''*

Will Merkel in spite of this concession reproach me further because I grant the possibility of '' limiting the state's power through judicial decisions '' only to a very limited degree and certain extent? Does he mean that what I say ''still remains a simple assertion?'' But if such a limitation of the state's power through '' constitutions and judicial decisions '' were possible, as Merkel asserts in the review, would not the problem of '' saving right from its dependence on might '' be solved, which, he says in the article, '' will continually present itself as unsolvable in spite of all progress?''

Merkel should not have referred me to his article; for in it he takes away the ground from the objections which he

* P. 20.

makes against me in the review.   Moreover he concedes, even in the review, that "it is true that the dependence of right upon might appears more palpable, intensive and direct in the sphere of public rights than in that of private rights;" only he considers "that no ground for denying the existence and even the possibility of the existence of real rights in the former sphere."

Well, that depends entirely upon the view a man has formed of "rights."   Whoever looks upon right as objective, throned high above the strife of parties, proclaiming its will in the form of statutory norms, must deny its existence and even the possibility of its existence where, even as Merkel concedes, "the problem of saving right from its dependence on might presents itself as unsolved."

As I hold the view mentioned I must of necessity draw the conclusion that public rights are entirely different from private rights.   Whoever on the contrary holds fast to the conception of "rights" even when "dependent on might" may, of course, discard my distinction.

But I think it has been proven in what precedes that there is at bottom no difference between the actual conception of the matter itself in Merkel's mind and in mine, between his conviction as to the real state of the case and mine, and that, throughout, the difference between us is not one of cognition but of tendency, in consequence of which Merkel lays more stress upon the fact that rights must tend to complete "release" (*Erloesung*) from might, while in my book, "*Rechtsstaat und Socialismus*," stress was laid on the fact that "release" was impossible and that we must make terms with the dependence of national right on might.

But whence, I ask myself, considering the similarity in the knowledge and conception of the matter itself, whence comes the difference of standpoint and emphasis, right in Merkel's case, might in mine?   I do not think I am wrong in referring it simply to the difference in the political situations of Germany and Austria in the seventh decade of the present century—for finally every political writer unavoidably reflects the political situation surrounding him however objectively he wishes and proposes to proceed.

No German of the seventh and eighth decades of this century has had need to be anxious about might under the régime of the Iron Chancellor.   On the other hand he has no doubt had some apprehension about "rights."   What is more natural than that both teachers of public law and philosophers in Germany have emphasized the pre-eminence of right over might and postulated the independence of the former from the latter.

Not so in Austria. We did not need to worry over "rights." They throve like an obtrusive weed in every path even where the direction "reserved for might" was to have been expected. At the helm sat a party calling itself the constitutionalist and fancying that the entire state could be subjected to the régime of right. In particular it expected to be able to attain this object by holding ready the universal remedy, a special tribunal constituted *ad hoc* for every possible political crime. It was content with this —for indeed the "eye of the law" in the form of a court of justice watched over the state. Recently this party has even proposed to submit certain actions of parliament, *e. g.*, those relating to election cases, to the jurisdiction of a particular court of justice created *ad hoc*.

This effort, which is certainly well meant, proceeds from the erroneous assumption, is controlled by the delusion we would like to say, that an ordinary mortal at once becomes an angel or at least an infallible pope upon sticking a judge's commission in his pocket. It needs but little experience, however, to learn that every judge above all else is and remains a man, and in spite of all the conscious objectivity which he industriously cultivates (and even that not always) is quite as much the slave of blind impulses, prejudices and efforts which have their source in his social, political, religious and national position as every other mortal and certainly not less than every representative of the people.

It must not be ignored that at some point in the state right must cease and might begin. The creation of a court for constitutional cases would only transfer the point from the representative body to the court. Would this be better?

The constitutionalists, so-called, who ought really to be called the "national rights" party (*Rechtsstaatliche*), because from the first they have labored under the delusion that the whole state could be represented in a juristic formula, have deeply atoned for their error. The power suddenly fell from their hands for mere right's sake; and nothing else could have happened, for the state belongs to might and not to right although it creates and forms the latter, develops and promotes it. This latter thought I have discussed in "*Rechtsstaat und Socialismus.*"

It is possible that this witches' Sabbath of "national rights," which raged in Austria in the same decade that Germany got a taste of the "might before right" theory of the Iron Chancellor, has a share in the Austrian's somewhat different standpoint in the question of might and right. The German reacts perhaps unconsciously against the all too powerful interposition of might. The Austrian, because right has been so emphasized, may have become a little anxious for national might. I can see no other difference between Merkel's standpoint and mine.

THE ACADEMY AND ITS WORK.

THE AMERICAN ACADEMY OF POLITICAL AND SOCIAL SCIENCE was formed in Philadelphia, December 4, 1889, for the purpose of promoting the political and social sciences, and was incorporated February 14, 1891.

While it does not exclude any portion of the field indicated in its title, yet its chief object is the development of those aspects of the political and social sciences which are either entirely omitted from the programs of other societies, or which do not at present receive the attention they deserve. Among such objects may be mentioned : Sociology, Comparative Constitutional and Administrative Law, Philosophy of the State, Municipal Government, and such portions of the field of Politics, including Finance and Banking, as are not adequately cultivated by existing organizations.

In prosecuting the objects of its foundation, the Academy has held meetings and engaged extensively in publication.

MEMBERSHIP.

"Any person may become a member of the Academy who having been proposed by a member shall be approved by the Council."—*Constitution, Article IV.*

Persons interested in the study of political, social and economic questions, or in the encouragement of scientific research along these lines, are eligible to membership and will be nominated upon application to the Membership Committee of the Council, American Academy, Station B, Philadelphia.

There is no Initiation Fee. Annual Dues, $5. Life Membership Fee, $100.

MEETINGS.

Public meetings have been held from time to time at which the members of the Academy and others interested might listen to papers and addresses touching upon the political and social questions of the day. The meetings have been addressed by leading men in academic and practical life, a wide range of topics has been discussed, and the papers have generally been subsequently published by the Academy.

The first scientific session of the Academy was held on March 14, 1890; three other sessions were held in 1890; seven in 1891; five in 1892; five in 1893; six in 1894; four in 1895; six in 1896; eight in 1897, and eight in 1898, or fifty-three in all.

PUBLICATIONS.

Since the foundation of the Academy, a series of publications has been maintained, known as the ANNALS of the American Academy of Political and Social Science and the Supplements thereto. These publications have brought home to members accurate information and carefully considered discussions of all the questions embraced within the field of the Academy's interests. The ANNALS is sent to all members of the Academy.

ANNALS.

The ANNALS was first issued as a quarterly, but since the second volume it has appeared as a bi-monthly. At the present time, the ANNALS comprises two volumes of about 500 pages each per annum. The thirteen volumes thus far issued comprise 52 numbers, constituting with the supplements 9,302 pages of printed matter which have been distributed to the members of the Academy.

Besides the larger papers contributed by many eminent scholars both at home and abroad, especial attention has been directed to the departments. All important books are carefully reviewed or noticed by specialists. The department of Personal Notes keeps the reader informed of movements in the academic and scientific world. Notes upon Municipal Government and Sociology preserve a careful record of events and other matters of interest in these subjects, which at the present time claim so large a share of public attention.

To persons not members of the Academy, the price of Vols. I.-V., including supplements, is $6.00 a volume, and of Vols. VI. XIII, $3.00 each. Separate numbers $1.00 each. Special rates to Libraries, Vols. I.-V., $5.00 each; Vols. VI.-XIII, $2.50 each.

Members are entitled to discounts varying from 16⅔ per cent to 20 per cent on orders for back numbers or duplicate copies of publications. All current publications are sent to members free of charge.

Essays in Economics and Sociology

BY

SIMON N. PATTEN, PH. D.

Professor of Political Economy in the University of Pennsylvania

---

COST AND UTILITY . . . . Price, 25 cents

COST AND EXPENSE . . . . Price, 25 cents

THE FORMULATION OF NORMAL LAWS . . . . . . Price, 25 cents

THE FAILURE OF BIOLOGIC SOCIOLOGY . . . . Price, 25 cents

RELATION OF SOCIOLOGY TO PSYCHOLOGY . . . . Price, 25 cents

THE ECONOMIC BASIS OF PROHIBITION . . . . Price, 15 cents

OVER-NUTRITION AND ITS SOCIAL CONSEQUENCES . . . . . Price, 25 cents

THE ECONOMIC CAUSES OF MORAL PROGRESS . . . . . . Price, 25 cents

ECONOMICS IN ELEMENTARY SCHOOLS . . . . Price, 25 cents

THE THEORY OF SOCIAL FORCES . Price, Paper cover, $1.00 ; Cloth, $1.50

A new and complete catalogue of over 240 publications on political, social and economic topics will be sent free on application.

American Academy of Political and Social Science

Station B, Philadelphia

Discussions of

Social Questions

Complete List of Publications Sent on Application

American Academy of Political and Social Science

STATION B, PHILADELPHIA

he Foreign Policy of the United States

POLITICAL AND COMMERCIAL

Addresses and Discussions at the Annual Meeting
f the American Academy of Political and Social Science,
pril 7, 8, 1899.

PAGES, 215.   PRICE, $1.00.   CLOTH, $1.50.

ADDRESSES BY

His Excellency the Chinese Minister, Wu Ting-fang.
Hon. Carl Schurz, New York.
Professor Theodore S. Woolsey, Yale University.
Worthington C. Ford, Boston.
Hon. John Bassett Moore, Columbia University.
Robert T. Hill, Washington.

DISCUSSION BY

A. Lawrence Lowell, Harvard University; Professor E. W. Huffcut, Cornell
lhiversity; Frederick Wells Williams, Yale University; W. Alleyne Ireland,
ondon; Professor L. M. Keasbey, Bryn Mawr College; John Foord, New York;
Ir. Talcott Williams, Philadelphia; Dr. W. P. Wilson, Philadelphia, and Professors
ii. R. Johnson and L. S. Rowe, University of Pennsylvania.

TITLES OF SECTIONS

HE GOVERNMENT OF DEPENDENCIES.
IILITARISM AND DEMOCRACY.
HE COMMERCIAL RELATIONS OF THE UNITED STATES WITH THE FAR EAST.
HE POLITICAL RELATIONS OF THE UNITED STATES WITH THE FAR EAST.

umerican Academy of Political and Social Science

STATION B, PHILADELPHIA

The American Academy

OF

POLITICAL AND SOCIAL SCIENCE

PHILADELPHIA

CPSIA information can be obtained at www.ICGtesting.com
Printed in the USA
BVOW05s1022100314

347178BV00019B/746/P

9 781313 45250